Social

The nature of social reality is a key problem in the philosophy of social science. This book outlines the major issues – historical and contemporary – raised by social reality and social facts. What, after all, are we talking about when we talk about social reality and the facts of social life?

Social science often asserts, and even more tacitly assumes, that social reality is generated by our 'interpretation' of it. Accordingly, social facts are claimed to lack an independent existence – rather, they are a product of the way they are conceived, explained and classified by social agents. This process is referred to as the social construction of social facts, postulated by social constructivists.

Social constructivism has become a very influential position, and Finn Collin reviews a number of traditional doctrines in philosophy and social science which support the constructivist position, whilst also exposing the excesses of that particular view.

This book has something to offer both philosophers and social scientists. To the former it shows how the well-worn topic of realism versus anti-realism (in the broadest sense) assumes new and interestingly varied forms when social reality is substituted for physical reality. For the social scientist, the book offers conceptual clarification of certain key issues in recent social science which are really philosophical issues. *Social Reality* is written for students of philosophy and the social sciences, and lucidly explains – in terms accessible to both disciplines – the problem of social facts and social reality.

Finn Collin is Senior Lecturer at the University of Copenhagen. He holds doctorates in philosophy from the University of California, Berkeley, and the University of Copenhagen. Dr Collin is the author of *Theory and Understanding: A Critique of Interpretive Social Science* (1985).

The Problems of Philosophy

Founding Editor: Ted Honderich
Editors: Tim Crane and Jonathan Wolff, *University College London*

This series addresses the central problems of philosophy. Each book gives a fresh account of a particular philosophical theme by offering two perspectives on the subject: the historical context and the author's own distinctive and original contribution.

The books are written to be accessible to students of philosophy and related disciplines, while taking the debate to a new level.

Social reality

Finn Collin

London and New York

First published 1997
by Routledge
11 New Fetter Lane, London EC4P 4EE
Simultaneously published in the USA and Canada
by Routledge
29 West 35th Street, New York, NY 10001

© 1997 Finn Collin

Typeset in Times by Routledge
Printed and bound in Great Britain by
Clays Ltd, St. Ives PLC

British Library Cataloguing in Publication Data
A catalogue record for this book is available from
the British Library

Library of Congress Cataloguing in Publication Data
Collin, Finn.
Social reality / Finn Collin.
p. cm. – (Problems of philosophy)
1. Reality. 2. Constructivism (Philosophy)
3. Ontology. 4. Philosophy and social sciences.
I. Title. II. Series: Problems of philosopy (Routledge)
BD331.C566 1991
301'.01–dc21

96–48387
CIP

ISBN   0–415–14796–4 (hbk)
ISBN   0–415–14797–2 (pbk)

For my parents

Contents

Contents

Part Two The Narrow Arguments

Contents

Preface

The present book is an essay in the philosophy of the social sciences. Its primary theme is an examination of the social construction thesis as applied to social reality itself. Like all work in the philosophy of science it occupies border territory between two major disciplines, and in consequence its viability is conditional upon its serving as an arena for communication and exchanges across frontiers. It follows from this claim that anyone proposing to embark on a serious examination of the social construction thesis as applied to social reality should adhere closely to actual work in social science; which is to say that the study should draw on the kinds of constructivist positions that have actually been presented in the social science literature, rather than starting out from vague philosophical speculation as to what a construction thesis might amount to in this field. In keeping with this precept I have sought to root my presentation of the topic firmly in problems that have exercised the minds of social scientists. Not all the ideas that have germinated in such contexts were originally conceived as contributions to the constructivism issue, but I attempt to show how they can be adapted to such a role.

A philosophical investigation is essentially a critical enterprise, however, and in the present work this critical dimension finds expression in a bifurcation of the subject matter that is critical in intent. A distinction is drawn between more radical positions, referred to as the Broad Arguments, which I claim are indefensible, and more moderate positions – the Narrow Arguments – which are held to be viable. The terms themselves are intended to be suggestive of why the former fail and the latter succeed: the Broad Arguments overreach themselves in purporting to apply to all of reality, whereas the Narrow Arguments prove to be sustainable in virtue of their more modest pretensions and their specificity: they apply only to the social world. The aim of the present essay is thus to show the attractiveness of the modest constructivist position, but also to expose the weaknesses of the radical position and the arguments supporting it, which currently enjoy a measure of undeserved popularity.

In the exposition of the views with which we shall be concerned the strategy followed is that of taking an argument developed in a social science context, recasting it to achieve the increment of theoretical refinement afforded by contemporary philosophical categories in order to assess it in a more perspicuous and persuasive form. But the connections between philosophy and social science are many, complex and varied so that the declared approach is not one that can always be implemented in a simple and straightforward manner. It works fairly smoothly when the views in question are traceable to a time not long since past when social science and philosophy were irresolvably interfused: this applies, for instance, when dealing with the hermeneutic and phenomenological views. It is feasible too when a social science position is influenced by a specific argument in recent philosophy: ethnomethodology, which is inspired by Wittgenstein's later philosophy, is a case in point. Often, however, forms of the constructivist argument have taken shape in total independence of any concrete philosophical influence, and in such cases their philosophical reconstrual becomes a more hazardous undertaking; care must be taken lest such a recasting seem to travesty the original view.

In the light of the many-strandedness of the relationship between social science and philosophy, the challenge to fit the present theme into a series which places philosophical problems in the context of their history is an exacting one. For the view we shall be examining does not have *one* history but many, owing to its having been nurtured by numerous historical sources, some belonging to the traditions of social science and others to pure philosophy. In order to take due account of this fact, presentations of relevant historical perspectives have not been concentrated in an initial chapter, or part, but have been related directly to the contexts to which they appropriately belong.

This essay has, I believe, something to offer both the philosopher and the social scientist. To the former, it shows how the well-worn topic of realism versus idealism offers new and refreshingly varied aspects when social reality is substituted for physical reality. To the social scientist, the book offers a clarification of certain key issues in recent social science that are in fact conceptual or philosophical although they are often misconstrued or given a deceptive empirical guise.

Preface

I have sought to strike a balance between philosophy and social science which will ensure that readers most at home in the one discipline will not find the contribution to the discussion made by the other inaccessible. I have no doubt, however, that the book bears the stamp of the fact that its author is a philosopher by training, not a social scientist. Still, I have sought throughout to keep the philosophy fairly simple, making no attempt to pursue the arguments into such fine-grained analyses of the issues that the social scientist might lose his way. Conversely, I have avoided making the examples drawn from social science more detailed than necessary so as not to overburden the philosophical reader. I have deliberately abstained from trying to attain full coverage or an up-to-date review of the social science literature from which the philosophical analyses take off. Instead, I often focus on a classic work in a given tradition, distinguished by its seminal presentation of a particular issue. This strategy seems preferable to any involving presentations of more recent discussions in which the original points have often been refined beyond recognition, or are buried underneath the fallout from decades of polemics. I believe the book to be accessible to readers with some grounding in one of the fields and an acquaintance with, and interest in, the other.

I wish to thank David Sachs, Peter Sandøe, Troels Engberg-Pedersen and Julie Zahle for critical comments on earlier versions of the manuscript, or parts thereof. Geoffrey Hawthorn and Ted Honderich offered moral support and practical assistance, for which I am deeply appreciative. Thanks are also due to two anonymous readers with Routledge, from whose comments the book has greatly benefited.

Lorilea Jaderborg, Susan Dew and Cynthia Grund undertook the task of enhancing my English, for which I am indebted to them. I am grateful to Jørgen Mikkelsen for initiating me into the finer points of word processing.

Clare Hall, Cambridge, provided a highly congenial environment and ideal working conditions during the period in which I started work on this essay; for this I remain indebted to them.

Finally, I want to thank the Danish Research Council for Social Science for its financial support, which enabled me to be relieved of my teaching duties whilst completing this book.

Finn Collin
Copenhagen, May 1996

Acknowledgements

I am grateful to the MIT Press for permission to quote from
Benjamin Lee Whorf, *Language, Thought and Reality* (edited by
John B. Carroll, 1964); to Blackwell Publishers for permission to
quote from Jürgen Habermas, *On the Logic of the Social Sciences*
(1988) and from Alasdair MacIntyre, 'A Mistake about Causality in
Social Science' (in Peter Laslett and W. G. Runciman (eds),
Philosophy, Politics and Society, 2nd series, 1962); to the University
of California Press for permission to quote from *Selected Writings
of Edward Sapir* (edited by David G. Mandelbaum, 1973); and to
Simon and Schuster, who requested that the following credit line be
used:

From *OUTSIDERS: Studies in the Sociology of Deviance* by
Howard S. Becker. Copyright © 1963 by The Free Press, a
Division of Simon and Schuster. Reprinted with permission of
the publisher.

The passages from *Georg Simmel, 1858–1918*, published by Ohio
State University Press (1959), are quoted by kind permission of the
editor, Kurt H. Wolff. The quotations from Peter L. Berger and
Thomas Luckmann, *The Social Construction of Reality*, (1967), pp.
13, 197–98, 210–11 (© Peter L. Berger and Thomas Luckmann) are
reproduced by permission of Penguin Books Ltd. and of Doubleday
Inc., as well as by permission of the authors.

A few paragraphs of Chapter 4 have previously appeared in an
article in *Danish Yearbook of Philosophy*, vol. 28 (1993). I am
grateful to the editors of that journal and to Museum Tusculanum
Press for permission to reuse this material.

Introduction

It is a truism that the reality in which the human species lives is of humankind's own making. The notion of *homo faber*, man the toolmaker, has iconic significance in our culture: human beings devise tools and, in using them to create and transform their environment, they make of the natural realm in which they evolved as a species a new order, one brought into being and sustained by themselves. The invention of hunting weapons and the rudimentary tools needed for the construction of dwellings was the beginning. The domestication of wild animals and the invention of the plough marked further advances in the taming of nature. For human beings are not compelled to submit to all the contingencies of the natural order, but have the resources to adapt circumstances to their needs. From the building of dwellings for human habitation to the moulding of larger geographical features to create appropriate living conditions for entire populations, such enterprises range from those on a small to those on a large scale. Wildernesses have been turned into fields and coastlines straightened. Swamps have been filled in and lakes introduced into deserts. The human species alone, then, among the animals, creates the entire biotope in which it lives. Human beings make their own world.

Now, clearly, man the toolmaker is not a solitary creature. Even when the individual caters primarily to his own private needs, the course his actions take inevitably criss-crosses with those of others pursuing their respective ends. Moreover, his more ambitious projects are, by necessity, ones that can only be achieved through working in partnership with his fellows. As a result, complex patterns of interaction emerge, with the behaviour of each individual influencing that of the others in a myriad of subtle ways. One patent example of this is the phenomenon of coordination: the members of a group observe each other's actions and modify their own accordingly.

In so regulating their activities, group members do more than bring about those changes in the physical environment at which they aim. In virtue of the resultant patterns of behaviour, they bring into being social relationships, social structures, and institutions – in brief, *social reality*. What is generated through this process is of a different order entirely from that of changes wrought in the physical environment or the impact of one person's behaviour on another's. For human actions do not make up social reality in any causal sense, but are instead identical with it in the sense of collectively *constituting* it. The hunt will produce a bag of game: its causal upshot, that is, will be the number of animals brought down by the hunters. But it will also generate something else, in a different sense: patterns of interaction will crystallise in the hunting party. A system of tacit norms will emerge specifying who does what; in particular, it will become clear who gives the orders and who carries them out. A minimal normative structure will have come into existence. Inasmuch as it forms the embodiment of this structure, human interaction *constitutes* social reality.

Thus, human beings produce a world of their own making, a distinctly human one, in two ways. First, they mix their labour (to use John Locke's apt phrase) with what the natural world supplies and transform it by so doing. Such transformations of the environment are typically the result of joint efforts and the behaviour of each agent is influenced by that of the others. In both cases we have examples of causal generation. But, second, in setting up patterns of coordinated interaction, human beings generate a new stratum of reality – namely, social reality. In this case, however, what is generated is not the outcome of some causal process but is rather what emerges when the patterns of human interaction assume a sufficiently fixed and permanent character as to acquire independent status in the form of a social framework existing over and above the concrete activities taking place within it. Taken together, this framework and the collective human action whose context it provides, constitute the social world.

SOCIAL FACTS AS CONSTRUCTIONS

In certain quarters of social science, we find yet another conception of social reality and the way it is made by man. This is the view that social reality is somehow generated by the way we *think* or *talk* about it, by our *consensus* about its nature, by the way we *explain* it

2

to each other, and by the *concepts* we use to grasp it. Social facts are thought to be a product of the very cognition, the very intellectual processes through which they are cognised, explained and classified, in so far as this cognition is a shared, collective one. This is not a causal mode of creation. What is being urged is not the trivial point that man translates his thoughts and schemes into reality through action, or that his ideas serve as blueprints for things that he proceeds to make real through his labour. It is the very intellectual activity that is thought to generate facts.

A simple illustration of the phenomena that inspire this line of thought is *money*. Money tokens are typically perfectly valueless in themselves; they are slips of paper or little metal discs. But we bestow a value upon these valueless tokens by collectively *believing them* to possess value. This belief involves a readiness to accept money in exchange for goods with a genuine value-in-use. In this way, the belief that money is valuable acquires a rational basis; each of us is warranted in thinking of money as valuable, since other people believe likewise and are actually willing to accept it in return for genuine goods. Thus, the collective belief that money is valuable is self-validating, creating its own reality. Note that the value does not await an actual exchange of goods against money to come into existence; it is established once the collective belief, and hence the common willingness to engage in exchange, are established.

The aim of the present book is to interpret, analyse, and evaluate the view that human thought, discourse, agreement, or concepts generate the social world in a non-causal sense. I shall try to show that there is indeed such generation – henceforth referred to as *construction*. I shall also try to show that its precise nature has often been misunderstood by its proponents and I will supply a more satisfactory way to construe it. Considerable space will indeed be devoted to giving a more precise sense to the social construction thesis – or rather, more precise *senses*, as several different versions will still remain after the vagueness has been cleared away. The various senses will emerge *pari passu* with an examination of the main arguments in favour of this view, for (as often in abstract inquiries) only the argument presented in favour of a position shows us what that position really is. The goal is to reach a maximally defensible version of the construction view; hence, faithfulness to the actual intentions of an author will be sacrificed on occasion to achieving a more viable position.

After having defined these various positions, I subject each to critical assessment. The constructivist positions, and the arguments provided for them, fall roughly into two groups. The first is more extreme, based largely upon philosophical arguments of a very general sort; by and large, I reject these arguments and the positions based upon them. The positions in the second group are more moderate and are based upon the distinguishing properties of social fact; I show that the construction thesis is true for these arguments.

Let us start by looking at some quotations in which the construction thesis is advocated. This will further define the position with which we shall be dealing.

> There is one division of nature where the formula of idealism is applicable almost to the letter: this is the social kingdom. Here more than anywhere else the idea is the reality.
>
> (Émile Durkheim 1915: 228)

> Knowledge about society is thus a realization in the double sense of the word, in the sense of apprehending the objectivated social reality, and in the sense of ongoingly producing this reality.... The sociology of knowledge understands human reality as socially constructed reality.
>
> (Peter Berger and Thomas Luckmann 1967: 84, 210–11)

> The distinctive features of the alternative perspective, which we offer here, reside in the proposal that the objective structures of social activities are to be regarded as the situated, practical accomplishment of the work through and by which the appearance-of-objective-structures is displayed and detected.
>
> (Don Zimmerman and Melvin Pollner 1971: 103)

> Once brought under scrutiny, the 'orderly structure' of the social world is no longer available as a topic in its own right (that is, as something to be described and explained) but instead becomes an accomplishment of the accounting practices through and by which it is described and explained.
>
> (Don Zimmerman and D. Lawrence Wieder 1971: 293–4)

> The way people think about people, themselves, is part of the reality about which they are trying to think in appropriate

ways. The concepts which we employ to grasp what we are become part of what we are; or rather that we use them in this way becomes part of what we are. Thus in social theory we are using concepts to understand beings who define themselves by means of their use of concepts, in some cases the concepts that we are using in trying to understand them.

(Alasdair MacIntyre 1962: 64)

A man's social relations with his fellows are permeated with his ideas about reality. Indeed, 'permeated' is hardly a strong enough word: social relations are expressions of ideas about reality.

(Peter Winch 1958: 23)

These are all programmatic statements, vague and metaphorical. They suggest several different ways in which social reality can be said to be generated by human language, thought, concepts, or agreement, and indicate the magnitude of the clarifying work that lies ahead.

The thesis I shall investigate is traditionally known as 'the social construction of reality', a phrase given currency by Peter Berger and Thomas Luckmann in a highly influential book of that title (Berger and Luckmann 1967), quotes from which were presented above. In what follows, I shall use the term 'construction' for the kind of generation I have in mind, but will modify the way in which the issue is traditionally conceived on three counts, one of which already has been foreshadowed above.

First, in the traditional conception, the scope of the construction thesis is not always clearly specified. Sometimes, both social and natural reality are encompassed. In the present work, we are concerned solely with the generation of *social* reality, and advance no claims about the status of the physical world. On the other hand, I shall use the term 'social' in a very liberal sense that does not mark a strong contrast between the social realm and the sphere of human facts in general. 'Social' here simply means *collective*: a phenomenon counts as social if it involves a plurality of human agents whose actions or plans are somehow mutually related. (We shall later see how exiguous this relationship may be.) Indeed, the investigation might well have been carried out under the caption of 'the social construction of human fact'. The point of the chosen formulation lies in signalling that the facts we shall deal with are

5

typically not about individual persons, but rather types or groups of people – that is, about social collectives. I shall have something further to say below about social facts, to set them apart from physical facts. Second, while the topic of our investigation is indeed the *social* construction of reality, 'social' here again simply means *collective* in the sense specified above. It is essential to the point of view we shall examine that reality construction is always the work of a plurality of social agents, never of single individuals. However, the possibility is left open that this collective generating agency and its activities can be analysed in individualistic terms. Third, in the following, I shall cease to talk about social reality and talk about social *facts* instead. The import of this modification will be discussed below.

Thus, the present work is about the *social* construction of *social* fact. In the following, I shall regard the former restriction to the social sphere as understood and talk simply of the construction of social fact. The second qualification is central to our topic and to my critical argument; it reflects my conviction that there are crucial differences between social fact (in my broad sense) and natural fact. The arguments for the social construction thesis will be successful only to the extent that they heed this difference. Certain arguments that have been advanced are such that, if they had been valid, they would support a construction thesis for natural fact as well. I shall try to show that they pay for this ambitious scope with a lack of validity.

CLARIFICATIONS OF THE CONSTRUCTION CLAIM

Let me say a bit more about the notions and qualifications just introduced. First, we must clarify the contrast between social facts and natural facts. The intuitive idea is that certain properties of man set him and the social life in which he partakes apart from inanimate nature. Social facts are facts that involve or depend upon such features, however indirectly.

The facts that distinguish man from inanimate nature (although not from all of his fellow creatures) are *intentional* facts. That is, they have to do with man's thought, volition, and desire being directed towards the world surrounding him. Evidently, this is intimately related to the traditional conception of man as being set off from the rest of creation by having a 'mind'. I want, however, to stay clear of traditional philosophical tangles concerning the nature

6

of the mind. I therefore adopt, for the purposes of this investigation, a purely pragmatic interpretation of the intentional vocabulary (for example, 'intention', 'goal', 'emotion', 'belief'). I simply wish to draw attention to the undisputed fact that human action is fruitfully described and explained in terms of these notions, which, in contradistinction, we need not invoke to explain the motion of sticks or stones. I refuse, however, to be drawn into discussions as to whether this difference reflects the presence, in man, of a special kind of entity, a *mind*.

Evidently, the feature of intentionality is shared both by collective and individual human phenomena. Hence, it does not serve to distinguish those two realms, a separation that was rather achieved by the reference to interrelated actions and plans as provided above. Thus, the reference to intentionality merely supplies a *necessary* condition – but a crucially important one – for the notion of a social phenomenon. According to the suggested condition, facts will not count as social if, although referring to human beings, they do not pertain to features that separate man from inanimate nature. Thus, a sentence about the rate of acceleration of persons falling off ladders does not express a social fact, as I define that notion here. To pick some more pertinent examples, neither do statistics about mortality rates, changes in average body weight in a population, or the incidence of somatic diseases. There are, no doubt, concerns that would make it useful to classify the last-mentioned facts as social, but they are not our present concerns. I work with a fairly narrow definition of 'social', tailored to the issues that will occupy us in the present book.

My definition of social facts as offered above makes such facts depend upon the existence of individuals, describable in intentional terms. This much I believe to be inarguable: there would be no social facts, no facts about collectives, if there were no facts about individuals. But this does not imply that collective, social notions can be reduced to ones referring only to individuals. I am not claiming that statements about social reality can be translated into statements about individuals, nor that facts about the former are in some sense 'nothing but' facts about the latter. On the other hand, neither does my conception of the social exclude such reduction. This point reflects the second of my modifications above of the traditional constructivist position, which is meant to make room for the possibility that certain reality-constructing processes might be susceptible to individualist analysis. An example is David Lewis's individualist, game-theoretical reconstrual of the notion of a social *convention*, to which we shall return in Chapter VIII.

When we define our issue in this more encompassing manner, we can accommodate both kinds of construction claims that have been advanced in the literature, one running in the individual-to-society direction and the other in the society-to-individual direction. The first version construes individual human facts as primary to social facts and sees social facts as somehow arising out of this individual level, although only when individuals form aggregates. The second views social facts as primary and irreducible and considers individual action to be a concretisation of the social sphere. Moreover, certain authors are actually committed to both points of view, much to their detriment. This is true, for instance, for the most renowned work in the tradition, Berger and Luckmann's *The Social Construction of Reality*. In the final part of the present book, we shall examine whether the moderate version of constructivism to which our investigations lead commit us either way on the individualism versus holism issue.

Standard formulations of the present issue are about the generation of social *reality*. The notion of social reality is rich in connotations hinting at issues other than the one I want to pursue; hence, as mentioned above, I choose to deviate from the traditional debate and talk instead about the generation of social *facts*. Generally speaking, the notion of 'fact' is less discriminative than that of 'reality'. In many situations, there will be no doubt about the facts (that there is a rainbow over yonder, that I had an unpleasant dream last night, or that there is a possibility of snowstorms later in the week), while the question as to the reality of items in the world will not have been broached at all. (Are rainbows, dreams, or possibilities real?) The question has not been answered, or even raised, just because a statement like those just cited is declared to be true, i.e. to express a *fact*.

From a logical point of view, the notions of facts and of reality belong to different levels of analysis. To say that a sentence expresses a fact (or is *true*) is to predicate a property of that sentence as a whole. When we raise questions concerning reality, on the other hand, we have moved to a more detailed level of analysis; we are now scrutinising the internal anatomy of sentences, locating their referential terms and asking whether there is something in the world corresponding to them.

However, this formal difference is not important. What is

important remains the differential fastidiousness of the two modes of description. As it happens, there exists, at the same level of analysis as that of 'real', a notion that is equally as permissive as that of 'fact': the notion of *existence*. According to a standard philosophical definition, to exist is to be referred to in a true sentence. This notion is less exacting than that of 'reality', but can be used to characterise the latter notion. For something to be real is for it to have existence of a particularly privileged kind; correspondingly, to deny its reality is not to declare it nonexistent *tout court*, but simply to deny it this ontological privilege. When we characterise a piece of jewellery as not *real* diamonds (they are paste), or Jones's teeth as not *real* teeth (they are dentures), or the notes in front of you as not *real* money (they are counterfeit), we are not implying that the items referred to do not exist. Costume jewellery certainly exists, though not made of real gems, and so do false teeth and counterfeit money. None of these things are mere sensory illusions.

What this privileged existence amounts to varies with the context; to describe something as 'real' is merely to bestow a honorific title upon it, without spelling out how it is earned. As John Austin pointed out (Austin 1962b: 64–7), asking whether the colour of a woman's hair is its real colour (as opposed to dyed) is very different from asking whether something is a real duck (as opposed to a toy or decoy, or a duck-like goose). To establish the import of claiming that something is real, in any concrete situation, one must examine the specific term that contrasts with 'real': 'fake', 'illusory', 'dummy', and so on.

The terminology of facts allows us to discuss the pros and cons of social constructivism without being entangled in the entirely different issues covered by the notion of 'reality'. It allows us to discuss to what extent the social realm is generated by the consensus of social agents, whether communities using radically different conceptual structures live in different social worlds, or to what extent the social sphere is a product of human convention, without being distracted by irrelevant issues.

To many speakers of English, 'fact' has some vague connotation of certitude or validation; fact is essentially *established* fact. If such a connection is espoused, constructivism might seem to follow as a matter of course. Certified facts are indeed social creations, in the sense that their certification is a social procedure. However, in the usage adopted here, the notion of a fact is tied to that of *truth*, not to the concept of *known* or *documented* truth. A fact is what is expressed in a true sentence; and it must be accepted on all sides that truth goes beyond what has been established as true at any given time. Hence, there is no quick proof of social constructivism, moving from the premise that fact, or truth, means established fact or established truth, to the conclusion that these phenomena are established by society.

In the following, I sometimes shall fall back upon formulations in terms of 'reality' instead of 'facts' when presenting the work of an author who uses this terminology. Occasionally, I shall also use it as a stylistic variant when expounding my own arguments. In the latter case, this mode of expression will always the translatable back into the canonical terminology of facts.

CONTRASTING ISSUES IN SOCIAL SCIENCE

I mentioned above that there are familiar issues within social science, different from the one we pursue here, that are traditionally formulated as questions about the 'reality' of the social. We might have a brief glance at some of these other issues, in order better to demarcate the one that concerns us.

One contrasting issue is that of the *reification* of social facts, a discussion that has its roots in the Marxian notions of fetishism and ideology and has later been developed within the schools of so-called 'critical theory'. According to this view, certain facts (e.g. that there is a current unemployment of 8 per cent, a difference in the job prospects for men and women in the upper echelons of management, a large income differential between certain regions of the country, or a gap between the educational opportunities for children of working-class parents and children born into the higher classes) do not represent a genuine social *reality*. The belief that they do is an illusion, fostered by the process of reification. This means that the facts in question are easily changed, should we so desire, and owe their persistence to certain political or economic interests that they serve and by which they are reciprocally sustained. In other words, to be real, as opposed to being a reification, a social item must display a certain 'robustness', or permanence. It must not occur only under a narrow range of conditions, especially not conditions controlled and manipulated by partisan interests.

The distinction between being constructed and having a more independent existence, which is the topic of this book, is different from the distinction drawn in critical theory between 'reifications' and genuine social facts. Marx himself was an anti-constructivist as regards social reality and would never have considered the reified (or 'fetish'-like) status of some feature of society to be constituted by a consensus to the effect that it was a reification. On the contrary, it would owe its existence as a reification to a general belief that is was an autonomous fact, hence *not* a reification. The very concept of a reification embodies a distinction between what the social world is really like, and what it is thought to be. On the other hand, some feature of society might be a robust one, not the result of reification, but still counting as a construct from the point of view of a sociological approach such as ethnomethodology. It would be generated by the consensus among social agents that it was robust, i.e. the consensus that that feature had proven resistant to societal efforts to change it. It is a characteristic claim of ethnomethodology that the objective character of social phenomena is an 'accomplishment' of the way in which we think about them.[1]

But are not the tenets of constructivism and those of Marxism intimately linked? If a constructivist position is adopted, we might seem to be committed to the view that *all* social facts are reifications, thus controverting the Marxist insistence upon the distinction between reifications and genuine social reality. Constructivist principles would seem to imply that human agents can shape social facts at will by agreeing on how to describe them. However, this interpretation is mistaken. The thesis that social facts are constructed does not mean that social agents have any liberty in generating them. This holds even if the construction view is based upon some radical position such as the consensus theory of truth, which we shall examine in detail in Chapter I. It is no part of such a view that social agents simply can agree upon anything they please. Obviously, any consensus theory must impose constraints upon the kind of agreement that generates fact (see Chapter I). Among these constraints might be one precisely to the effect that the participants should somehow feel compelled to decide as they do. That is, a consensus would only count as genuinely fact-generating to the extent that the participants felt that the moves they made in reaching it were somehow forced – not by external factors, but by the very issue under debate, as it were. True, if the consensus theory is correct, this feeling is somehow an illusion, at least if it is taken to reflect the constraining force of an independently existing object of inquiry. Still, this feeling might be taken as the criterion that the consensus was of the proper kind and that the reflection that had gone into it was sufficiently thorough. Hence, it does not follow from the consensus theory of social fact, properly understood, that social reality is (as it were) at the mercy of a society-wide conspiracy to generate facts arbitrarily. The social construction view does not allow us to enrich ourselves through an arbitrary mutual agreement to the effect that we are all millionaires.

There is another related social science issue with which our present concerns must not be conflated. The construction view is not in the same line of business as Durkheim's thesis of the *thing-like* quality of social phenomena; more specifically, it is not in contradiction of that view. Unfortunately, the mere introduction of the notion of 'fact' does not protect against this conflation – for Durkheim availed himself of that very terminology in expressing his view (as, famously, in his first rule of sociological method: 'Consider social facts as things' Durkheim 1938: 14). One might well feel that some violence is being done to language and logic here: incompatible categories are being forced together. Durkheim would have done better by urging us instead to treat social facts in the same way as physical facts, or to consider social 'things' (social entities) to be like physical things. Be this as it may, Durkheim's slogan has become a classic, and we cannot use a purely terminological criterion to separate his concerns from our present ones, but must provide a more substantial account.

In calling social facts 'thing-like', Durkheim was drawing attention to several distinctive features of such facts, the most important being their independence of human consciousness and will. Durkheim characterises this property in a dual way. In the first place, social facts are such that no individual person's desire that they be different, and his resulting efforts to change them, will make them go away. This is a very modest condition for factuality – much less demanding than that which a Marxian theorist requires to grant that a certain social fact is other than a reification (as indicated above, this would require that that fact will not change, even if everyone desires that it do so and takes appropriate action). Second, Durkheim points to the constraining, compulsory character of social facts. Social 'things' are not merely there, but are somehow mandatory, being backed up by sanctions in case of deviation. The fact that people in Great Britain drive on the left side of the road, whereas people in the USA drive on the right, is no mere accident, but is something inculcated and enforced. There are sanctions against deviating from this 'regularity'.

Durkheim's concerns, too, diverge from those pursued in the present work. The distinction between constituted and non-constituted facts cuts across that between thing-like and non-thing-like facts. Let us suppose that some specified social fact were not thing-like, as it could be changed by some particular person's will. (Say, some trivial feature of that person's everyday conduct. Think of a cult revolving around a particular aspect of the guru's daily habits.) That fact still might be socially constructed, in the sense that its existence would consist in the community-wide consensus that the individual conducted his life in the given manner and that this conduct reflected his own will. Conversely, if some fact is social and hence thing-like, in Durkheim's sense, and thus cannot be changed by any individual act of will, the issue is still open with regard to whether the fact is socially constructed (i.e. formed by the consensus of the total community of agents) or whether it is a 'hard' fact, possessing a sort of reality that transcends what everyone would agree to be the case.

ANOTHER PROGRAMME OF SOCIAL CONSTRUCTIVISM

There is a programme that is currently being pursued with great vigour within social science, from which it is important to keep our present topic distinct. That programme, too, goes by the name of 'social constructivism', a tag applied by some of the protagonists to themselves, whereas others are so labelled only by their critics. Representatives of this brand of social constructivism are Harry M. Collins and Steve Woolgar in Britain, Bruno Latour and Michel Callon in France, and Karin Knorr-Cetina in Germany.[2]

There are two chief differences between the position of these social constructivists and the one discussed in this essay. First, the 'other' social constructivists – let us call them 'science constructivists' for reasons that will appear directly – have been primarily concerned with the construction of *natural* fact, whereas our present topic is the generation of *social* fact. Second, the generation of (physical) reality is seen as an achievement of (natural) *scientific* knowledge, rather than of our everyday ways of understanding the physical world. Correspondingly, the focus is on the scientific community and on scientific research. The social constructivists we examine in the present work, on the other hand, view social reality as a product of the cognitive efforts of ordinary social agents, not of social scientists. Social constructivism as the topic of our present investigation is more democratic, one could say, whereas the science constructivists are rather elitist. Reality generation is held by them to be the privilege of specialised groups of agents, although it is a crucial point for the science constructivists that in this process of generation, the scientific community is conditioned by various factors of a general societal nature.

There are obvious similarities between the argumentative strategies of the social constructivists examined here and the science constructivists, however; in particular, the science constructivists rely on modes of reasoning that are closely related to what I call the 'Broad Arguments'. This is no cause for surprise, since at least one of the schools to be examined works in both fields; I am referring to ethnomethodology. This means that the science constructivists face the same problems that, as I shall prove, bedevil strong versions of social constructivism, based upon the Broad Arguments. I shall return briefly to these issues in Chapter III.

CONSTRUCTION AND CAUSAL GENERATION

So far, I have characterised the construction of fact as the generation of fact by social consensus, by description, or by conceptualisation. This is a rather meagre characterisation, but nothing better can be given in advance of the detailed examination that makes up the bulk of this book. However, a few further points can be made at this early stage to distinguish this kind of generation from the more familiar causal one.

First, questions about causal generation are purely empirical matters. They pertain to regularities in the patterns of events that may be discovered and expressed in scientific laws. On the other hand, the status of social reality as a social construction is not an empirical discovery, in particular not a discovery based upon observed regularities. It is not as if we have been struck by certain correlations between social facts and certain societally distributed ways of thinking about them or explaining them, and venture the hypothesis that the former must be generated by the latter. The relation between the two is not the same as, say, the relationship between labour's push for higher wages and an ensuing inflation. It would make no sense to prove the former correlation in terms of such technical statistical devices as regression analysis. Second, if the construction thesis is true, it must be true everywhere and always. It would make no sense to speculate that perhaps the relationship between social facts and the way we conceive them holds good in the current decade, but may lapse in the next. But such a concern is always in order with purely causal–empirical regularities; remember the fate of the Phillips curve, which articulates a connection between the rate of change of money wages and the rate of unemployment and which for some time was taken to be one of the long-sought-after laws of social science. It turned out to be merely a trend, which eventually was broken. The construction thesis, if true, tells us something about the nature of social reality as such, something that cannot be changed by social developments.

We are well advised, therefore, not to ask questions about construction that come naturally in the context of causal genera-tion, such as how construction comes about, what are the mechanisms involved, or how long it takes to construct a social fact. To the extent that such questions make sense at all, they will, I hope, be answered by the arguments in favour of the various positions that I shall present later. The import of such queries, however, is radically different from the similarly-worded questions about causal generation. Construction is not a shadowy counter-part to causal generation, with its own mechanisms and its own energies. It is called 'generation' only by virtue of satisfying the minimal common denominator in that notion, i.e. the idea of a process through which a fact comes to prevail at a certain time, prior to which it did not. We may refer, even more neutrally, to a process through which a sentence comes to possess a truth value that it did not previously possess. This is what happens in construction: by virtue of human agreement (and other mechanisms of construction), it comes to be true that, say, a certain piece of metal possesses value, a statement that was not true prior to that agreement. I do not believe that it is possible to characterise construction more fully here, but shall introduce a crucial refinement in Chapter I.

The distinction between construction and causal generation is especially important, since the thesis that belief and agreement generate reality, in a *causal* sense, is hardly in need of defence. This thesis is part of the truistic picture that I presented at the opening of this Introduction. For, of course, the picture of *homo faber*, man as the maker of his world through his actions, shows us only the outside of things. Those external transformations of the world spring from – that is, are caused by – human thoughts, plans, and desires; man transforms the world in accordance with his mental projects. The external activities are just a reflection of these thoughts and plans. Thus, it is a truism that man's thought changes the world – including that part of it consisting of his fellow men's actions – when this is read as a claim about a causal nexus between thought and reality, mediated by human action.

We may, while still not going much beyond truism, add the point that human beliefs will change the world even when they are largely mistaken. In particular, beliefs about social reality are likely to influence social reality in a way in which it matters little whether those beliefs are true or not. If it is generally held that certain individuals are witches, then the fate of these hapless people will be the same as if they really had been witches. To take a slightly different kind of example, if there is a widespread, although completely unfounded, suspicion that a certain presidential candidate will not be able to gather sufficient support, people will not vote for him out of fear of wasting their vote; hence, he will lose the election, although he may be everybody's favourite choice for the job. This is a case of a self-fulfilling prophesy. Such cases bring out the truth of W. I. Thomas's dictum, 'If men define situations as real, they are real in their consequences' (Thomas 1928: 586); Thomas, of course, had *social* situations in mind. But this slogan has only a limited range of validity: the case of the election immediately brings the opposite kind of case to mind, that is, in which voters are so convinced of the victory of a particular candidate that they do not bother to go to the polling place; hence, the favourite loses. This is a self-defeating prophesy. Both kinds of prophesy exemplify the *causal* impact of beliefs about society upon society. They involve causal feed-back loops between the social world and beliefs about it and thus differ from the non-causal connections we shall be dealing with.

PHILOSOPHICAL ISSUES IN CONSTRUCTIVISM

We have seen that the claim that a certain segment of social reality is constructed springs from reflection upon the logical interconnections between the notions of (*social*) *fact*, (*social*) *reality*, *cognition*, *meaning*, *agreement*, and others. The social construction issue is not a purely empirical one, to be adjudicated by experiment or controlled observation. It cannot be solved by investigating the statistical correlation between societal events. Instead, illuminating those interconnections is a task of philosophical analysis. This is not, of course, to imply that it is something to which social scientists are not entitled, only to say that it differs from the purely empirical parts of their endeavours. Indeed, most arguments put forth about this matter are philosophical, although they occur in the writings of social scientists; tacit assumptions of a philosophical nature are even more frequent. In my opinion, these arguments and assumptions are often bad ones, or at least insufficiently worked out. Hence, an important task of the present book will be one of criticism and reconstruction, eliminating invalid arguments for the construction view and providing better formulations of the sounder ones. I shall also try to develop entirely new arguments in favour of the construction view. My aim is to build the strongest possible case for that view and then subject it to critical examination; for a critique of the social construction view will have limited interest unless the version assessed is the most defensible one.

The claim that the construction thesis involves philosophical presuppositions may be controversial. An objection might be that constructivism precisely represents the abnegation of philosophical pretensions in social science – notably the pretension of being able to adjudicate between the rival world views of different societies. Social science is in no position to decide, for instance, whether witches exist, or whether the scientific explanation of diseases in modern Western civilisation is superior to the magical one of preliterate societies. This would call for professional qualifications – *inter alia* philosophical ones – that go beyond those of social scientists and besides would presuppose that social science has some platform outside of any culture from which to adjudicate the claims of diverging cultures. The only tenable policy for social science is to adopt a studied neutrality with respect to those claims; it must consider them all equally true and the things referred to in them equally real. This is all there is to the claim of the 'social construction of reality' – viz. the methodological principle that social science must take all existence claims and other factual claims made inside of a society at face value, at least as long as they are part of a going concern, a functioning practice, in that society.

I do not think this suggestion will do. First, it is doubtful if it genuinely expresses the constructivist stance. The doctrine that (social) reality is socially constructed is often presented (with considerable fanfare) as a substantial insight, and alternative conceptions are rejected as naive. Such attitudes would be inappropriate if the construction thesis were purely methodological. Second, the constructivists underestimate the logical strength of the core notions used to express their position, notably 'true', 'fact', 'real', 'knowledge', etc. These are all absolute notions, in their ordinary use, not relative ones. The idea that there is only one truth and only one reality is not a fiction dreamed up by philosophers, as constructivists are fond of insinuating, but is deeply embedded in these perfectly ordinary notions and their critical function in everyday discourse. Hence, when the social scientist follows the precept of going along with the way a community talks about the world, calling certain things real and others unreal, he faces a dilemma if it turns out that society A declares some kind of thing X to be real, while society B denies this. Apparently, he cannot go along with both societies. The sociologists may try to suggest that, contrary to what is normally believed, 'truth' and 'reality' are not absolute notions, but are implicitly relative to a society; hence, such apparently contradictory claims can be reconciled by saying that X exists in society A but not in society B. However, to articulate a relativist reading of existence claims and to defend it against familiar difficulties is a squarely philosophical task; social constructivism will now have moved beyond an innocuous methodological stance. In any case, the presence of philosophical arguments in the constructivist arsenal is indisputable, as I hope will be clear from the following investigation.

IMPLICATIONS FOR PHILOSOPHY AND THE SOCIAL SCIENCES

The present work is addressed to philosophers of social science and to social scientists. To the former, it offers a demonstration that the fundamental philosophical question concerning the relationship between thought and reality – the question, that is, to what extent reality is independent of the way we conceive it – assumes a somewhat different form when applied to social knowledge rather than physical knowledge. Or perhaps one should say, it assumes different *forms*; for it turns out that not only one but many questions arise about the relationship between social reality and the way we think about it. The overall issue I hint at here is often referred to as the struggle between realists and anti-realists, in the broadest sense. When transferred to the social realm, this debate is seen to be much more multifarious than is normally appreciated and does not fit, for example, the single mould into which Michael Dummett has tried to fit it; nor is it much illuminated by the discussion about the reality of theoretical entities that has been going on in the philosophy of physics. Indeed, the debate is not about the reality of certain entities postulated by science, but of entities known to and considered real by everyday agents. (Or, as couched in the alternative terminology, it is not about the truth of theoretical facts, but about everyday facts.) Moreover, the strongly realist intuitions that most philosophers harbour with respect to physical reality are significantly attenuated in the social field; social reality is somehow felt to be closer to the way we think about it.

Turning now to the social scientists, what can they learn from a book that engages them in a debate about various philosophical problems about existence? The answer is that science, while essentially an empirical enterprise, is always inextricably intertwined with conceptual issues of the kind that, when treated in a sustained fashion, we may refer to as 'philosophical'. Reflections about what is required for something to be a fact, or to be real, are central instances, in social as well as in natural science. Think of the debates about the reality of theoretical constructs in physics and the way they have been integral to the development of particular disciplines, quantum mechanics being the most famous example. As Thomas Kuhn points out, this need for science to ponder its conceptual presuppositions is particularly great in times of foundational crisis. It would be no exaggeration to say that social science, since its inception more than a hundred years ago, has been locked in a perpetual crisis over foundations. This indicates that our investigation is quite called for.

Moreover, as I indicated in the previous section, I believe that many of the social constructivist positions are even more intimately related to philosophical doctrines. At their core, they have certain standard philosophical positions; they are, at least in part, philosophical views presented in a social science dress. This is particularly true with respect to what I call the 'Broad Arguments' below. Since many of these philosophical positions are deeply flawed, it is important that they be criticised from a properly philosophical point of view.

Are there any implications for the practical conduct of social science? I believe the answer is yes. In the first place, the social scientist will be warned of dangers to avoid: taking certain extreme formulations of the constructivist view as guiding tenets would have repercussions on the explanation of the genesis of social agents' beliefs about social reality. In a traditional, realist point of view, we explain agents' beliefs by pointing to an independently existing reality that is held to cause people's beliefs about it, directly or indirectly. In the constructivist point of view this is no longer possible, and we have to find another pedigree for such beliefs. I believe that the constructivist position will lead the researcher into dead ends here, dead ends that I touch upon briefly in discussing Peter Berger and Thomas Luckmann's work in Chapter III. The problem is closely related to the regress problem, which I treat at great length in the following chapters and which in the end forces us to abandon the strong versions of constructivism. This leaves us with other, more moderate versions, one of them being to the effect that the agents' definition of the situation generates social reality by being a *component* of it. This position has methodological implications, too, but this time of a more constructive sort. The chief one is that we cannot do social science without heeding agents' definition of the situation, since to do so would be to fail to come to grips with the social reality in which they live.

The account of social facts I provide in this book is meant to stake out a middle ground between two extremes. I try to avoid, and counteract, the tendency of much constructivist work to make social reality excessively fluid; indeed, to the point (as I show) of threatening to dissolve it altogether. There is a need in social science for a respect for social facts that, although essentially constrained by the way we think about them, still forever transcend our conception. Social facts are 'out there', something we come up against and that we may understand more or less adequately; they do not necessarily coincide with our conception of them. On the other hand, it is equally important to avoid a total assimilation of social fact with natural fact, and to oppose the refusal to differentiate in the methods of scientific investigation applied to either. Social facts are inescapably bound to the way we describe the world of collective human action; this circumstance must be reflected in the methodology of social science. I see 'social constructivism' as a convenient label under which to exhibit and celebrate the distinctiveness of social fact, in particular that which springs from its embodiment of human thoughts, plans and desires. The present work is thus meant to inculcate both a respect for the hardness of social fact and an appreciation of its *sui generis* nature.

OUTLINE OF THE BOOK

In closing this Introduction, I offer a brief outline of the structure of the book. The arguments for the construction view fall into two main groups, which I term *Broad Arguments* and *Narrow Arguments*, respectively. A discussion of the Broad Arguments comprises the first part of the book. These arguments are based upon certain general premises of an idealist nature, to the effect that we generate reality as the object of our cognitive activities. The arguments in principle pertain to natural as well as social fact, which is why I refer to them as being 'broad', but here we examine them only as they apply to the social realm. I go through a number of variations on this common theme and argue that the Broad Arguments and the constructivist positions based upon them are mistaken. A weakness shared by most, although not all, of these arguments is that they do not lead to a constructed reality, but to a failure to get any reality constructed. On the assumptions on which the arguments are based, there is no source from which social reality could ever arise. The construction view, as based on the Broad Arguments, leads to massive non-determinacy of social fact; to put it more plainly, it implies that there is no social reality. I regard this as a *reductio ad absurdum* of those arguments.

The second part of the book deals with the Narrow Arguments, which are premised upon features peculiar to social facts. These would seem to offer a more promising starting-point for the constructivist position and their potential is explored in a number of different lines of argument. Social reality encompasses human actions, which have two crucial characteristics. First, they are 'meaningful', insomuch as they possess an 'inside' made up of the thoughts with which the agent accompanies his external bodily movements. Such thoughts determine the nature of the action and, when conjoined with the actions and thoughts of others, are ultimately determinative of social fact. The significance of the meaningful 'inside' of action is seen particularly clearly in the case of *symbolic* action, whose whole point is precisely that of giving expression to this 'inside' aspect. Second, human actions often assume the patterned and regular forms known as *conventions*; conventional facts are projections and extrapolations from the social practice on which they are based. They are in a true sense social constructions. Thus, the Narrow Arguments succeed in vindicating a constructivist position.

The third and final part of the book treats certain methodological corollaries of the moderate constructivist position defended in Part Two. That position calls for social science to approach social reality through the agents' way of conceiving it, yet it does not impose an individualist–reductionist methodology upon social science. Although certain aspects of the construction view favour the individual-to-society direction in the determination of social fact, considerations will come to light in the course of our investigation that definitely argue against a reduction of constructed social facts to facts about individuals.

Part One
The Broad Arguments

By Broad Arguments, I mean certain loosely related ways of supporting the social constructivist position that bring general idealist lines of reasoning to bear on the narrower issues of social fact. Idealism is the doctrine that human thought creates its object, in any realm of being. The purpose of the Broad Arguments is to show that this holds for social facts as a special case – and how it does so. The detailed arguments are of somewhat varying kinds and are taken from different regions of social science. I shall introduce the different points of view by first presenting an advocacy of the view in question from some social science source and then identifying and elaborating the philosophical roots of that view.

In the present book, social constructivist views are evaluated from a restricted, philosophical angle. Needless to say, the positions examined are not advanced by their proponents primarily as contributions to conceptual analysis, but to social science; in all of them, the metaphysical element is interwoven with empirical theorising and is combined with exploration of a particular corner of the social world. Hence, some injustice is done to those views when we adopt the narrow angle; they will still have interesting theoretical and empirical contributions to make, even though we cast doubt on their conceptual claims. But we have to bypass those contributions in the present context, apart from incidental remarks.

In my treatment of the social science sources of the constructivist positions, I do not aim at surveying all the pertinent literature within each particular school or at presenting the most recent developments. Our purposes are better served by an examination of a few classic statements of the view in question, where the position in question is laid out more clearly than is often the case.

Part One

The Broad Argument

CHAPTER I

Ethnomethodology

The line of reasoning to be examined first is found in its most pronounced form in the writings of social scientists who label themselves *ethnomethodologists*, but may be encountered elsewhere as well. It should be stressed at the outset that ethnomethodology is only a loosely-defined approach; its adherents vary greatly among themselves, *inter alia* in the extent to which a constructivist position is adopted. Here, I examine the most extreme version to be encountered, not only because this is the one that most clearly represents constructivism, but also because it is the one that best safeguards the distinctiveness of ethnomethodology. Weaker versions will be found to overlap with related positions such as symbolic interactionism. But it should be stressed that the position examined is probably not shared by the majority of ethnomethodologists. Its merits lie in the clarity of the position, which is what interests us here, whereas a detailed empirical mapping of the current convictions of social scientists (an opinion poll of the discipline's practitioners, as it were) is not our concern. Those who object to identifying ethnomethodology with this position may simply substitute the phrase 'the radical constructivist wing of ethnomethodology' wherever I write 'ethnomethodology'.

Let me start by listing a few distinctive passages:

> From the member's point of view, a setting presents itself as the objective, recalcitrant theater of his actions. From the analyst's point of view, the presented texture of the scene, *including* its appearance as an objective, recalcitrant order of affairs, is conceived as the accomplishment of member's methods for displaying and detecting the setting's features....
>
> The distinctive features of the alternative perspective, which we offer here, [i.e. ethnomethodology, FC] reside in

the proposal that the objective structures of social activities are to be regarded as the situated, practical accomplishment of the work through and by which the appearance-of-objective-structures is displayed and detected.

(Don Zimmerman and Melvin Pollner 1971: 95, 103)

Thus, the program of inquiry sketched by the preceding remarks does not treat the accounts of patterned action achieved by laymen or professional sociologists as revealing a pattern of events having an existence independent of the accounting practices employed in its 'discovery'. Indeed, that such accounts display the property that they are accounts of independent events is a feature of the phenomenon of members' accounting practices of critical interest to ethno-methodology.

(Don Zimmerman and D. Lawrence Wieder 1971: 293).

Thus, ethnomethodologists view social reality (social fact) as generated by the processes through which social agents think about, describe and account for it, and the consensus they reach about it. This is not just a philosophical appendix to ethnomethodological doctrine, a metaphysical conviction that ethnomethodologists happen to share but which does not interact with the empirical concerns of ethnomethodology; on the contrary, it has direct repercussions upon the research interests of that school. A crucial slogan of ethnomethodologists is that social science must turn something which traditionally has been used as a *resource* into a *topic* of research – namely, the methods through which human beings in everyday situations cognise social events and pass verdict upon them. Mainstream sociology is reproached for relying on unanalysed, everyday methods of action interpretation in establishing its data, typically (for instance) when using the agents themselves as sources of information through questionnaires or interviews. Often, the agents' conception of what goes on is simply appropriated by social science, if perhaps in a slightly tidied-up version, and the actual cognitive work performed by the agent to reach that verdict is made invisible. Mainstream social science is parasitical upon a phenomenon that it ought to treat as an object of study.

It is obvious that this criticism of traditional social science and the recommended reorientation of research are closely linked with the constructivist aspect of ethnomethodology. The minute it is claimed that social facts are generated through agents' cognitive efforts, the investigation of everyday cognitive procedures becomes the paramount concern of social science. The focus of interest naturally shifts from the putative facts, which have been revealed to be derivative and ephemeral, onto the processes through which those facts emerge and the methods that govern them. These methods now become the chief topic of social research. Besides, an examination of those methods will teach us something about the facts generated.

This shift is what the name 'ethnomethodology' is meant to convey. Introduced by Harold Garfinkel in a series of works from the late 1950s and 1960s, including the book *Studies in Ethnomethodology* (1967), it is constructed on the model of such labels as 'ethnobotany' and 'ethnomedicine', which are social anthropologists' terms for the body of native lore in the realms of botany and medicine. Similarly, ethnomethodology is a discipline that examines the general cognitive methods through which 'natives' – ordinary societal agents – understand their world and decide how to manoeuvre through it. Focus is upon practical rationality, the reasoning that sustains decision and action.

Thus, in their research, ethnomethodologists are determined to go beyond traditional concerns of sociology. These are largely seen as pseudo-problems that dissolve once the man-made nature of social reality is appreciated. In particular, ethnomethodologists are critical of traditional sociology's preoccupation with the problem of *order*. This is often termed 'Hobbes's problem', bequeathed by him to all later social science. The problem is this: how do social order and predictability arise out of the actions of thousands or millions of people, of which only a very small part know each other personally and of whom only a small number are in a position to coordinate their actions through explicit agreement? To this question, Hobbes answered, 'Through the dictates and prescriptions of an all-powerful ruler, backed up by the use of force or the threat thereof'. Later social science has adopted other, less bleak answers. Spencer claimed that the more developed societies were ordered through a web of contractual relations between their members. Durkheim criticised this conception, pointing out that the possibility of entering into contracts already presupposes social norms, viz. minimally, norms to the effect that contracts are to be honoured. Contracting cannot be presented as an autonomous foundation of social order. Instead, this distinction goes to shared social norms. Continuing the tradition of Durkheim, such authors as Talcott Parsons have claimed that it is the possession of a system of shared values that generates coordination and stability in society. This remains the preferred solution of modern sociology to the 'problem of order'.

A major influence upon the ethnomethodologists comes from the social metaphysics of Alfred Schutz; yet the ethnomethodologists' attitude to Schutz is not unambiguous. The ethnomethodologists follow Schutz in adopting a 'cognitive' stance in social science, seeing its aim as that of laying bare the cognitive processes through which social agents conceive social reality. For Schutz, these cognitive processes are centred upon the phenomenon of *typification*. The primordial sphere of social reality, as viewed from the perspective of the individual agent, consists of the circle of people with whom he has currently face-to-face contact. In the encounters he has with them both he and they enjoy a full and direct grasp of each other's individuality, apprehended intuitively without any need of conceptual mediation. Outside of this privileged zone, social reality is organised around the subject in circles of diminishing concreteness and sensory vividness the more remote they are from the subject in the dimensions of space, time, or personal commitment. The inhabitants of such more remote regions cannot be grasped in their full individuality, but must be conceived as representatives of general types. These types, or typifying concepts, are generated by abstraction from and the conferring of anonymity on the subject's immediate experiences of the Other in social interaction.

Implicit in Schutz's theory of typification lies an answer to the problem of order. Order in society can be maintained because people relate to each other for the most part, not in the spontaneity of direct face-to-face contact, but in the predictable and controlled manner made possible by typification; it is a case of one type interacting with another, as it were. Type concepts often take on the nature of roles or norms; they dictate how people are to behave in social exchanges, thereby imposing predictability upon social intercourse. Provided that the roles are suitably integrated with each other and mutually agreed upon, typification makes for smooth and harmonious social interaction. Moreover, many social roles fulfil certain social *functions* and thereby further the perpetuation of society in the long term.

The ethnomethodologists reject both the phenomenon of order and the rule-following invoked to account for it, however; they even dismiss Schutz's theory of typification. The order that social science sets out to explain does not exist in the substantive sense in which, for example, Parsonians take it to, nor even in the rather more subjective sense in which phenomenologists such as Schutz understand it. Instead, order is an 'accomplishment' – an artefact resulting from the way we describe and think of society. Here are a few quotations to illustrate the point:

> [I]t would seem that the notion of action-in-accord-with-a-rule is a matter not of compliance or noncompliance per se but of the various ways in which persons satisfy themselves and others concerning what is or is not 'reasonable' compliance in particular situations. Reference to rules might then be seen as a common-sense method of accounting for or making available for talk the orderly features of everyday activities, thereby making out these activities as orderly in some fashion.
>
> (Don Zimmerman 1971: 233).

How can norms or symbols become topics of study? The first step is to suspend the assumption that social conduct is rule governed, or based on and mounted from shared meanings or systems of symbols shared in common. The second step is to observe that the regular, coherent, connected patterns of social life are described and explained in just such terms, or close relatives of them, by laymen and professional sociologists alike. The third step is to treat the appearances of described and explained patterns of orderly social activities as appearances produced, for example, by and through such processes as analyzing an event as an instance of compliance (or noncompliance) with a rule. . . . The ethnomethodologist is not concerned with providing causal explanations of observable regular, patterned, repetitive actions by some kind of analysis of the actor's point of view. He is concerned with how members of society go about the task of seeing, describing and explaining order in the world in which they live. . . .

Once brought under scrutiny, the 'orderly structure' of the social world is no longer available as a topic in its own right (that is, as something to be described and explained) but instead becomes an accomplishment of the accounting practices through and by which it is described and explained.

(Don Zimmerman and D. Lawrence Wieder
1971: 288, 293–4)

This metaphysical stance has direct impact upon the empirical research interests of ethnomethodologists. Ethnomethodologists have been especially attracted to the study of institutions, with an eye to the way such institutions manage to uphold the illusion (as ethnomethodologists see it) of being strictly bound by rules and working procedures. Thus, they have investigated the work that goes on at police stations and probation offices to reduce the complexity of social life to a number of simple legal categories. This work itself must be hid, to make it appear as if social life is inherently ordered and law enforcement practices merely a reflection of that order. Ethnomethodologists have examined the way that coroners produce verdicts concerning the mode of death of the deceased persons who are brought in. There is a great concern that their verdicts should appear incontrovertible and grounded in clear-cut decision procedures, whereas the truth is often quite the opposite. Ethnomethodologists have examined the practices of psychiatric clinics in diagnosing patients and prescribing the proper treatment, again recording the efforts put into creating an appearance of an objective procedure, strictly rational and rule-governed, which infallibly produces an objective diagnosis. The emphasis of ethnomethodological research is always on the way that the order of such institutions is a constructed or 'accomplished' one and that the work of creating this order is not only hid from outsiders, but is somehow made invisible to the participants themselves.

In their empirical work, the unique attitude of ethnomethodologists to the reality-generating powers of negotiated agreement shows itself in the greater attention devoted to the *retrospective* as compared the *prospective* use of rule deliberations and other practical reasoning. That is, ethnomethodologists are not primarily interested in the rule thinking (and rule negotiation) that agents engage in prior to action in order to decide which rule interpretation is to govern the subsequent action; they are not concerned, we might say, with thinking and negotiation as the cause of action. They are more interested in the retrospective deliberations undertaken in order to make sense of an action already performed. Often, such thinking is initiated by others than the author of that action or those otherwise directly involved. Thus, the stress is on rule thinking as used to make sense of social reality, not as the motivational basis of action (Zimmerman and Wieder 1971b). We might describe this as a third-person rather than a first-person approach to social reality and to the problem of order in particular.

Rule thinking creates social order by imposing upon actions already performed a description or classification that makes them out to be regular and rule-governed. Here, the constructivist feature of ethnomethodology is clearly in evidence.

THE ETHNOMETHODOLOGICAL ARGUMENT RECONSTRUCTED

Reconstructing and reorganising the ethnomethodologist position somewhat, and disregarding individual differences among its advocates, we may present that position as resting upon two premises. The first articulates what is called, in ethnomethodological jargon, the *indexicality* of rules, including linguistic rules. Rules are necessarily abstract and always fail to reach all the way down to the individual case. To establish such contact, appeal must be made to concrete, 'situated' features of the instance in question. This process is not in itself rule-governed, which would only raise the very same problems all over again. It is decided on the bases of *ad hoc* judgement – not individual judgement, but collective judgement, arising out of negotiations in the group.

I believe it is illuminating to distinguish between two levels in the first premise of the ethnomethodological argument, representing two different degrees of strength of that premise. The first and weaker level is that the dictates of *normative* social rules are, in the final analysis, a product of agreement between the parties involved. This claim is not very controversial – social rules, such as traffic codes, the house rules of institutions, etc., are normally taken to be largely conventional and hence subject to discretionary decision by the participants. (We shall return to this later in the chapter.) This feature is often manifest in the very wording of legal and other provisions, which may call for persons to take *reasonable* care in handling dangerous substances, to charge only a *fair rate* for their services, or to give *due attention* to the safety of employees. Such formulations clearly leave a gap in the provision, to be closed by discretionary judgement in light of the concrete features of the case. Moreover, it is commonly recognised that even where such linguistic devices are not employed, legal rules and other social norms involve implicit *ceteris paribus* clauses that have the same effect; for instance, motorists are only required to drive on the left side of the road in Great Britain as long as doing so will not place them in immediate danger, as when that lane is occupied by a careering truck. The scope for such *ceteris paribus* clauses is a matter of discretion and negotiated agreement between agents. Legal reasoning is rife with such considerations and with the negotiations they invite.

The second level, on the other hand, is controversial. It emerges when the ethnomethodologists support the first-level claim by pointing to the 'indexicality' and vagueness of *all descriptive terms*, that is, of the semantic rules that define them. All descriptive terms are inherently 'indexical' or 'situated', it is claimed; that is, whether or not they apply to a particular thing or situation always depends upon concrete, local features of the situation and cannot be inferred from some abstract general definition. Thus, there is no way to dispose of this indexicality through more careful and elaborate specification of rules. No amount of detail will bridge the gap between the general rule and its concrete application, as that gap is founded in the very nature of linguistic meaning. Nor is there a way in which the use of a descriptive term can be projected from the sum of previous applications on to the new application, for such projection can always be undertaken in countless different and incompatible ways. Hence, the application of a term or a rule emerges as a creative, *ad hoc* accomplishment in the concrete situation of use, fundamentally unconstrained by general principle or precedent. However, to repeat, this is not to be seen as some act of individual creativity. Ethnomethodologists stress the social character of the application process. The application emerges from a negotiation between the parties involved.

Evidently, this vagueness clings to descriptive terms not only when they are used to formulate normative principles, but even when they are used to describe concrete events. For instance, exactly which acts are prescribed by an ordinance that dictates special precautions in the disposal of toxic waste may be vague because (*inter alia*) of the indexicality of the concepts of 'toxicity' and 'waste'; hence, precisely what acts we must avoid if we want to abide by that ordinance may be subject to negotiation. Obviously, this vagueness is equally present when we try to decide if some action already committed was an act of toxic waste disposal. The decision on this factual matter, too, is subject to negotiation between the parties involved.

It is important to appreciate that the ethnomethodologist claim is not merely a contribution to cognitive psychology, or to the sociology of group decision-making. It does not merely say that the procedure described is how people actually reach a verdict about the dictates of social rules, but makes a point about the *logic of rules* as well, to the effect that there is no other substance to the question of what a rule dictates or how a term applies than the outcome of a process of negotiation. There is no ulterior reality to which that application can be compared, no further court to which it can be appealed and possibly rejected as invalid. The agreement between agents not only fixes the actual application, but even the *correct* application.

The second premise in the ethnomethodological argument is the constructivist premise proper. It says that what is generated by these social negotiations is not just the correct extension of the rule to a new case. Rather, it is a determination, or construction, of the very *reality* to which the rule applies; or, as I should prefer to say, it is a construction of social *fact*. What this further step amounts to is especially clear in the case of semantic rules for descriptive terms. It means that in agreeing that a term T is correctly applied to a concrete object O, the group also establishes the fact that O possesses the property specified by that predicate. That is, agreement between the participants of some social encounter not only fixes what is to count as a correct application of their shared language, but also fixes the facts expressed in that language.[1]

As mentioned, the ethnomethodologists base their view of the negotiated character of action description upon fundamental features of the meaning of linguistic terms. This is where their position enters the borderland between social science and philosophy – more specifically, the philosophy of language. Indeed, references to philosophical semantics are ubiquitous in the works of ethnomethodologists. Not surprisingly, Ludwig Wittgenstein's reflections upon rule-following and meaning in the *Philosophical Investigations* (Wittgenstein 1953) are among the sources from which ethnomethodologists draw.[2] In many ways, ethnomethodological reflections upon rules and semantics read like Wittgenstein's rule-following considerations transposed into an empirical key, as it were, and turned into a topic for social science. Let us cast a brief glance at Wittgenstein's critique of the phenomenon of rule-following.

Before we start, a caveat is in order. I have adopted the reading of Wittgenstein's rule-following argument that was given prominence through Saul Kripke's *Wittgenstein on Rules and Private Language* (Kripke 1982). This interpretation is disputed by other Wittgenstein scholars, who deny that Wittgenstein adopted a 'community-solution' to the problem of correctness; this exegetical issue is likely to remain moot. Fortunately, we are not committed to a canonical interpretation of Wittgenstein here, since we use Wittgensteinian ideas merely as a foil to develop and deepen the ethnomethodological case for social constructivism.

In the *Philosophical Investigations*, sections 185–242, Wittgenstein takes us through a convoluted path of reasoning designed to answer the deceptively innocuous question, 'What is it for someone to follow a rule?' There is in particular one aspect of the notion of rule-following to which any answer to this question must do justice: to wit, the *normative status* of rules. Following a rule means doing that which is *correct* according to the rule. An analysis of the notion of rule-following must make room for a distinction between what a person actually does and what is the correct thing to do, according to a rule that applies to his actions.

To follow a rule is, *inter alia*, to do that which follows from that rule. Now that which follows from a rule is not determined by the rule – i.e. the rule formulations – in a causal sense. When we say that my answer of '1002' follows from the rule of addition as a response to the order 'add 2 to 1000,' we are not saying that the rule of addition, as formulated in terms, say, of counting units along the number axis, causally determines that answer. We are talking about a *logical* determination, with the rule logically fixing the correct answer to the question. Similarly, when we say that it follows from the definition of English geometrical predicates (combined with certain facts about the world) that 'rectangular' is the correct answer to the question, 'What shape is a soccer field?', we are not referring to a causal determination, but to a *semantic* one.

This non-causal determination is not the work of the linguistic signs themselves (the verbal formulae defining 'addition' and 'rectangular', respectively), but of the *meanings* they possess. The linguistic signs are mere noises or scratches on paper and, as such, are inert. But what are these meanings and how do they determine what follows from the meaningful expression? It is not helpful to view them as Platonic entities, existing in some transcendent realm of objective ideas. Even if we grant that such items exist, it is not clear how we interact with them intellectually, nor how they assist us in giving the correct answer to questions like the ones cited above. Nor does it help to construe a meaning as a mental item, a picture in the mind's eye, as such a picture would just be another sign. A sign is no less inert for being painted on the canvas of the mind, as it were, rather than on paper or on a blackboard. Nothing *follows* from a mere sign or symbol, but only from its meaning or interpretation; but then the interpretation cannot be construed as one more sign.

Another suggestion is that what follows from a rule is determined by the sum of its previous applications, when combined with the notion of doing *the same* in the new application as was done in the previous ones. As a matter of fact, this is the way rules are typically learned: one is shown a number of applications and is then told to go on in the same way. So, in a sense, this answer has to be right. However, Wittgenstein admonishes us, we must not misconstrue it; it is not as if there is some independent notion of 'sameness', some Aristotelian essence, dictating what to do when we are told to 'go on in the same way'. It is rather that, as a result of having been exposed to a number of previous applications of a rule, a person simply feels that a certain way of going on is the right one. This way he will dignify with the epithet 'doing the same'. However, the feeling of rightness is prior to the sameness and hence not guided by the latter. It is not as if there is some objective notion of sameness that tells an agent, on any concrete occasion, what constitutes 'doing the *same thing*', which is then the correct way according to the rule in question. It is the other way about: what strikes the agent as the right way is, *eo ipso*, what we call 'doing the *same thing*'.

The conclusion so far is that nothing, no independent instance, guides a person in following a rule. The person just does what strikes him as being right, as a result of the drill through which he learned the rule. However, this seems to threaten the normative status of rules. If action guided by a rule is simply the action that seems right to the agent, it is impossible to criticise an action as being incorrect as assessed by that rule, as long as the agent sincerely strives to abide by it. (Of course, there would still be room for the charge that a person deliberately neglects the dictates of the rule.) So, according to Wittgenstein, the only way we can find a foothold for the normative status of rule-following is by defining correct application as that which the *collectivity* adopts. Only by comparison with what others do can any individual person's action be described as in accord or not in accord with some rule. The correct application is that which conforms with what the community does, whereas the incorrect is the deviant, idiosyncratic one.

This point holds for rules of language as a special case – one in which Wittgenstein himself took particular interest. What counts as a correct use of a term is not determined by an abstract definition, nor fixed by previous applications. Only the agreement of the community lays down the correct use.

Wittgenstein's argument gives us close counterparts to the essential elements of the ethnomethodological position on rule-following, including the following of linguistic rules; all we need to add is the point that the community verdict as to what follows from a rule does not spring from some simple counting of noses, but from some process of negotiation between its members. The ethno-methodologist position adds some sociological detail to the bare bones of Wittgenstein's philosophical account.

The above excursion into Wittgensteinian philosophy was designed to support the 'indexicality' premise of the ethnometho-dological argument. We may be much briefer with the second premise, which at first glance does not appear to need any elaborate philosophical defence. This premise, you will recall, says that what is generated by the negotiation over the application of a semantic rule to a new case is not just the correct extension of the rule. Rather, it is a determination, or construction, of the very *fact* to which the rule applies. Agreement between speakers not only fixes what is to count as a correct application of their shared language, but also fixes the facts expressed in that language. This premise seems simply to spell out certain truistic connections between the notions of 'correct application of a term', 'truth', 'reference', 'fact', and 'reality'. Assume that P is a predicate (a linguistic term), p is the property referred to by this term and O is an object. Now the correct application of P to O is not to be distinguished from O having the property p. From the recognition that a predicate is correctly applied to a thing, we may infer that that thing possesses the property denoted by that predicate. It is one and the same thing for an object to have the property p, and for the predicate P to be correctly applied to that object. What, for instance, could be the difference between admitting that the terms 'jealous' or 'civil servant' apply to a person, and admitting that this person is indeed jealous, or a civil servant? It does not seem possible to drive a wedge between these two specifications. (We shall see shortly, though, that this apparent truism harbours a fatal ambiguity.)

THE ETHNOMETHODOLOGICAL ARGUMENT CRITICISED

I have detailed and reconstructed the ethnomethodological position using an argument inspired by ideas from Wittgenstein's late philosophy. It is now time to present considerations showing that this position, as presented above, is flawed. In fairness to Wittgenstein, we must stress that the constructivist conclusion was not one he himself endorsed. In a pair of characteristically cryptic passages in *Philosophical Investigations* (sections 241–2) Wittgenstein repudiates the suggestion that 'human agreement decides what is true and what is false'. Agreement in verdicts is rather a precondition for the *meaningful* use of language. One reason why Wittgenstein would resist the idealist conclusion, and the argument that led to it above, is evident in his later philosophy: this is his scepticism with respect to the notion of 'fact' and the construal of assertion as 'fact-stating discourse'. In the *Philosophical Investigations*, there is adumbration of the view that assertoric sentences are not defined by any 'correspondence with the facts', but rather by being associated with conditions of correct assertion. When this conception is substituted in the ethnomethodological argument, as this is reconstructed above, the second premise of that argument will become unavailable. The following considerations will show that Wittgenstein was correct in dismissing the argument and its conclusion.[3]

Grant first, for the sake of the argument, the ethnomethodologists' view that definite classification and determinate fact only emerge through a negotiation between the participants in a social encounter. A difficulty immediately becomes apparent: that the parties to a negotiation are in agreement is in itself a social fact. So this fact, too, only becomes determinate once an agreement exists between certain social agents, perhaps not necessarily the same ones, that the exchange between the original parties constituted an agreement. Unfortunately, this second-order agreement itself is in need of an agreement to bestow determinate existence upon it, and so on *ad infinitum*. The result is that social fact becomes utterly and totally indeterminate: since the ethnomethodologist analysis calls for an infinite number of agreements for there to be determinate social facts, and since there is not and could not be such an infinite series of agreements, social facts become totally indeterminate. For most putative facts, there will not even be a ground-level consensus about them – after all, in everyday social life, not much time is wasted on pronouncing upon obvious features of the social setting. Even where such consensus exists, it is not likely to be many-tiered. At some stage – and presumably a quite early one – we reach an agreement that is not certified by a higher-order agreement to the effect that the former agreement is a fact, rendering the former fact indeterminate. From this point, the indeterminacy spreads back downwards, eventually to reach the fact that was the object of the first agreement and making even this ground-level fact indeterminate. The conclusion is that there simply are no determinate social facts. No sentence expressing a social fact may be asserted to be true. If we revert for a moment to talking about social reality, we may express our conclusion by saying that social reality does not exist. For we may plausibly define (social) reality as the sum total of *determinate* (social) facts. If there are no determinate social facts, there is no social reality. This conclusion clearly amounts to a refutation of the position that led to it.

It is crucially important to appreciate that the regress is not brought about by an epistemological problem, i.e. the difficulty of establishing facts with certainty, but by the necessity to fix the meaning of terms; hence, the problem cannot be sidestepped by the observation that, after all, there could hardly be serious doubt as to whether some prevailing attitude in a social group amounted to a consensus or not. The regress does not arise because we need to call in our fellows to back up our individual judgement if we are ever to know anything for certain. Instead, as you will recall, the regress comes about because the meanings of even the plainest descriptive terms, including 'consensus', are held not to be fixed in their application to a new item until the community has agreed that they do or do not so apply. The regress is generated by a consideration of the nature of linguistic meaning, not by a worry over the certainty of our knowledge.

To make plain that our argument does indeed have the force of a *reductio*, we must appreciate the extent of the indeterminacy. No doubt any empirical fact suffers from indeterminacy to some degree, due to the ineradicable vagueness of descriptive terms: there is a thin layer of fuzziness around every empirical fact, as it were. In the case of social fact, this indeterminacy is compounded by another one reflecting the existence of issues about which social agents have simply not made up their minds. Such limited indeterminacy is compatible with there being, for any empirical situation or setting, a large class of sentences that are determinately true or false with reference to it. For instance, it may be a determinate fact that a majority of voters want the current government to step down, without there being a determinate answer as to which government they want in its stead; the people in question have simply not considered the matter. Or, it may be a fact that industrial leaders expect the economy to pick up during the next six months, while there is no determinate fact as to how much they expect unemployment to go down, since they lack the expertise to have any confident opinion upon the matter. Here, however, we are talking about something on an altogether different scale. What follows from the above argument is that for any situation or setting, there is *no* sentence that is determinately true about it and *no* sentence that is determinately false. We cannot tie down social fact at all, not even by declaring that this or that sentence is definitely false. If reality is defined as the sum total of determinate facts, this is as much as to say that there is no social reality at all. Social constructivism will have revealed the social world to be a perfect fiction.

The above argument might seem to be of the quick, logic-chopping kind, and there are several ways in which one might hope to counter it. However, I believe that it can defeat all such defensive manoeuvres. One defence might be to claim that a genuine agreement reached in a face-to-face situation is a privileged sort of interpersonal event, in which the participants are particularly transparent to each other. Alfred Schutz, the grandfather of ethnomethodology and other phenomenological positions, stressed the particular fullness of the experience that social agents possess of each other in the face-to-face situation. He referred to this, rather poetically, as the two persons 'growing older together'. In more technical fashion, one might describe this transparency in terms of David Lewis's concept of 'common knowledge' (Lewis 1969, ch. 2). Whenever two persons, A and B, agree about something in a face-to-face situation, A will know that B agrees with him; will know that B knows that A knows that B agrees with him; will know that B knows that A knows that B knows that A knows that B agrees with him, and so on. B has a corresponding hierarchy of knowledge states. These knowledge states will not all be explicit, of course, but will be implicitly present, since they follow logically from information that is available to each of A and B in the face-to-face situation. Now it might be said that at any level L in this hierarchy, A and B's knowledge of the lower-ranking states, when viewed on the background of the higher level states which have L as their object, amounts to a *tacit agreement* between A and B that the lower level states L1 . . . Ln-1 exist. If A and B both know that alter has a knowledge (belief) that p, both know that alter knows that ego has this belief, and does nothing to change that belief, this might be interpreted as a tacit agreement or consensus that p obtains.

An example: suppose I believe that the ice is safe and that you know about this belief; this knowledge on your part is known to me, and so on. Suppose, furthermore, that you are the local expert on the thickness of the ice, and know that the ice is not safe. If you do nothing to communicate this fact to me in a face-to-face situation in which I air a plan to go ice-skating, I could then afterwards, having got drenched, not just blame you for not warning me about the danger; I could even blame you for having *implicitly endorsed* my belief that the ice was safe. In a face-to-face situation, characterised by the agents' full mutual knowledge of each others' mental content, failure to disagree spells endorsement. The argument can be repeated at each higher level. Thus it might be said that agreement in face-to-face situations has infinite intentional depth, the same kind of depth that Lewis claims to find in language and other social conventions.

Now one may have all sorts of doubts about this argument; one would concern the reality of these complex hierarchical intentional structures postulated by Lewis. However, I shall not pursue this line here. Instead, I want to point out another difficulty. No sane theory of the social generation of reality will endorse the claim that a bare agreement suffices to constitute reality. The agreement must somehow be a qualified one, reached in the proper way and satisfying certain further constraints. If not, we get the corollary warned against in the Introduction, that we could all make ourselves wealthy by arranging a meeting in which we declare in unison that we are, indeed, rich. Clearly, such an agreement must satisfy the trivial condition that it is sincere on the part of the participants, as well as many other conditions concerning the way it is reached. For instance, an agreement must ensue at the end of some kind of investigative procedure – and not just any kind of procedure will do. Gazing into a crystal ball is not good enough; observation of the people concerned and careful interrogation of them is a more promising suggestion.

Clearly, this consideration opens up a regress of another and less benign kind. In the social construction view, there is only a determinate fact concerning any of these subsidiary elements in the original agreement – such as the fact that it was correctly carried out – provided there is a consensus that this was the case. However, this higher-level agreement stands in need of a similar investigation and consensus concerning its credentials, and so on *ad infinitum*. Clearly this new regress cannot be blocked through the Lewisian device. There is no plausibility in claiming that two persons who agree that p is the case (where p expresses a social fact) will thereby implicitly have gone through all the preliminaries to establishing p; that they must, moreover, be agreed that they have done so; that they must implicitly have gone through the procedures to establish the credentials of this agreement, and so on. Indeed, the meaning of these things having been done *implicitly* is not clear.

The last reflection also shows that it will not help to require mere *consonance* in verdicts, instead of *agreement* (i.e. the mutual recognition of such consonance); such a shift would in any case represent a major deviance from ethnomethodology, which stresses the role of negotiations between the people concerned. The point of the modification would be that, although an explicit agreement will not always be forthcoming, there will normally, for any issue, be a consonance of verdicts; at least, this will be so if we do not require a consonance among all the individuals who have a view on the matter, but only a majority of them. Thus, truth would be defined as the majority view on any issue. The problem is that, for reasons we have touched on before, those views have to be arrived at in a *proper manner* – as certified, of course, by a majority opinion, the credentials of which have to be certified in their turn, and so on. We may safely assume that after a few steps down this path we reach a point where nobody has any determinate opinion on the matter any more. For instance, there may be a majority opinion, at a given time, that the world economy is currently in a slump, and there may be a corresponding majority opinion that the former opinion was formed in the proper manner (for example, that it was based upon reliable economical statistics). But it is highly doubtful whether anybody would have any opinion as to whether the latter opinion was based upon proper data, or, if so, whether this new opinion was so based. At any rate, by repeating this question a couple of times, one would soon draw a blank from even the most conscientious observer of society. Thus, social truth is once more rendered indeterminate.

THE THEORY REFINED: INTRODUCING
HYPOTHETICAL AGREEMENT

A critic might object that we have overlooked a way to save the idealist argument. We have established that, if determinate social fact requires actual human agreement (or consonance), then social facts are utterly indeterminate. For the determinateness of social fact requires an infinite series of such agreements. And no such series can exist. However, it might be claimed, the position does not necessarily call for *actual* agreement. All that is required is *hypothetical* agreement; that is, such agreement as *would have occurred* if human beings had taken the matter up for explicit consideration.

A position of this kind has actually been advocated by philosophers of social science, notably (among others) by Jürgen Habermas. In the article 'Wahrheitstheorien' ('Theories of Truth'), Habermas launches an attack upon traditional conceptions of truth and introduces his own alternative, called the *consensus theory* of truth (Habermas 1974). In his formulations of this theory, the hypothetical element is much in evidence – the truth of a statement is said to consist in the *potential* agreement of that statement with those of other individuals. Indeed, Habermas puts such stringent conditions upon the kind of agreement that defines truth and the setting in which it may occur, that it is highly doubtful if such conditions can ever be realised. Habermas actually describes the hypothetical setting in which truth can be attained as rather of the nature of a *regulative ideal* – something towards which actual discussion may strive, but which can never be fully realised.

I do not believe that the social generation view can be saved by this manoeuvre, however. It is highly uncertain that such radically hypothetical assumptions possess a determinate truth value at all, and hence can serve as the basis of determinate social fact. The most potent source of indeterminacy is the difficulty of specifying what counts as ideal conditions for the genuineness of a consensus. The conditions specified by Habermas all revolve around the idea of the equality of the participants to the discussion – they must all have equal chances of having their arguments heard. Habermas is at pains to stress that these equal opportunities are not purely formal ones, but have substantive content. He does not go into detail about this in 'Wahrheitstheorien', but we know from other writings that he considers inequalities in economical conditions, educational background, etc. to be inimical to the equality of participants in a free discussion. Moreover, not all impediments to a person's participation in dialogue are external ones. A person may also be hampered by internal factors, such as neurotic tendencies that impede his rationality. These, too, must be removed in order to achieve a rational, truth-generating dialogue.

I believe that there is simply no *a priori* answer as to which such constraints define rational dialogue and hence bestow the virtue of Truth upon its outcome. Must the participants in a dialogue have undergone psychoanalytic therapy, liberating them from their repressions? Or is the truth rather, as enemies of psychoanalysis will suggest, that the very belief in psychoanalysis is a commitment to irrationality? (The writer Karl Kraus, a contemporary critic of Freud, once wrote that psychoanalysis is the disease for which it claims to be the cure.) How similar must people's social and economic conditions be for them to be fairly matched in a truth-finding discussion? Only a rash man would claim that these questions have firm, *a priori* answers. Still, the consensus theory, and the use of it made here, presuppose that a precise answer can be given.

Habermas's consensus theory of truth embodies an idea that has been a crucial element of Western thinking since the enlightenment – to wit, that human understanding is bound to converge towards agreement once superstition and bias are cleared away. The consensus theory owes its initial attraction to this circumstance. In its hypothetical version, however, it abolishes a crucial component of that view, namely a realist conception of reality. In the enlightenment view, reality is represented as an independent instance against which man can measure his theories, as well as his methods for testing them – his canons of rationality. With reality serving as a touchstone, faulty theories and methods will in due time be weeded away and we shall be guided towards a conception of reality that somehow mirrors that reality. This entire picture collapses, however, once the constructivist view is adopted. All forces that might serve to propel the cognitive process towards convergence must now somehow come from *within* that process, in the form of inherent, *a priori* constraints, since there is no independent reality from which they could spring. Once this is realised, the consensus view loses whatever plausibility it may have (illicitly) gained through its association with the enlightenment view, and we realise that there is no reason to expect the cognitive process to display convergence. That process will come to look to us more like, say, the development of *art*, which we see as taking twists and turns, some of which we may want to designate as 'progressive', but which we do not see as converging towards consensus among artists. This is because we do not (any longer) see art as *representing* an independent reality, which would impose constraints upon it and channel its development in one particular direction.

THE FLAW IN THE CONSTRUCTIVIST ARGUMENT

Above, I have tried to show the untenability of the ethnomethodologist position by a *reductio ad absurdum*. Clearly, such an argument does not in itself pinpoint the flaw in the reasoning that led to the refuted position, nor is this my concern in the present context. However, I would like to offer a reflection on the conditions of using language and to indicate how the idealist argument conflates two kinds of language use.

The ethnomethodologist argument for the social construction of reality was based upon two premises. I want to show that the premises are only true if the core terms in them are read in different ways in each of the two premises, with fatal consequences for the soundness of the argument.

The two premises were as follows:

1. What is commonly agreed to be the correct application of a rule to a particular case, *is* indeed the correct application; there is no higher court of appeal. As a special case, this holds for rules for the use of linguistic terms.
2. In laying down the correct use of a linguistic term on a concrete occasion, we simultaneously establish a fact about the world: that (that segment of) the world possesses the property signified by that term. For any descriptive term 'P', our agreement that 'P' correctly applies to an object O is tantamount to establishing the fact that O is P.

Unfortunately for the ethnomethodologist, the phrase 'laying down the correct use (or application) of a term' is used in different and mutually exclusive senses in the two premises. Hence the soundness of the argument cannot be saved. Remember that, according to the ethnomethodologist position and the Wittgensteinian argument that we used to support it, the correct application of a term is unconstrained by its previous uses as well as by any explicit definitions that might be provided, or by any other symbolic content that the users may associate with that sign. This is as much as to say that the term is *undefined* as far as its use in any novel situation is concerned. What happens, then, when the linguistic community agrees to apply a certain term to an object or situation is that that term *gains semantic determinacy* on a point where it possessed, until then, none. What gets fixed is not a fact about the nature or properties of the thing, but a fact about the meaning of the word applied to it. (Of course, this is sort of a fact about the thing, too, but not the kind for which we were looking.)

Now, the following seems to be a fundamental truth about language: no instance of language use can be one in which some term is being *used* to predicate a property and simultaneously be a *definition* of that term. In the former case, the term is doing some work; in the latter, it occurs in quotation marks, explicitly or implicitly. It is being displayed and operated upon, but is not used to say anything. If you point to a tomato and say, 'This is *red*,' this sentence cannot both serve to define the term 'red' and to impute a property to the tomato (at least not the property *red*); we should add, it cannot serve both purposes with respect to the same audience.

The predicament of the ethnomethodologist argument is this: for the first premise to be true, we have to take the notion of fixing the correct application of a term in the sense of laying down a *definition* of that term. In the examples that ethnomethodologists typically offer us, this takes the form of extensional definition, i.e. definition by providing (or adding to) a list of items falling under the term: through a process of negotiation, agreement is reached that some novel item should be included in the extension of the term. On the other hand, if premise 2 is to be true, the phrase 'correct use of a term' has to be taken in another sense; we are now talking about the correct use of a term that is already defined and thus comes along with a baggage of linguistic meaning.

Thus, for the argument to have true premises, the reference to 'agreeing on the correct use of a term' must be understood in different senses in the two premises. In other words, the argument exploits an ambiguity of terms and is hence invalid.

This shows, by the way, that the abstract characterisation of generation that we adopted in the Introduction needs modification. Generation can only be characterised as the process in which a sentence receives a truth value that it did not possess before, provided that all the expressions occurring in the sentence *already possess a determinate meaning*. Or, more briefly put, generation is the process by which a *meaningful, non-ambiguous, non-vague* sentence receives a truth value it did not possess before.

CHAPTER II

The Cultural Relativity
Argument

The cultural relativity argument might also be termed the social anthropology argument. At the core of the argument is the observation that the ways of men vary endlessly across societies; this is the very fact upon which social anthropology was founded. Social anthropology is the study of *culture*, a concept designed to capture those aspects of human existence that are variable across societies, set over against those features that are biologically fixed and hence constant. In the present argument, we shall focus upon differences in conceptions of rationality in particular: the argument from cultural relativity is essentially an argument based upon the *cultural relativity of standards of rationality.*

In thus moving from ethnomethodology to social anthropology, we also shift our attention from small groups to entire societies. While the ethnomethodological argument represented fact-generation as the work of small groups, the present one sees it as the accomplishment of entire societies. Where the previous argument tried to give substance to the notion of generation by seeing social fact as a function of cognitive group processes, the present one represents it as a function of varying cultural contents, a variance that is itself explicable by reference to social configurations.

THE ARGUMENT PRESENTED

Very crudely put, and subject to refinement in what follows, the cultural relativity argument goes like this: standards and styles of reasoning vary from one culture to another. This variation is a dual one. First, it is a purely ethnographic datum: societies vary in the canons of rationality actually subscribed to, as an empirical fact. Second, it is also a variation at the normative level. Certain norms are *valid* in our culture, but are invalid in another; this is due to the overall differences between the two cultures.

Add a second premise to the effect that rationality is deeply intertwined with our cognition of the world. Most of our thinking is infested with theory, i.e. with abstract assumptions, leaving only a tiny and uninteresting part of our cognition (if any) to deal with pure observations. General principles of rationality must be invoked to decide between different theoretical interpretations of reality. Hence, principles of rationality are involved in most or all human cognition.

Add, finally, a premise to the effect that facts extend as far, but only as far, as the human capacity to establish them. Facts are never transcendent, going beyond man's capacity to know. This is an assumption that defines a philosophical stance of anti-realism, for which there have been powerful arguments in recent Anglo-American philosophy.

When we combine all these premises, they lead to the conclusion that there is no such thing as one common body of social fact, corresponding to a shared human standard of cognition. Instead, there are several bodies of fact, each relative to the standards valid in a particular society. Social fact becomes a function of the identity of the society in question. We might go so far as to say that social fact is a social creation.

Let us add some individuality and detail to this anonymous picture by examining a passage in which a social anthropologist espouses such a view. Mary Douglas writes:

> It is part of our culture to be forced to take aboard the idea that other cultures are rational in the same way as ours. Their organisation of experience is different, their objectives different, their successes and weak points different too.
>
> Relativism is the common enemy of philosophers who are otherwise very much at odds with one another. To avoid its threat of cognitive precariousness, they shore up their theory of knowledge by investing some part of it with certain authority. For some there is fundamental reality in the propositions of logic or in mathematics. For others, the physical world is real and thought is a process of coming to know that real external reality – as if there could be any way of talking about it without preconceiving its constitutive boundaries. . . . The disestablishing anthropologist finds in W.

V. O. Quine a sympathetic philosopher. Quine's whole 'ontic commitment' is to the evolving cognitive scheme itself. This implies a theory of knowledge in which the mind is admitted to be actively creating its universe. An active theory of knowledge fits the needs of a radicalized Durkheimian theory. But active theories of knowledge seem to be especially vulnerable to seduction. Instead of being seen as a process of active organization, knowledge... is taken to be a matter of stubbing a toe on or being bombarded by solid reality or being passively processed by the power of real ideas, a matter of discovering what is there rather than of inventing it.

(Douglas 1975: xvii–xviii)

The commitment to a constructivist position is clear, although one may want to quarrel with the reading of Willard Van Orman Quine, who, after all, adopts a staunchly realist position in certain areas.

Since penning the lines above, Douglas has even more explicitly committed herself to the social constructivist position in a debate of these very passages with John Skorupski (Skorupski 1979a,b; Douglas 1979). Douglas's contribution to this debate is interesting in ways other than as a demonstration of her constructivist leanings, since it goes some way towards identifying the philosophical foundations of her position. Let me mention in passing that Skorupski's reading of Douglas is significantly different from the one I propose here. Whereas Skorupski sees Douglas as concerned to support relativism, using constructivism as a premise, I view her as engaged in the converse project of establishing constructivism on the basis of relativism. Very possibly, both directions are operative at the same time in Douglas's reasoning, which is somewhat fragmentary. Hence, like Skorupski, I believe that the reader is entitled, and indeed forced, to undertake a certain amount of reconstruction of Douglas's text; I shall propose such a reconstruction below. But first, a word about Skorupski's gloss on the argument.

Skorupski makes play with Wittgenstein's epistemological reflections in *On Certainty* (Wittgenstein 1969), especially the notion of 'core sentences'. These are sentences the truth of which we uphold, come what may in the area of experience or abstract critical reasoning. They serve as the fixed points relative to which we describe and explain the rest of our experience; they are points of origin, as it were, in the theoretical system of coordinates we impose upon reality. Now, if these fixed points are differently located in two different world views, embraced by different societies, then so are the entire descriptive systems based upon them; hence, relativism ensues.

Skorupski offers this interpretation of Douglas only as one possibility among others; while Douglas goes along with it to a certain extent in her reply, other passages in her commentary point in rather a different direction. Here is one such passage, in which she is concerned to argue that there are ways of comparing and assessing core sentences across world views:

> I am interested in what can be understood about the grounds for believing and about core statements. There certainly can be judgement from one core as to the value of the other world views, so long as the objectives to which the choice is angled are made explicit. There are plenty of ways of specifying a particular level of technological control and comparing world views on their success in achieving it. Or they could be compared according to the scope for emotional maturity, or for developing the memory or the sense of smell or for other strengths. Comparison between world views poses no specially thorny problem for an anthropologist who is not interested in maintaining one is as good as another. Rather the contrary if anything: I am interested in finding criteria for agreeing, within our world view, that among other core structures some are not as good as others.
>
> (Douglas 1979: 180)

From this passage, it transpires that core statements are not the ultimate ground of a world view, nor hence of the world it creates. Core structures themselves are subject to assessment in the light of certain value standards, be they technological control, emotional maturity, or others.

The view that reality is generated by certain broad, but socially determined and hence variable, canons of collective thought is a familiar theme in recent philosophy. The most celebrated example is Thomas Kuhn's doctrine of 'paradigms' and the claim that partisans of different paradigms 'live in different worlds' (Kuhn 1972: 118), but we encounter the same line in Michel Foucault's thesis that human thought moves within a determinate cognitive framework, an 'episteme', which somehow creates the reality it is about (Foucault 1972). Neither doctrine is compellingly clear, however, and they are of doubtful use in illuminating Douglas's position above. To find a more useful philosophical model, we should turn to Mary Hesse's account of the logic of theory choice, and the role of value standards therein, as presented in *Revolutions and Reconstructions in the Philosophy of Science* (Hesse 1980). I believe it represents a lucid and carefully worked out rendition of the same ideas that are put forward in a somewhat ambiguous way in Douglas's argument. Hence, I shall substitute Hesse's version in the subsequent discussion, trying to determine whether a viable social constructivism can be based upon the relativist position contained therein. I shall first provide a very brief sketch of Hesse's position, to serve as a basis for our investigation.

Hesse starts out by observing that in our current, so-called 'post-positivist' epistemology, theory, including social theory, is now generally conceded to be underdetermined by observation; not just actual observation, but all possible observation. Any body of empirical data will be consistent with a number of different and mutually incompatible theories devised to explain those data. To jump the gap between data and theory, we thus need general principles of theory choice, referred to by Hesse as *coherence conditions*. This is precisely where cultural relativity creeps in, since these coherence conditions will embody culturally specific values and metaphysical commitments. Examples from physics are the Renaissance scientists' penchant for circular motion, or the preference for a cosmology that places man at the centre of the universe.

According to Hesse, the scope for such coherence conditions is especially large in social science, where they are relatively secure against external criticism. In natural science, the facts exert some kind of selective pressure upon the principles of theory choice, although only in the long run, since, if particular principles of selection consistently pick theories that are later falsified, eventually these principles will be discarded. This is what happened to the principles urging us to select theories that depict celestial motion as circular, or that place man at the centre of the universe. Hesse suggests that in social science, it is much harder for data to attain critical mass, so that we shall perhaps never see well-entrenched coherence conditions being overturned; this is due to the familiar obstacles to data collection in social science such as the complexity of the object and the difficulty of performing experiments.

In social science, values thus enjoy considerable autonomy *vis-à-vis* conformity with the data as selection criteria of theories. Imposition of those values becomes an independent goal of science over and above that of prediction and control. Examples of these so-called *value goals* might be the concern for social stability in the face of man's disruptive impulses, a concern so visible in Hobbes and Durkheim, or the contrary call for social change in Marxism. In embracing the legitimacy of such goals in science, Hesse is very close to the position advocated by Mary Douglas, above.

In her presentation of this view, Hesse combines it with substantial borrowings from Habermas's consensus theory of truth. The coherence conditions valid in a particular society are held to be chosen through consensus. Here, I shall disentangle those two lines. If the Habermasian position is adopted, we immediately land in the same predicament in which we found ourselves in the last chapter. That is, we shall be caught in a regress or vicious circle that affects the determinacy of all truth and, hence, renders social reality incurably indeterminate. For the discussion through which coherence conditions emerge is not sufficiently tightly circumscribed by rationality constraints to render the outcome determinate. Hence, the rationality standards will be indeterminate and will transmit their indeterminacy to reality. (I shall argue that we eventually end up in this patch of quicksand anyway. But there is no reason to court immediate disaster by directly following the previous argument.)

What distinguishes the line offered in the preceding chapter from the one suggested here is that, in the latter, the constraints upon theory choice are supposed to be *autonomous* with regard to the modes of thinking available in the society in question, although they are still culture-relative. They are not supposed to be fixed through a discussion, not even a hypothetical one, in the community in question, or by any other cognitive effort by the members of the community. Instead, they are a function of other features of society.

This means that, in order to determine what the (right) principles of theory choice for the society in question are, we do not have to identify the criteria that are actually used in that society, or would be used under specified hypothetical circumstances. There may thus be some divergence between the methods actually adopted and the valid ones (for that particular community). Admittedly, for anti-realism to be consistent, the standards of rationality in question must presumably be recognis*able* for members of the society in question. If not, they become transcendent, thus contradicting the fundamental verificationist axiom of anti-realism. At any particular stage, however, they need not yet be actually recognised, and may indeed by positively misconstrued. In brief, social facts are constructed on the basis of principles of rationality that are somehow *valid for*, but not necessarily *endorsed by*, the society in question. By introducing this distinction, the adherents of the present argument hope to avoid the regress that beset the previous one.

The relativity of rational standards to societies justifies the appellation of a 'social constructivism' to the present position. Anti-realism as such is not a species of constructivism; to say that facts are only determinate to the extent that they are within the compass of human cognition is not to say that facts are generated by human cognition, but merely that all facts are subject to an epistemological constraint: they have to be testable. There should be no temptation to take this to mean that facts are generated by the tests – for the principles of testing are not generated by human cognition in their turn. They are taken to be objective, timeless principles that define what counts as human cognition in the first place. The minute it is granted that canons of rationality are relative to human societies, however, it becomes natural to say that facts are socially generated, although perhaps in a somewhat attenuated sense. The canons are now no longer purely external to human or social activity, but are somehow a function of the nature of particular societies. Thus, we are allowed to say that social reality is a social construction.

A PRIMA FACIE OBJECTION TO THE ARGUMENT

Before we move on, we must clear away a prima facie objection. The argument we have just examined reaches its constructivist conclusion via a relativist assumption, to the effect that protagonists of different canons of rationality live in different worlds. As a matter of fact, many social constructivists see some independent attraction in that view, which undermines absolutist pretensions (cf. Mary Douglas's remarks above). Still, that view creates insuperable difficulties. Evidently, members of different societies may engage in dispute about the relative merits of their world views. In which reality does this encounter take place? How can the parties communicate, if they are placed in different worlds? And how can the different realities fail to constitute one, overarching world, thereby giving the lie to the notion of different worlds (cf. Trigg 1985: 72)?

The constructivist may object that the critic puts an unbearably naive interpretation upon his view here. The different worlds are conceived as rather like different islands in an archipelago, the inhabitants of which are too far apart to establish contact. But this is clearly not the way his doctrine is meant, the constructivist will insist. And we may grant that it is not. But the constructivist owes us a positive account of how we are to take his theory. A suspicion may grow that it is just a metaphor, one that cannot be given any coherent literal reading.

I believe that the best strategy for the social constructivist is to adopt a *relationist* construal of his relativist premise. Normally, claims that some properties of things are relative to certain other things do not create difficulties. We are not puzzled to be told that an individual is heavy as compared to an average person, but is still light as compared to a hippopotamus. In particular, we do not feel forced to conclude that the individual in question leads a double life as a denizen of two worlds, one of his incarnations being light and the other heavy. The constructivist's relativist claim may be understood in a similar manner: as referred to the rationality standards valid in one society, the (social) world is such-and-such, in terms of the standards of another, it is different. This is not to say that members of either society live in different worlds, but merely that they view it from different cognitive perspectives. They are like people who observe the same landscape from different mountain peaks.

It seems that relativism of rationality, and the social constructivist position that is built upon it, can survive the first clash with a standard counter-argument. From the point of view of the cultural relativity argument, however, it is not enough to show that relativity is philosophically coherent; societies must be shown to be actually different. Here we touch upon a classic dispute in social anthropology concerning the proper way to characterise the difference between traditional and modern thought. Do natives really differ from us in rationality, or do they actually employ the same canons of rationality as we do, only on the basis of a sparser body of data? Or, are the natives in a different line of business altogether, for which our concepts of rationality are simply irrelevant? This question has been the source of intense dissension in anthropology and we cannot omit a brief discussion.

THE CONCEPT OF RATIONALITY IN ANTHROPOLOGY

The history of social anthropology has witnessed a steady evolution in the attitudes of its practitioners on the topic of rationality. There has been a constant movement away from ethnocentrism and towards a more universalist perspective. By and large, this change has been motivated by concerns that are not directly relevant to our present subject, namely a strongly egalitarian attitude. Non-universalist interpretations have normally taken a highly invidious stance towards native patterns of thought, dismissing them as somehow inferior. This way of construing the issue will be echoed in my presentation of the opposing views below. However, the normative aspect is irrelevant to present concerns: here, it is the bare fact of a difference in rationality that matters, not whether the difference can be viewed as a question of superior or inferior.

Anthropology started out with strongly ethnocentristic attitudes. In the works of Tylor, 'the father of anthropology', and his fellow Victorian anthropologists, natives are assessed as deeply irrational. Tylor and contemporaries such as Frazer adopted what later came to be called an 'intellectualist' interpretation of the dominant native mode of thought, that is, *magic*, construing it as primitive science or technology, a way of understanding and controlling reality. Viewed in this way, native beliefs must be deemed irrational, since they are not based upon the systematic collection of evidence that is the hallmark of science. Rather, they spring from haphazard generalisation and analogical thinking. As a consequence, native 'laws of nature' are largely false, as is strikingly illustrated by magical thinking.

A generation later, this view was given more precise, but also more balanced expression, by Evans-Pritchard. In his celebrated studies of the Azande, Evans-Pritchard (1937) makes a point of showing that native beliefs are not illogical (as had been claimed by Lévy-Bruhl). Still, they are unscientific and, hence, irrational, since they deal in explanatory agencies – gods and spirits – that in principle escape empirical detection. Evans-Pritchard improves upon the Victorians in two respects: he stresses that the verdict of inferior rationality applies to native ways as *collective*, not as individual phenomena. The individual native is no less rational than the modern European, since both acquire their beliefs in the same way, namely by giving credence to what is believed in the society around them. The native is as rational in accepting magic as the modern European in accepting theoretical physics, since neither is in a position to assess his intellectual heritage critically. Second, Evans-Pritchard stresses that the native ways often have practical validity; their major deficiency is *theoretical* explanation.

A revolt against the 'intellectualist' picture was instigated by the 'symbolists', including Edmund Leach and others who were building upon Durkheimian ideas. According to the symbolists, it is an ethnocentric mistake to see magic and the lore that supports it as satisfying an explanatory urge, or, derivatively, as serving practical ends. Instead, it is *symbolic* – it aims at somehow *representing* reality, in particular social reality. The intricately related cohorts of gods and spirits that occur in native lore should not be taken as descriptions of a distinct ontological realm, but give metaphorical expression to mundane social facts instead: the interrelationship of the different castes, the intricacies and conflicts of kinship ties, the mutual relations between the sexes, and so on. Moreover, 'expression' should not be taken in a purely referential sense here; rather, it is a case of indicating *allegiance* to or *affirmation* of the reality represented.

The symbolist interpretation embodies an implicit answer to the question of rationality. To the extent that their orientation to reality is predominantly symbolic, natives do indeed differ from us in rationality. Although the symbolic attitude is far from unknown in modern industrial society – after all, we do engage in symbolic celebrations of all sorts on national or religious holidays – it is distinctly subordinated to more practical attitudes. Thus, the natives are different, but not inferior, in rationality: the symbolist interpretation makes it possible to maintain that the natives are simply doing something else and hence are not to be judged by the same standards. In this way, the interests of equality are served.

Among philosophers, a slightly different reinterpretation of magic has been advanced by Peter Winch. According to Winch (1964), it is a mistake to see native magic as directed towards practical goals. Magic is not a different way to control reality than that of science – it is not an instrument of control at all. Instead, it is a way to come to terms with reality; man accommodates himself to reality rather than the other way around, as is characteristic of science. Magic is a way of divining what the powers that be have in store for one, in order to accept the verdict. It does not involve the idea of trying to change the order of things, but instead to acquiesce in it. In this, Winch claims, it is much closer to a religious attitude, in particular to the institution of *prayer*. Prayer is not a method of influencing or manipulating the deity, indeed this very thought is slightly blasphemous. Instead, it expresses acquiescence in the divine decision.

Matters have been taken one step further by Charles Taylor. Taylor (1982) believes a residual ethnocentrism is found in Winch's insistence on a sharp division between magic and practical modes of thinking. True, this is the way the two look to us today, as viewed from the vantage point of a society in which practical, manipulative thinking has come to exist in a pure form. In primitive societies this is not yet the case, however: natives simply do not possess, in theory or in practice, the distinction between the two modes of thought. Instead, magical thinking is symbolic thinking *and* practical thinking rolled into one; it is the activity of simultaneously influencing the world and expressing an attitude to it, doing one by means of the other.

Both Winch's and Taylor's construals of native thinking support the idea that the natives operate a different system of rationality. The notion of means–end rationality either plays a much smaller role in native society than in modern industrial ones (Winch), or occurs in a state of conceptual fusion with the notion of symbolic action (Taylor).

Robin Horton has pointed to another difference between the native and the modern mind, in part as a corrective to the above picture. Horton[4] writes on the basis of a more sophisticated conception of scientific method than Taylor and Evans-Pritchard, according to which it is precisely characteristic of science to postulate entities that cannot be directly experienced; in this respect, the world of native gods and spirits has a standing similar to that of subatomic particles. As a matter of fact, this feature points precisely to their common function, which is to provide explanation and prediction of observable events. But this leads on to the true difference between natives and modern Westerners – that is, the differential awareness of alternatives to one's current ways of thinking. Awareness of alternatives is acute in modern man, since he knows that his current theories are just a stage in a historical process; moreover, at any given time, numerous rival theories compete for his favour. Traditional thought, on the other hand, knows only one interpretation of reality, to which it is deeply committed. From these two basic intellectual stances, which he dubs the *open* and the *closed predicament*, respectively, Horton deduces the familiar surface differences of traditional and modern thought. The magical, symbolic character of native thinking reflects the identification of word and object that is inescapable as long as only one framework for describing the world is available. The object and its name become fused, whence the idea comes naturally that you can manipulate the former by manipulating the latter; here lies the roots of magical symbolism. The characteristic patience of native thought with inconsistency and incoherence, and the lack of urge to find a superior understanding, become understandable, too, in their contrast to modern thought with its constant willingness to question established dogma and replace it with something better. As long as one is immersed in a single conceptual framework, one cannot radically question that framework; to do so would be to invite intellectual chaos and is bound to provoke highly emotional reactions. These are what we know as *taboos*.

Summing up, at least a fair case seems to exist for the claim that modern and native societies do indeed differ in their concepts of rationality, which is all we need in the present context. With this result, we secure the last premise of our philosophical reconstrual of a version of social constructivism, based upon the relativity of rationality. It is a version that is recognisably similar to suggestions actually made by such anthropologists as Mary Douglas, while avoiding the most obvious standard counter-arguments to which such suggestions are vulnerable. It is time now for a somewhat more exacting assessment of the argument.

ASSESSING THE CULTURAL RELATIVITY ARGUMENT

There are two ways to go about the task of assessment, one of which is to develop more sophisticated variants of the standard objections of the kind we examined above. I believe that such a strategy would ultimately prevail. In particular, I suspect that the relationist construal of relativism will not survive close scrutiny. In the uncontroversial examples of relational facts upon which this construal is modelled, the items related are not themselves thoughts or cognitions, but, for example, particulars about the observers' motion or location, when they describe the motion or position of other things; these are features that are themselves solidly non-cognitive. In the present proposal, on the other hand, facts are made relative to features of the very intellectual process through which they are cognised, namely the canons of rationality invoked. Thus we are not dealing with a cognition with a relational *object*, but with a cognition that is *itself* relative. This invites all the doubts about such a construal back in again.

However, to explore fully such arguments would call for very extended epistemological and semantic investigations, leading far beyond the topic and scope of this essay.[5] Hence, I shall adopt a second angle of attack, choosing a simpler argument that is closer to the concerns of the social anthropologist. I shall develop the argument by first considering a version that is open to rebuttal and then present a more sophisticated and complicated version that is not.

The simple version is as follows: cultural relativism claims not only that rational standards vary across societies, along with other elements of culture, but that they vary *as a function* of traits of those societies. These traits might for instance be socio-political organisation; different standards of rationality would apply in a tribal society based on kinship relations than in one built upon abstract social relationships, such as explicitly-defined legal rights, membership of political parties or special-interest organisations. Alternatively, rationality might be a function of the developmental stage of the means of production. Rationality canons valid in agricultural and rural societies will then differ from those in capitalist, industrial ones.

However (the simple version continues), this relativist position is vulnerable to the objection that there is no fact as to which developmental stage a given society occupies, so long as the social facts constituting that society are not yet fixed. Social facts are claimed to be generated through communal cognitive and symbolic processes embodying differential standards of rationality; these standards, in their turn, are a function of certain features of the societies in question. But the latter features, being themselves part of social reality, have no determinate nature prior to the constitutive process through which social reality is generated; that process, however, is totally unconstrained until the rationality canons governing it are fixed through features of social reality. Once more, constructivist reasoning is caught in a circle, or regress. Certain cognitive communal processes are supposed to generate social reality, while in their turn being constrained or determined by that reality. There is no hope that determinate social fact can ever emerge from this circle.

As indicated, this objection can be countered. It is not obviously true that the rationality-fixing features of a society cannot be identified independently of a full description of that society, including features that only emerge through social construction. Although the argument from relativity of rationality covers natural as well as social fact, we are really only interested in its application to the social sphere. We could simply make this restriction explicit and allow physical facts to enjoy an autonomous, non-relativist existence. Such a restriction would not be completely *ad hoc*, since it corresponds to an intuition about the differential degrees of autonomy of the physical and the social sphere. Given this modification of the argument, the 'hardware' of a society may now be allowed to exist independently of construction; if, for instance, a Marxist position is adopted, it will be possible to identify the features on which rationality is supposed to depend, namely the machines and tools that define a particular mode of production. The horse-driven plough will identify the feudal nature of society as effectively as the cotton gin and the assembly line will signal an industrial society and, in the process, fixing the character of the corresponding rationality concepts. Admittedly, the mere presence of these items is not enough; it must be established that they can actually be put to productive use. Here again, however, this seems to be open to determination prior to social construction. The sight of a rich harvest in the field or of a batch of shiny cars rolling out from the assembly line testifies that people know how to use the hardware. But no particular social concepts need to be applied, such as (for instance) those specifying the ownership of the means of production.

The argument can be repeated for the other dimension of rationality, the open/closed predicament introduced by Horton. In *The Domestication of the Savage Mind* (1977), Jack Goody argues convincingly that the difference between the open and closed mentality, and the historical development from one to the other, hangs essentially on the appearance of the printing press and the book. The critical attitude and willingness to consider alternatives that is characteristic of the open predicament presupposes that the rival options can be fixed in a medium different from, and more capacious than, memory. This is where the printing press and its products come in. It would seem possible to establish the fact that books are found in a given civilisation and are used productively, without first establishing any social facts – in the strict sense involving intentionality – about that society. For instance, the contents of the books, and the nature of the discussion conducted with their assistance, would not have to be fixed at this stage, but would rather depend upon the identification of the proper standards of rationality for their own fixation.

However, while this rejoinder may be effective against the objection as its stands, a little modification will render it powerless. We must take into consideration the fact, often overlooked by philosophers who engage in speculative anthropology, that societies do not come neatly labelled as representatives of well-defined types, nor packaged into clearly separated units, temporally and geographically. Historically, one societal form will melt imperceptibly into another; moreover, anthropology provides many examples in which, through various historical accidents, two different societal forms exist simultaneously, although normally they succeed each other as stages of a historical development. (For a pertinent discussion, see Gellner 1968.)

The challenge to the above counter-argument should be obvious. That argument presupposes that there will always be a fact, in the historical case, as to *precisely* when a society ceases to be, say, feudal, and enters into the industrial stage, whereupon the standards of rationality change abruptly. Similarly, in the anthropological case, there has to be a *precise* answer concerning which mode of rationality a given society is committed to – even a society that combines, for example, basic tribal features with elements borrowed from modern industrial societies, such as large-scale use of advanced technology or medicine. There cannot be allowed a grey zone, or transitional period, in which neither the one nor the other is dominant. In such a grey zone, there would be no answer as to which canon of rationality is valid and hence defines social facts; thus, there would be no determinate answer as to what those facts were. The social world, once more, would become utterly indeterminate.

To insist that such precise answers must always be available just strains credulity, however. Developing countries often present a striking syncretism in combining archaic and modern elements; sober observers of our own society might say that the same point is illustrated by the way that religious and semi-magical practices exist side by side with science and technology. Is it to be supposed that clear, determinate answers exist as to whether such societies are to be classified as tribal/traditional or industrial/modern, with correspondingly determinate answers concerning which principles of rationality are valid in such societies – those of the previous societal stage, or of the one to come, or perhaps a third one? This is hardly credible.

It will not do to object that this is just the familiar problem of the vagueness of classifying terms, for which there is a similarly familiar remedy: we just draw a sharp line as the need arises. But who are 'we'? Are 'we' the author and readers of the present book and others with an interest in the foundations of social science? Hardly – this group of people is not likely ever to congregate to pronounce upon the epochal division of a particular historical process. It would be far more plausible to say that the privilege of drawing lines in the historical continuum falls to the people involved in the transition in question. They are in the best position to decide when a societal form has ceased to exist and a new one arisen in its place. Unfortunately, this suggestion suffers from the problems besetting the ethnomethodological position, which the argument from relativity of rationality was precisely designed to avoid. The consensus in a society that an epoch has come to an end and a new one has emerged is very much a *social* phenomenon; it is something going on *within* the society under examination. Hence, it is not a brute fact, but is constructed on the basis of certain principles of rationality, commensurate with the stage of development of the society. But *ex hypothesi*, this stage can only be identified on the basis of the social agents' own sense of historical continuity and change. Once again, we have a vicious circle, with two things mutually relying on each other for determination and total indeterminacy as the result.

The situation cannot be saved by suggesting that the conceptions of rationality that are valid in such transitional societies may themselves be hybrids between the pure forms, for the pure forms are often mutually antagonistic in a way that precludes hybridisation. There is no compromise between magic, which sees symbolic representation as a mode of affecting things, and scientific rationality, which considers pure representation as powerless. It is no accident that the relationship between religious and scientific modes of thought in our culture has been one of intense rivalry and, at one stage, of open hostility and persecution. Today, where scientific thinking has emerged victorious, its attitude to its opponent is one of benign neglect. No compromise or hybridisation has taken place.

In other words, when the romantic fiction of societies as discrete, homogeneous entities is given up, the idea of a unique fit between social units and (discrete and incompatible) standards of rationality must be abandoned as well. Once we see societies no longer as smoothly functioning organisms, clearly separated from each other and from their surroundings, but rather as the outcome of historical *bricolage*, societies constantly borrowing from and otherwise interacting with their neighbours, we are immunised against this misconception.

But this means that the notion of a construction of social fact, based upon the argument from relativism of rationality, must also be rejected. That argument will not survive the realisation that societies are permanently in transition, forever located somewhere in between those 'pure types' that are the only ones for which the suggestion of an *a priori* linkage between societal type and rationality makes sense. For such transitional societies, there is no determinate canon of rationality that can be identified *a priori* as the one fixing the reality-generating cognitive processes going on in them. The price of applying the argument from the relativity of rationality is, once more, the utter indeterminacy of social reality.

It is important to appreciate the magnitude of the resulting indeterminacy. Otherwise, a critic might suggest that the constructivist is right: when societies are in transition, social reality *is* indeed in a state of indeterminacy and flux. But while this may hold for such global, institutional features as, for instance, the political or legal structure of a society in metamorphosis – think of Russia after the collapse of the Soviet system – it certainly will not hold for simple aggregative social facts such as, for instance, that 45 per cent of the population believe that they are better off than before the upheaval, or that 1 per cent of males under 30 years of age have emigrated. In the present argument, all such concrete facts partake fully of the indeterminacy. Not only will global social institutions disappear, concrete statistical facts will as well.

The outcome is that if social fact is generated by applying certain autonomous, although relative, coherence conditions (standards of rationality) to bodies of non-social data, then social facts are once again rendered radically indeterminate. We are in the same predicament as before: social constructivism lacks a non-constructed basis from which social reality can arise. Instead, it leaves social reality completely free-floating and indeterminate. This constitutes a refutation of the version of social constructivism that is based upon the relativity of rationality.

CHAPTER III

Social Constructivism and the Sociology of Knowledge: Berger and Luckmann

There are social scientists who combine the basic commitments of constructivism with a doctrine that might seem to draw the teeth of the refutations adduced in the two previous chapters. The resultant position is a version of the sociology of knowledge that claims that we can explain human knowledge in social terms. Such a doctrine purports to show whence the determinacy of knowledge derives: human knowledge is *causally* determined by various social factors. Hence, human knowledge, including that commanding communal agreement or consensus, is not dependent for its determinate content upon some infinite hierarchy of negotiated agreements, nor is it fixed by standards of rationality that are themselves relative to the social settings in which knowledge evolves. Instead, determinacy is derived from certain laws specifying the *causal*, social determination of cognitive processes. Such laws spell out how social cognition is a product of certain other factors, such as class interests, or the power structure of the group.

The italicised words are crucial lest we miss the difference between the position we are about to examine here and the one treated in the previous chapter. There, we discussed the view that (social) reality is constructed (i.e. generated in a non-causal manner) within each community in the sense of emanating from standards of truth, reality and rationality that differ from one community to another, each set of standards being distinctive of a given community. The alleged correlation between a community and a specific set of standards was a highly abstract one that did not imply that the standards associated with each society were necessarily embraced in that society. In a rather speculative (and somewhat highhanded) fashion, the possibility was left open that the standards of truth and rationality appropriate to a society at any particular stage of its development might diverge from and be at variance with the standards actually endorsed in that society – a theme familiar from social theorising in the Hegelian and Marxian tradition where it is expressed in terms of the concept of *ideology*. The present chapter, on the other hand, is concerned with those constructivist theories that maintain that social reality is generated by the actual and empirically ascertainable habits of thought prevalent in a given society; and these, in turn, are claimed to be fixed through being the causal product of certain other aspects of social reality.

I shall address this view by examining the most celebrated text in the social constructivist tradition, namely Peter Berger and Thomas Luckmann's *The Social Construction of Reality* (1967). This book is distinguished by its attempt to combine constructivism with a sociology-of-knowledge stance. Social reality is claimed to be a human construction; but conversely, man and his habits of thought are said to be shaped by social factors. Berger and Luckmann put it succinctly: '*Society is a human product. Society is an objective reality. Man is a social product*' (ibid.: 79, authors' italics).

On the constructivist side, the book presents an argument that combines several distinct strands of reasoning, all of them familiar from our present exposition in which a separate chapter has been devoted to each. One such strand is the argument from cultural relativity, which we examined in the previous chapter. Another is the phenomenological argument, which will be introduced, in a significantly less radical version, in Part Two. Berger and Luckmann were deeply influenced by the phenomenological thinking of Alfred Schutz and his doctrine of 'multiple realities', such as are constituted by the different attitudes which agents may adopt to their experiences. Strong affinities with the argument from convention (also to be assessed in Part Two) are exemplified too in the two authors' account of the genesis of institutionalisation. They show how humans create social institutions as their iterated and typified social actions gradually congeal into a fixed form, supported by a sense that this form is somehow mandatory.

On the sociology-of-knowledge side, there are extensive borrowings from the Marxist tradition. Berger and Luckmann operate with a distinction reminiscent of the Marxian duality of substructure and superstructure, with the former comprising the fundamental economic features of human society, the latter its legal and political system as well as the intellectual and cultural life of society. According to Marx, the former factors largely determine the latter.

Berger and Luckmann accept this general framework, but soften it to accommodate the fact that two-way determination obtains here: social reality indeed determines man; but man also determines social reality.

I shall argue in this chapter that the combination of social constructivism and the sociological determinism expounded in Marxism and other sociologies of knowledge does not resolve the problems of the former, but rather throws the problem of determinacy into stark relief.

THE SOCIAL CONSTRUCTION OF REALITY INTERPRETED

Before we go on, however, a few exegetical remarks on *The Social Construction of Reality* are called for. This book is a bible for social constructivists and has given this school of social science its name. Yet, surprisingly, a close scrutiny of the book reveals that its commitment to constructivism is not unequivocal. A crucial source of ambiguity lies in the fact that, early in the book, the authors present a disclaimer that might seem to render their account of the nature of social reality irrelevant to the entire issue as defined here. On page 13, they write as follows.

> What is real? How is one to know? These are among the most ancient questions not only of philosophical inquiry proper, but of human thought as such.... It is, therefore, important that we clarify at the beginning the sense in which we use these terms in the context of sociology, and that we immediately disclaim any pretension to the effect that sociology has an answer to these ancient philosophical preoccupations.
>
> If we were going to be meticulous in the ensuing argument, we would put quotation marks around the two aforementioned terms ['reality' and 'knowledge': FC] every time we used them, but this would be stylistically awkward. To speak of quotation marks, however, may give a clue to the peculiar manner in which these terms appear in a sociological context.... the philosopher is driven to decide where the quotation marks are in order and where they may safely be omitted, that is, to differentiate between valid and invalid assertions about the world. This the sociologist cannot

possibly do. Logically, if not stylistically, he is stuck with the quotation marks....

It is our contention, then, that the sociology of knowledge must concern itself with whatever passes for 'knowledge' in a society, regardless of the ultimate validity or invalidity (by whatever criteria) of such 'knowledge'. And in so far as all human 'knowledge' is developed, transmitted and maintained in social situations, the sociology of knowledge must seek to understand the processes by which this is done in such a way that a taken-for-granted 'reality' congeals for the man in the street. In other words, we contend that the sociology of knowledge is concerned with the analysis of the social construction of reality.

In these passages, Berger and Luckmann take their stand on a controversial issue within the sociology of knowledge, namely the scope of this discipline. Some sociologists of knowledge (among them Karl Mannheim) insist that sociology can do no more than explain human error, that is, such deviations from right thinking as are brought about by distorting societal factors; Marx held that natural science and mathematics were immune to the influence of social determination in virtue of their methodological rigour. This approach makes it incumbent upon sociology to decide, somehow, which views are erroneous or irrational and which are not, so that the appropriate method of explanation may be applied to each. (Of course, any such decision might emerge as a result of the discovery that the views in question invite a certain kind of explanation, more precisely, sociological explanation). In declaring that the sociology of knowledge should treat impartially everything that is accepted as knowledge in a given society, Berger and Luckmann reject this position. The implication is clearly that sociology of knowledge must explain all bodies of doctrine, and must do so in a non-discriminatory manner.

Thus sociologists of knowledge are urged to regard all socially endorsed knowledge claims as being on a par, and to consider all occurrences of such terms as 'knowledge', 'fact', 'truth' and 'reality', encountered in the course of their investigation, as coming furnished with invisible quotation marks. However, in setting out this principle, Berger and Luckmann render their views irrelevant to the discussion we are engaged in here, if we take their claim at face value. For the view we are examining is precisely none other than the claim that societal cognitions create social *fact*, not merely social 'fact' – i.e. what is *believed* to be fact. Indeed, the alternative view hardly deserves consideration, since it is a tautology that social consensus determines what is believed to be a fact in society. After all, 'social consensus' is merely a synonym for 'what is universally believed to be a fact in society'; hence, it is obvious that the one 'determines' the other.

Still, I think it correct to classify Berger and Luckmann as social constructivists. Later in their book, the authors make statements that seem to indicate that their initial deferential remarks about philosophy were somewhat disingenuous. Once having discarded the quotation marks (allegedly as a purely stylistic measure) the two authors frequently express positions that only make sense if we take the absence of quotation marks at face value. For example, they write:

> [A] psychological theory positing demoniacal possession is unlikely to be adequate in interpreting the identity problems of middleclass, Jewish intellectuals in New York City. These people simply do not have an identity capable of producing phenomena that could be so interpreted. The demons, if such there are, seem to avoid them. On the other hand, psychoanalysis is unlikely to be adequate for the interpretation of identity problems in rural Haiti, while some sort of Voudun psychology might supply interpretive schemes with a high degree of empirical accuracy. The two psychologies demonstrate their empirical adequacy by their applicability in therapy, but neither thereby demonstrates the ontological status of its categories. Neither the Voudun gods nor libidinal energy may exist outside the world defined in the respective social contexts. But in these contexts they do exist by virtue of social definition and are internalized as realities in the course of socialization. Rural Haitians *are* possessed and New York intellectuals *are* neurotic. Possession and neurosis are thus constituents of both objective and subjective reality *in these contexts*. This reality is empirically available in everyday life. The respective psychological theories are empirically adequate in precisely the same sense. The problem of whether or how psychological theories could be developed to transcend this socio-historical relativity need not concern us here.
>
> (Berger and Luckmann 1967: 197–98, authors' italics)

This passage is hardly a paradigm of philosophical lucidity; but it does seem to assert the existence of both Voudun demons and neuroses, though granting each reality only within its particular social context. Such ascriptions of existence, however, would be perfectly tautological, and the emphases in the text utterly redundant, were the authors to stick to their declared policy of using 'real' and 'exist' with invisible quotation marks. The assertions would be very circuitous ways of saying that members of different cultures hold different beliefs. Instead, what is offered here, I think, is genuine cultural relativism, not sociology-of-knowledge neutralism (cf. p. 17). It is important to keep the difference between those two stances firmly in focus. Often, writers in the constructivist tradition move directly from the observation that the sociology of knowledge must be neutral about the truth value of the cognitive systems under scrutiny, to the conclusion that these systems are all equally true, from the sociological vantage point, and the items they comprise equally real. However, to say that they are 'equally true' can only mean that their truth values are equally in abeyance.

The ontological relativism of *The Social Construction of Reality* becomes even clearer at the very end of the book. Here, the authors appear to renounce their declared neutrality and to turn their attention to the philosophical issue of the constitution of reality. They write:

> The sociology of knowledge understands human reality as socially constructed reality. Since the constitution of reality has traditionally been a central problem of philosophy, this understanding has certain philosophical implications. In so far as there has been a strong tendency for this problem, with all the questions it involves, to become trivialized in contemporary philosophy, the sociologist may find himself, to his surprise perhaps, the inheritor of philosophical questions that the professional philosophers are no longer interested in considering.
>
> (Ibid.: 210–11).

It is not clear what the problems and questions are that are purportedly 'trivialized in contemporary philosophy'. In any case, in so far as 'reality' is furnished with invisible quotation marks in the cited passage, it is far from evident why philosophy should have anything to say on the matter. 'Reality' in quotation marks means 'what is *believed* to be real'; and it is no part of philosophy as traditionally conceived to deal with empirical issues concerning the factors that shape people's conception of reality – this is precisely the task of the sociology of knowledge. It is true, on the other hand, that philosophy traditionally addresses itself to the problem of the constitution of *reality* (the genuine article, without quotation marks), in particular to the relationship between reality and the way we conceive it. One issue here is precisely that of whether reality is independent of our conception of it, or whether reality is essentially reality as conceived by us; beginning with what Bishop Berkeley wrote on this topic in the eighteenth century, there has been a thoroughly radical answer to this question, to the effect that reality is a product of our cognitive processes. It is hard to avoid the impression that at this point, in approaching the end of the book, Berger and Luckmann have shifted their interest to this genuinely philosophical question, having effectively and not only stylistically discarded the quotation marks around 'reality'. Here, at last, the issue being broached is whether *reality* is a social creation, not whether 'reality' is. And we are not, I think, mistaken if we read the above passage as pointing towards a relativist notion of reality. The idea being suggested is clearly that there are multiple realities, constituted by different societies.

THE ARGUMENT ASSESSED

The version of constructivism expounded here is one with which we are already familiar: it is based on the argument from the relativity of rationality, which we examined in the previous chapter. Individual societies subscribe to differing standards of reasoning, reality and truth. As there is no neutral, supra-cultural vantage point from which such divergent world views can be compared directly with reality and possibly be found to misrepresent it, differing standards engender their several realities. Such strong divergencies as obtain between the cognitive standards of rural Haitians and of urban New Yorkers make it the case that demons are real in Haiti but are quite devoid of reality in New York City; and vice versa for subconscious wishes and libidinal energy. The example chosen by Berger and Luckmann to illustrate their claim, however, brings out very clearly the weakness in this position, to which attention was directed in the previous chapter. It presupposes that humankind can be exhaustively divided into clearly demarcated social groups, each of these being assigned a distinctive conception of rationality on a pattern of neat one-to-one correspondence. But this presupposition is not satisfied, as their own example amply demonstrates. Grant for the sake of argument that inhabitants of the Haitian countryside are the bearers of a clearly defined, homogeneous culture making unequivocal the appropriate choice of standards of rationality and truth in interpreting their behaviour; consequently, on constructivist principles, we are compelled to accept the reality of the demons that they claim assail them. But how about the Haitians who have fled the political turmoil of their native island and currently live in New York City? These individuals will gradually become encultured in a new life-style and get acquainted with different ways of thought; still they are likely to cling to their native ways for a while. Now are we compelled to take their claims at face value if they go on asserting that they are being assailed by evil demons, even as they live in the heart of New York City? And if the answer is yes, will the same commitment apply if their grandchildren, otherwise totally immersed in American culture, were to make the same claim fifty years hence? The Haitians' privilege to have their actions construed in conformity with voodoo metaphysics can hardly be one attaching to their biological inheritance forever; as one generation of descendants is succeeded by the next, there will come a time when it can no longer be incumbent upon us, in the name of ontological impartiality, to accept their claim that their sufferings are the work of evil spirits.

My objective in making these remarks is not to point to any particular place where the line between domains of rationality should be drawn; rather the opposite: it is to suggest that no matter how such principles of demarcation are defined, a large grey zone will remain where neither of two rival standards of rationality is *a priori* preferable to the other. This means that a constructivist position which claims that reality emerges as the local correlate of relativistic principles of rationality, as applied in the interpretation of social action, will leave large tracts of social reality totally indeterminate.

We have satisfied ourselves, first, that Berger and Luckmann's position is indeed a social constructivist one, and, secondly, that it has so far added nothing new to the discussion in which we have been engaged in previous chapters. In particular, it has done nothing to deflect the criticism that social fact threatens to become wholly indeterminate on a social constructivist position – at least in its ethnomethodological and social relativist versions – since a stable non-constructed source from which determinacy could spread is nowhere to be found. In particular, there was no way that determinacy could be assigned to those cognitive processes which, according to the social constructivist view, generate determinate social facts.

SOCIOLOGY OF KNOWLEDGE TO THE RESCUE?

It is at this stage of the argument that the sociology-of-knowledge component of Berger and Luckmann's position might be called in to fill out the cracks we have exposed in the foundations of constructivism. The sociology of knowledge might well be expected to provide the determinacy that has been lacking so far. This branch of sociology supplies us with laws in terms of which the outcome of hypothetical cognitive processes can be determined. They are fixed, we are told, not by the objects of cognition, nor by a consensus, but by the social context of the cognitive process. Thought processes are shaped by conditions in the society within which they occur, in accordance with laws that the sociology of knowledge uncovers.

This pledge cannot be delivered, however: the distinctive tenets of the sociology of knowledge are in fact incompatible with a global social constructivism. On a consistent social constructivist view, scientific laws, including those of the sociology of knowledge, will themselves be constructed, thereby presupposing the existence of a consensus that such laws hold (or presupposing instead the existence of some other mechanism of social construction). This consensus (or other mechanism of construction) may obtain in actual fact, but will typically be hypothetical. Thus, we are beset by problems no less serious than those discussed above from which we sought to escape.

According to the proposal under investigation, the validity of a scientific law consists in the truth of a hypothetical sentence stating that the law would be generally accepted in a society in some specified set of circumstances. Now, there are indefinitely many such hypothetical sentences, each formulating a scientific law and correlating it with a particular set of social, cultural, technological and organisational conditions under which that law would be accepted as true. By way of illustration, consider two very simple examples taken from natural science. First, there is a law to the effect that massive things on or near the surface of the earth strive to reach the centre of the earth, which is their 'natural place'. Other things, such as flames, rise upwards to reach *their* assigned place, which is somewhere beyond the starry heavens. This picture is likely to be endorsed in a society that (for religious reasons, perhaps) views the earth as the centre of the universe and which conceives of the remainder of the universe as being composed of an entirely different kind of matter. The reader will, of course, have recognised this example as the cosmological conception of the Middle Ages. According to another picture, however, all bodies in the universe act upon each other by gravitational force. This position is likely to be endorsed in a more secular society that has relinquished the idea of its occupying a privileged region of space and that, besides, has devised better means of observation; this is, by and large, our present-day picture of the cosmos.

As these simple examples illustrate, the laws accepted under alternative societal conditions are likely to be mutually incompatible. Such incompatibility will not merely obtain in respect of the scientific theories of radically different societies, but even within individual societies, when certain salient parameters of those societies are varied. By the same token, mutual incompatibility will inevitably be a feature of relations between sociology-of-knowledge laws where each claims to specify which beliefs people are likely to form about the workings of society under differing societal conditions. Hence, we have to make a selection from among these laws when we appeal to such (hypothetical) beliefs as a way of fixing social reality. Which ones should we adopt? The only sound policy will be to pick those laws that emerge under conditions most conducive to the attainment of scientific truth: conditions, for instance, in which rational discussion and investigation flourish. We recognise immediately that we have been down this path before, with inconspicuous results: the occasion was our examination of Habermas's consensus theory of truth, which defined truth as that conception that would be formed as the conclusion of an idealised, hypothetical process of investigation. The problem is that we cannot pick out, *a priori* and in the abstract, a social setting in which an inquiry is guaranteed to produce truth. Or, putting it the other way around, we cannot define truth in terms of the results which would command consensus at the limit of some hypothetical investigative process, since we cannot, in advance, single out and justify a unique truth-generating procedure.

To sum up the argument so far, we cannot define social fact as the product of a hypothetical societal discussion, whose precise outcome we leave to the sociology of knowledge to determine. On constructivist principles, the laws on which the sociology of knowledge would rely for this hypothetical prediction are themselves social constructions, the outcome of societal consensus. The way to break out of the circle would seem to be to accept such consensual verdicts, and hence such laws, as spring from specific privileged, idealised conditions of investigation and discussion. Unfortunately, there is no uncontroversial way of specifying conditions under which an investigation is likely to produce truth. This is the familiar and intractable problem of defining a notion of scientific procedure that is uniquely rational, and able to be effectively demarcated from all non-scientific enterprises. Today, most philosophers of science have given up this project. Thus, the addition of a sociology-of-knowledge component to the basic constructivist position does not solve the problem of indeterminacy of social fact. Rather, the facts and laws supplied by the sociology of knowledge are themselves drawn into the all-engulfing regress of construction.

An alternative reading of the social constructivism-cum-sociology-of-knowledge position is one providing for the suspension of the principle of construction with respect to the factors involved in the social conditioning of knowledge. The causal nexus between a belief and its social determinants is granted some kind of brute existence and need not itself to be constituted through communal agreement or otherwise. This allows determinacy to permeate social reality in virtue of a combination of causal and non-causal generation, with social processes causally bringing about social facts of a particular kind, namely beliefs, and these beliefs, in turn, generating further social facts by construction. I think we find hints of some such view in Berger and Luckmann. As was mentioned above, the sociology-of-knowledge component of their position makes play with the Marxian distinction between substructural aspects of society, which enjoy a substantial mode of existence, and superstructural ones, whose reality has a merely derivative status. Social constructions figure primarily in the latter category. Berger and Luckmann call them 'legitimating universes', and they comprise those abstract metaphysical speculations that societies will produce to justify the current social order. The distinctive character of Berger and Luckmann's work resides precisely in this marriage of a Marxian and a phenomenological approach, the latter being part of the legacy of Alfred Schutz. While social facts – social conditions – are claimed to generate certain knowledge structures, the converse also holds: knowledge structures generate social facts by bestowing certain 'meanings' upon them. The determination runs both ways.

The trouble with this suggestion is its capriciously hybrid character. Certain social facts are allowed to enjoy brute existence; others exist as the determinate causal effect of the former; yet a third kind exist only *qua* social constructions. What is the principle of categorisation? It will hardly do to say that the only social facts enjoying brute existence are those which do not embody cognitive states (intentional contents or 'meanings'), since this class is empty. As Berger and Luckmann themselves emphasise, all social facts somehow include, directly or indirectly, elements of human thought, understanding or 'meaning'. Thus, no brute social facts would exist to set in train the process of social construction. Before we need feel committed to taking it seriously, the hybrid view must offer us some coherent and plausible formula that specifies which segments of society enjoy what kind of existence.

The constructivist position argued in *The Social Construction of Reality* is quite ambiguous and many-faceted; the discussion above was not intended to exhaust this rich and suggestive work, nor was the criticism meant as a rebuttal of all readings of its constructivist tenet. Another thesis advanced by Berger and Luckmann under the 'construction' label is that human beings generate the social world by their *actions*, especially in so far as these actions are institutionally fixed and thereby 'objectified'. Human action, considered in terms of its dependence upon specific normative and institutional constraints, *makes up* social reality and hence 'constructs' it. I have no quarrel with this position, which in fact I referred to briefly at the beginning of this book, but put aside as a truism scarcely worthy of further attention. It is, however, possible to put a more interesting gloss on this argument which would stress the intentional content of institutional action, its meaningful 'inside', and would insist that this aspect is what gives institutional action its distinctive nature in contrast with, for instance, purely habitual action. This argument would generate a moderate version of the construction claim that would be immune to the above criticisms. I shall actually examine a position on these lines in Part Two under the heading of 'the argument from convention'.

There is also evidence of a purely causal interpretation of the construction thesis in Berger and Luckmann, to the effect that certain structural features of human society cause certain specific beliefs in social agents, which in turn causally generate further social facts. Berger and Luckmann refer to this phenomenon as the 'dialectics' of social reality, a process in which social facts affect and condition human beliefs and vice versa. The authors here signal their opposition to certain vulgar interpretations of Marxism, which have it that determination runs uniformly from social structure to human beliefs; the 'substructure' uniquely shapes the 'super-structure'. The criticism I advanced above was not directed against this causal interpretation of the construction thesis, but only against a constructivist position in the sense adopted in the present work. This, to repeat, is one that takes social reality to be generated in a *non-causal* way by the very cognitive processes (in a broad sense of the term) in which we grasp it.

In Part Two of this book, we shall return to the phenomen-ological tradition which figures prominently in the theoretical framework informing Berger and Luckmann's work. We shall see that it makes room for another, weaker version of the construction claim that is not beset by the difficulties I have pointed out above. It is a moot point whether that position would be strong enough to support the broader conclusions which Berger and Luckmann infer from constructivism in *The Social Construction of Reality*. In any case, it remains a fact that there are numerous formulations in this work that go beyond the moderate position and are, indeed, incompatible with it. Hence we are not being unfair to the authors in attributing a radical view to them. (I shall return to the difference between the two positions in Part Two.)

THE 'SCIENCE CONSTRUCTIVISTS' REVISITED

This is an appropriate place to make a few critical remarks about the school (or rather, the loose affiliation of individuals) in social science that I dubbed 'science constructivists' in the Introduction, a group numbering such writers as Harry M. Collins, Steve Woolgar, Bruno Latour, Michel Callon and Karin Knorr-Cetina. They are representatives of a recent revival in the sociology of knowledge that has been promoted under such labels as 'Sociology of Scientific Knowledge' (SSK), the Edinburgh 'Strong Programme', and others; the science constructivists might be said to represent the extreme left wing of this 'new' sociology of knowledge.[6] Not all the positions represented here are radical to the same degree, nor is the type of reasoning exemplified in every case the same, but like Berger and Luckmann, all subscribe to the dual claims that cognition is socially determined (typically in a causal sense) and that reality is generated through such cognitive processes (in a non-causal sense). There is indeed a historical link between Berger and Luckmann and current workers within the new social studies of science, and the science constructivists often pay tribute to those two authors as their precursors.

On closer inspection, however, important differences between Berger and Luckmann and the science constructivists appear. In part, they reflect the general difference spelled out in the Introduction between science constructivists and constructivists in the sense used in the present essay. First, the former are primarily interested in the construction of facts about the *physical* world – facts concerning quasars, gravity waves, microbes, and so on – whereas Berger and Luckmann are (predominantly but not exclusively) concerned with the generation of *social* fact. Second, the generation of physical reality is seen as the upshot of *scientific* activity, rather than of our everyday interaction with and discourse about the natural world. Correspondingly, it is the scientific research process that is the topic of investigation, rather than our common-sense understanding. Berger and Luckmann, along with the other social constructivists under scrutiny in this essay, view social reality as a product of the cognitive efforts of ordinary social agents, not of social scientists. (This is not to deny that social scientists and other specialists are held to play a role in social construction, but this is seen as being primarily achieved through their impact on the broad mass of ordinary social agents.) Third, the science constructivists are typically concerned to pinpoint the role played in social construction by the power structure and by class and group interests, whereas Berger and Luckmann are more interested in the basic structural properties of the generation of social reality, for instance such features as objectification and reification. Berger and Luckmann study the processes through which reality is generated from the highly abstract vantage point of a philosophical anthropology.

Despite these differences, the two forms of social constructivism are sufficiently alike for the science constructivists to feel the heat of the criticism that I have just levelled against the ethnomethodologists' version (and even more so against Berger and Luckmann's); in fact, some ethnomethodologists have done work in both fields. The problem may not be apparent as long as the science constructivists focus narrowly on natural science and claim only that *physical* fact is a social construction. Such was the case in early social constructivist studies, where social facts were treated naively, as an unproblematic resource for the explanation of natural fact. It was unavoidable, however, that science constructivists would soon be confronted with the question concerning the ontological status of the social facts thus invoked. Once this issue was broached, the arguments that persuaded the constructivists that natural facts are social constructions would have to be recognised as applying to social reality as well. At this point, social constructivists in the sociology of science find themselves trapped in the very same regress that I have already shown to afflict the constructivists above: the social items that are claimed to generate social facts must themselves be understood to be generated by other social items, and so on *ad infinitum*. Since there can be no such infinite chain of social fact generation, total indeterminacy ensues.

In fact, science constructivist have recently begun to recognise this problem, although so far only confusedly and without a full appreciation of its gravity. They have deployed a number of strategies designed to obviate it. One is to adopt a bipartite approach to natural and social facts, being a realist about the latter while a constructivist about the former; this position has actually been advocated by Harry Collins (Collins 1992: 187–9) and by Steve Fuller (Fuller 1993: xiv). But such a move is highly implausible and *ad hoc*, at least to the extent that the science constructivist position is based upon reasonings akin to the Broad Arguments, since these are entirely nondiscriminatory and leave no room for any such distinction. Another strategy is to grant that both natural and social facts are socially constructed, but then postulate a stratum of non-physical and non-social facts out of which the other types of facts emerge. This doctrine has been adopted by Latour and Callon, who see the realm of primordial facts as composed of 'actant networks' from which the other strata of facts emerge (cf. Callon and Latour 1992; Latour 1993). This manoeuvre seems to be a purely terminological one, however, as long as there is a reliance on one or another of the Broad Arguments; such a reliance will inevitably introduce the problem into the new segment of reality, no matter how it is designated.

It is a safe prediction that a crisis concerning the theoretical foundations of science constructivism is inevitable on account of this problem; indeed the indications of such a crisis are clearly visible in the literature.[7] The sole solution lies in abandoning the idea that science creates fact, and stick with the thesis, held in common with less radical members of the 'new' sociology of science, that societal conditions determine the contents of scientific theories.

Let me end this brief note on the science constructivists by observing that, fortunately, the problems attaching to their metaphysical stance has not prevented these authors from producing valuable empirical work. A number of penetrating case studies have been presented which must henceforth be taken into account by any writer on the history, sociology or philosophy of science.

CHAPTER IV

The Linguistic Relativity Argument

The ancestry of the linguistic relativity argument can be traced back to certain ideas that were widely influential in Germany in the late eighteenth and early nineteenth centuries. In the nationalistic, romantic spirit of the German counter-enlightenment, such thinkers as Johann Georg Hamann and Johann Gottfried Herder celebrated the uniqueness of the spirit (*Geist*) possessed by each individual people (*Volk*). They considered language to be the major source of this uniqueness as well as being the medium to afford it the richest possible expression; in literature and poetry in particular, this *Geist* was thought to achieve its supreme manifestation.

The most influential figure in this movement was the Prussian polymath Wilhelm von Humboldt. In his works on linguistics, Humboldt stressed the organic connection between language and thought: a language is not just a nomenclature, a set of labels affixed to an already existing structure of concepts in the mind, and introduced only to facilitate their communication. Rather, language contributes essentially to the very constitution of this conceptual structure. It does so in a thoroughly holistic manner, such that a difference in one area will have repercussions in every other. Accordingly, every language has a unique essence, its 'inner linguistic form' which comprises semantic as well as grammatical elements and which distinguishes it from all other languages. In virtue of this distinctive form, its shapes the entire 'world picture' of the population whose native language it is. A true child of the nineteenth century, von Humboldt identifies the linguistic community with the '*Volk*', the people. As his famous pronouncement has it, 'Language is, as it were, the outer appearance of the spirit of a people, the language is their spirit and the spirit their language; we can never think of them sufficiently as identical' (Humboldt 1988: 46).

80

In the present century, the linguistic relativity view has primarily been associated with the names of two American linguists, Edward Sapir and Benjamin Lee Whorf. A historical link ties the German and the American arguments together, since Sapir and Whorf knew of von Humboldt's work through the German-born linguist–ethnographer Franz Boas. It was Whorf who coined the phrase 'the principle of linguistic relativity' to designate the view that languages differ in their fundamental lexical and syntactical structure and that these differences lead to corresponding differences in thought. This thesis has occasioned considerable debate in social anthropology, especially in the subdiscipline known as *cognitive anthropology*. While linguistic relativity was glorified by the German romantic thinkers as a crucial element in their nationalistic philosophies, it turns into something of an embarrassment when we look at empirical linguistics and empirical anthropology as these disciplines are conducted in the present century. Linguistic relativity is a threat to the comparative linguist's aim of developing a unified conceptual framework in which to describe the semantics of diverse languages, and raises a powerful challenge to the ethnographer's professed ability to penetrate the native mind and to convey the results of the inquiry in the researcher's own language.

In our present context, however, we are only interested in this doctrine to the extent that it serves as a premise of a constructivist position. What I refer to here as 'the linguistic relativity argument' draws upon the principle of linguistic relativity, but conjoins it with the doctrine that the language-induced differences in thought generate different realities. We must now examine these ideas more carefully.

The first premise in the linguistic relativity argument is the tenet that language shapes thought; more specifically, that differences in language translate into differences in thought. Language is not a set of labels that come to be attached to a range of previously-existing mental contents in man. The situation is rather the reverse: man thinks the thoughts that language puts into his head. Whorf expresses the point as follows:

> Actually, thinking is most mysterious, and by far the greatest light upon it that we have is thrown by the study of language. This study shows that the forms of a person's thoughts are controlled by inexorable laws of pattern of which he is

unconscious. These patterns are the unperceived intricate systematizations of his own language – shown readily enough by a candid comparison and contrast with other languages, especially those of a different linguistic family.

(Whorf 1956: 252)

We saw in Part One that, in linguistic and mental phenomena, significant behavior [is] ruled by a specific system or organization, a 'geometry' of form principles characteristic of each language. This organization is imposed from outside the narrow circle of the personal consciousness, making of that consciousness a mere puppet whose linguistic maneuverings are held in unsensed and unbreakable bonds of pattern.

(Ibid.: 257)

A second tenet is that, via our thoughts, language determines the way reality is divided up:

As I said in the April 1940 *Review*, segmentation of nature is an aspect of grammar – one as yet little studied by grammarians. We cut up and organize the spread and flow of events as we do, largely because, through our mother tongue, we are parties to an agreement to do so, not because nature itself is segmented in exactly that way for all to see. Languages differ not only in how they build their sentences but also in how they break down nature to secure the elements to put in those sentences. This breakdown gives units of the lexicon. 'Word' is not a very good 'word' for them; 'lexeme' has been suggested, and 'term' will do for the present. By these more or less distinct terms we ascribe a semi-fictitious isolation to parts of experience. English terms, like 'sky, hill, swamp', persuade us to regard some elusive aspect of nature's endless variety as a distinct THING, almost like a table or chair. Thus English and similar tongues lead us to think of the universe as a collection of rather distinct objects and events corresponding to words. Indeed this is the implicit picture of classical physics and astronomy – that the universe is essentially a collection of detached objects of different sizes.

(Ibid.: 240)

According to Whorf, the most fundamental formative influence of language operates not at the level of individual words (the lexicon), but of syntax. For instance, a crucial aspect of the way Indo-European languages shape reality is not by imposing this or that lexical segmentation upon it – although this is significant, too – but rather by imposing a subject–predicate structure. This makes the world appear as composed of discrete objects, possessing various qualities. Another important feature is the way our language projects agenthood upon nature. Certain kinds of events are, in English and related languages, described by sentences such as, 'A light flashed' or 'It flashed,' conjuring up a wholly fictitious actor, the flash or 'it', to perform the 'action' of flashing. Other languages, such as that of the American Indian Hopi, avoid any such fiction, but instead use a sentence whose literal translation would simply be, 'Flash (occurred)'.

Thus language serves to define an otherwise amorphous reality, cutting entities out of this continuous substrate. Sometimes, it even projects wholly fictitious entities on to nature, such as the category of agent as applied to certain subjectless processes. In these ways, language generates a reality of a particular nature.

The preceding paragraph expresses an essential step in the linguistic relativity argument, as I define it here, but is less securely grounded in Whorf's writings than those earlier. Although this paragraph seems to capture an element in Whorf's thought, he also occasionally expressed the view that languages reflect the world more or less adequately, thus apparently presupposing that we can speak of the way reality *is*, as opposed to the way we conceptualise it. Indeed, one of Whorf's favourite ideas was that Indo-European languages, with their rigid subject–predicate structure, are inferior to certain American Indian languages, which are better suited to do justice to the 'processual' nature of reality: reality is essentially a patterned *process*, rather than a structure of permanent, discrete objects. Hence, reality, at least physical reality, apparently possesses a nature independent of language that language ought to reflect.

To find a less equivocal commitment to the construction view, we must turn to Edward Sapir. In the article 'Linguistics as a Science', he wrote:

Language is a guide to 'social reality'. Though language is not ordinarily thought of as of essential interest to the students of social science, it powerfully conditions all our thinking about social problems and processes. Human beings do not live in the objective world alone, or alone in the world of social activity as ordinarily understood, but are very much at the mercy of the particular language which has become the medium of expression for their society. It is quite an illusion to imagine that one adjusts to reality essentially without the use of language and that language is merely an incidental means of solving specific problems of communication or reflection. The fact of the matter is that the 'real world' is to a large extent unconsciously built up on the language habits of the group. No two languages are ever sufficiently similar to be considered as representing the same social reality. The worlds in which different societies live are distinct worlds, not merely the same world with different labels attached.

(Sapir 1973: 162)

THE LINGUISTIC RELATIVITY ARGUMENT IN THOMAS KUHN'S WORK

The past couple of decades have witnessed a resurgence of interest in the linguistic construction view owing to the work of Thomas Kuhn. We must briefly mention this work here in order to cast some additional sidelight on the argument from linguistic relativity, although Kuhn's concerns are significantly different from the ones that preoccupy us in the present essay. Kuhn is a 'science constructivist' in the sense I defined on p. 13, only to set the topic aside as irrelevant to our present undertaking. He is interested in the way in which *physical reality* is generated through the way in which it is conceived by man. Kuhn holds this construction to be the work of scientific communities, not a mere product of commonsense thinking.

For Kuhn, the framework within which the community of scientists constructs the natural world is that given by the *paradigm*. A paradigm is a set of shared assumptions and an array of recognised techniques, centred around an 'exemplar', an instance of the successful use of these techniques and serving to demonstrate their efficacy in practice. Prominent among the shared assumptions is a language that is unique to those subscribing to the paradigm. Each such paradigm-related language offers its distinctive classification of the objects encountered in the world. For instance, in the Ptolemaic system the earth enjoyed a unique status in the universe, poised motionless at its centre; in the Copernican system, it orbits the sun and is merely one planet among others. Conversely, in the Ptolemiac system the moon was a planet, whereas in the Copernican system it is a satellite of the earth.

According to Kuhn, such differences in classification are not to be distinguished from differences in the *meanings* of the terms in two different paradigms. This blocks the translatability of languages across paradigms, and renders theories which are couched in different languages rationally incommensurable. For there is no neutral observation language to which scientists may have recourse to settle their differences; no pure language untainted by theory into which theories may be translated and assessed according to some neutral yardstick. Thus, in a sense, every theorist is trapped inside his own theoretical universe. Another way of putting this is to say that the paradigm creates its own reality. This is indeed what Kuhn implies when he says, for instance, that scientists before and after a paradigm shift live in different worlds (Kuhn 1972: 118). Kuhn's position, in other words, is a constructivist one.

I shall not go any further into the exegesis of Kuhn's work, nor shall I attempt to review the large literature that has emerged, debating the pros and cons of the incommensurability view. This literature occasionally touches on Whorf and Sapir's position as well.[8] For our present purposes, we need not try to adjudicate the thorny issue as to whether such languages really are incommensurable or not, or resist 'calibration', as Whorf puts it in making the same point. We can bypass all these problems here and focus instead on the second premise of the argument from linguistic relativity, since this is by far the most controversial assumption of the entire reasoning. This is to the effect that if languages are indeed incommensurable, multiple realities will be engendered as a result.

AN EXAMPLE

To conduct this investigation, we should now leave the historical sources of the linguistic relativity view and focus on a concrete example instead. Here is a case from social anthropology that illustrates and supports the thesis of linguistic relativism. In Dyirbal, an aboriginal language of Australia, correct linguistic use requires all nouns occurring in a sentence to be preceded by one of four words, *bayi*, *balan*, *balam* or *bala*. These expressions thus serve as classifiers, placing all nouns (and hence the items they signify) in one of four categories. According to R. M. W. Dixon (1982), who has examined Dyirbal, the resulting categories are as follows:

1 *Bayi*: Men, kangaroos, possums, bats, most snakes, most fishes, some birds, most insects, the moon, storms, rainbows, boomerangs, some spears.
2 *Balan*: Women, bandicoots, dogs, platypus, echidna, some snakes, some fishes, most birds, fireflies, scorpions, crickets, the hairy mary grub, anything connected with water or fire, sun and stars, shields, some spears, some trees.
3 *Balam*: All edible fruit and the plants that bear them, tubers, ferns, honey, cigarettes, wine, cake.
4 *Bala*: Parts of the body, meat, bees, wind, yamsticks, some spears, most trees, grass, mud, stones, noises, and language.

When a Westerner reflects upon this classification, he may well be unwilling to grant that the property of (being) *bayi* or *bala* is something found in the world, independent of Dyirbal classification. He will be inclined to say that these properties only came into existence with the appearance of Dyirbal speakers. In an influential book that derives its title from the Dyirbal classifiers, the linguist George Lakoff (1987) uses this and other examples to discuss linguistic classification and its relationship to reality. He ends in a position not unlike Whorf's; specifically, he claims that social reality is a construction out of linguistically-embodied thought patterns.

A brief digression: why distinguish (as I have done) between the argument based upon the relativity of rationality, and that based on the relativity of language? Are we not dealing with alternative formulations of the same point, given the way that linguistic forms and rationality are interwoven? A closer inspection will reveal, however, that there is no involvement with rationality in the present reasoning. This is precisely what renders it immune to the objection that disposed of the previous version. The role of rationality in the earlier version was as part of the epistemic process through which predicates are applied. But the present argument is silent about the process through which a predicate is applied to a given thing; *eo ipso*, it is noncommittal with regard to the role played by *rationality* in this process. All that matters is that the predicate *exists* in language at all. The argument also avoids the objections directed against the ethnomethodological argument, since the present reasoning does not assert that the fact of S being P only comes into being once the predicate P has *actually been applied* to S, but, once more, only requires that P be *available* in the language.[9]

Undeniably, the linguistic relativity argument would at first seem to be vulnerable to an objection related to the one raised against ethnomethodology, namely, the resulting paucity of determinate fact. If facts are only definite to the extent that things are subsumable under appropriate classificatory terms available in language, this would seem to imply, for instance, that bacteria did not exist until advances in optics had made them visible to, and describable by, Leeuwenhoek and others in the late seventeenth century, or that viruses only appeared in the 1920s. But does this mean that a disease such as the common cold did not occur until that late date? Or did it occur, but not *as* a viral infection, but as something else – say, a reaction to cold weather, as the etymology suggests? Or did it exist as a mere cluster of (linguistically tagged) symptoms, but without any uniform aetiology?

Perhaps the social constructivist can sidestep this problem in the present context, however. Remember that in this part of the book, we are examining what I called the Broad Arguments in favour of the construction view. These are general arguments that, if sound, would support a global constructivism, valid for the natural world as well as for the social world. However, what concerns us is really only the thesis that *social* fact is socially constructed; hence general weaknesses in the Broad Arguments should not be taken as a reason for dismissal if special considerations neutralise them when applied to social reality. It would seem that there are such special considerations with respect to the linguistic relativity argument, nullifying the objection just raised. The social constructivist may point out that social and other human events are never devoid of a description. Social events are made up of human actions, which are essentially associated with a description, namely the one which the agents themselves apply to the actions. It is essential to the notion of human action that the agent can always provide an answer to the question, 'What are you doing?' If no answer is forthcoming, we must conclude that the individual in question did not really act, but was just fidgeting or was in some state of mental disorder that precludes his classification as an agent. In brief, the linguistic relativity argument seems not to be threatened by the difficulties that undermined the ethnomethodological point of view.

THE LINGUISTIC RELATIVITY ARGUMENT
RECONSTRUCTED

Let us now clarify and reconstruct the Sapir–Whorf thesis in a philosophical light. Here is an attractive argument to support this thesis. Classification is a question of grouping things together in sets, the members of which are more similar to each other than to the items outside the set. However, all things are similar in some respects and dissimilar in others. Things that are like each other from one point of view, and hence belong in the same class, could have been placed in different classes if another dimension of comparison or another measure of similarity had been used. Thus, classifications are not objective divisions, inherent in the nature of things, but are structures we impose upon the world. A *kind of thing* only emerges when we decide to emphasise a certain dimension of similarity between objects, thereby generating a determinate class of items. A crucial way to emphasise a particular dimension of similarity is precisely by introducing a linguistic term to denote it or the class of things that it generates. To this extent, *kinds* of things are indeed created by the classificatory categories of our language. However, if *kinds* are social constructions, then so is every fact involving a kind. But this means any fact at all, since any fact about the world consists in the assignment of one or more things to a specified kind. Any description can be recast as the subsumption of the thing described under a kind-term. It seems as if social constructivism has been vindicated.

I believe that this reasoning is mistaken. What follows from the premises is a less radical conclusion. It is true that the way the world divides into classes of similar things depends upon the respects in which things are compared and the measures of similarity adopted. Things that are similar from a physical point of view (for example, by being all made of steel) may be different from an economic one (some of them are produced abroad, while others are of domestic origin). The similarities of things may depend upon the measure used – all proteins, or birds, will be alike from the point of view of a very general classification. From a more specific point of view, however (for instance, a nutritional one), certain proteins will be classified very differently from others, as will some birds – say, if you want to start an egg farm. It does not follow, however, that these similarities, or the properties they define, are somehow man-made and therefore not real. They do not wait to pop into existence until somebody actually notices them, or captures them in a verbal description. They were there all the while; what has been shown is merely that we cannot talk about things being similar or dissimilar *tout court*, but must always add, 'in this or that respect', or 'given a similarity measure of such-and-such a kind'.

In the face of this counter-argument, the constructivist might radicalise his position. It is not true, he might insist, that things are objectively similar, *even in particular respects*, prior to and independently of the cognitive attitude we adopt towards them. Similarities are not something we detect in objects, but are created by our classificatory activities. They are produced when we *treat* things in the same way (of which application of the same linguistic label to them is only a minor aspect). What makes all instances similar of a disease like malaria, or of a colour like red, or of artefacts like chairs, is the fact that we respond to them in the same way. We apply the same treatments to diseases labelled as 'malaria'; we react in the same way to certain colours when we observe them, say, in traffic lights – for instance, by applying the brakes; and we use certain pieces of furniture in the same way – by sitting on them, for example. The similarities are constituted by the attitude and behaviour we adopt towards the things said to be similar and, hence, so are the predicates (properties) that are defined by the similarity relations.

This analysis appears quite attractive until we start inquiring into the nature of the sameness of behaviour that is claimed to generate similarity. Clearly we are not talking about *quantitatively* the same reaction being manifested towards different cases of disease, or towards patches of colour, or pieces of furniture. We are talking about *qualitative* sameness – that is, about *similarity* of reactions. Nor are we talking about quantitatively the same sign token being applied to different cases of malaria, or red patches, or pieces of furniture, but about quantitatively distinct but phonetically *similar* tokens. The word 'red' that you apply to the tomato today is not the same token as the one I used to describe the sunset yesterday, but is merely similar to it. The same goes for the word 'bayi' that one Dyirbal speaker applies to a particular woman, and the token 'bayi' that his fellow applies to a fire. We now must ask if these similarities are objective. If the answer is positive, we must conclude that objective similarities exist after all; if it is negative, the conclusion is that similarity is not so much a construction as an *illusion*. The critique of objective similarity will have eliminated the very notion we need in order to make sense of similarity, even as a social construction. We can no longer say that similarity is constructed out of a certain feature of people's reactions to things, since, when queried as to *which* feature, we could only answer, 'The *similarity* of the reactions'. We would be caught in a vicious circle, an outcome that refutes the assumption upon which the argument was based – that is, that similarity is not an objective property of things.

However, what has been demonstrated is that *some* objective, intrinsic similarities (and the properties they define) must be allowed to exist, since they are presupposed by constructed similarities (and the associated properties). It was not established that *all* classifications reflect intrinsic similarities. The argument leaves room for a restricted version of the construction thesis, to the effect that *some* (but not all) similarities between things are constructed. As a consequence, so are the properties defined by the similarity classes and the facts embodying those properties. The mechanism of construction would be the one suggested above. A property would belong to a set of things by construction when a predicate is attributed to those things, solely for the reason that human beings manifest (objectively) similar reactions to them, but in the absence of intrinsic similarities among those things. The constructivist would have to grant that the similarity between human classificatory actions is an intrinsic one and not in itself constructed, but he would still get most of what he bargained for if he could show that a large proportion of the similarities among things are not intrinsic, but are precisely constructed on the basis of the (similar) acts through which people classify them.

It would seem as if the constructivist could make some headway with this task. Linguistic classification is rarely just a theoretical exercise, but is typically preparatory to *doing* something with the items labelled. This goes for classification of social as well as natural items. Anthropological literature is replete with studies of the way native classifications reflect and articulate fundamental structural aspects of the native world view, with associated differences in conduct. According to an influential tradition in anthropology, represented by such figures as Durkheim and Mauss (1963), and carried on recently by Mary Douglas (1975) and others, native classifications of the physical world are projections of classifications salient in the social world. These social classifications are associated with differences in conduct with respect to the classified items, dictated by social norms. The differences in conduct are transferred, by various considerations of analogy, to the items of the natural world. Classifications of the natural world thus reflect divisions and distinctions that are socially salient; they go together with differences in conduct.

As it happens, the Dyirbal classifiers would seem to fit neatly into this familiar picture. Although Dixon does not tell us anything about this, we have reason to assume that things that are identically labelled in terms of the four Dyirbal classifiers are also identically *treated*, and that, obversely, things differently labelled are also differently treated. And we may suspect that those differences reflect socially salient distinctions. For instance, we spot a gender-like distribution in the Dyirbal labels of *bara* and *bala* and may expect the labelled items to belong within female and male domains of Dyribal social life, respectively. A strict separation of social activities and social status into male and female spheres is a dominant theme of native societies, as is the way that this division is projected on to the universe at large. Certain things in the natural world have an affinity to the female sex, others to the male, and are treated accordingly.

The constructivist would conclude that his position is vindicated to the extent that at least *some* properties of things do not reflect intrinsic similarities among them, but are a product of the way that the items in question are classified. The classification reflects the role that the items in question play in the social practice of the people involved. Hence, the sameness of the items in question – the sameness that makes them belong to the same kind of things and thus makes them what they are, generically – is a social creation. The things in question are social constructs, as far as their generic properties are concerned.

The constructivist's conclusion would not be warranted by the premises, however. Constructivism remains the thesis that (social) reality is constructed by the way human beings think and talk about it, by the way they describe it and explain it, by the agreements they reach about it, and so on. In brief, (social) reality is a product of the cognitive processes with which social agents grapple with it; in the present context, we examine classifying processes in particular. The position to which our examination leads, however, is rather that social reality is created by people's *actions* – specifically, their behavioural reactions to certain things.

The alternative conclusion just proposed needs to be put with some care, lest it be misunderstood. It is not the trivial claim that social reality is generated by people's actions in a causal sense, the way that a potter's actions generates a vase; instead, it directs attention to a more subtle connection between action and social facts. Many predicates of things are defined by reference to the reactions those things engender, rather than by any intrinsic properties of the things themselves. Good examples are such natural science predicates as 'toxic' or 'carcinogenic', which classify substances in terms of their effects on biological organisms, while referring to no shared intrinsic features. A thing's relationship to another thing is conceptualised as a property of that thing (appropriately called a *relational* property). Special cases of such relational properties are those that accrue to a thing by virtue of its being related to human action as its object and/or cause. Thus, certain social entities are called 'scapegoats', 'deviants', 'opinion leaders', 'role models', 'inmates', 'bank notes', 'traffic lights', and so on – terms that all indicate a response that the items in question engender in people confronted with them. The constructivist's argument above directs attention to these properties and the fact that the items possessing them need have no intrinsic similarity. He uses this observation to argue that the 'sameness' of these things is imposed by the act of classification.

In none of these cases, however, are the facts in question generated by linguistic labelling in itself. The objects classified would possess their (relational) properties even in the absence of suitable classificatory terms in the language. Strychnine is toxic, whether or not people have a term for toxicity; certain individuals are opinion leaders, even though the people who follow them may lack a label for this role. A traffic light by any other name, or even by no name at all, would still be a traffic light as long as it controls people's driving. We are not dealing with mysterious fact-creating powers of linguistic classification here, but with the way new facts emerge when things or people enter into novel relationships, including causal ones, with each other; relationships for which linguistic labels may only subsequently be devised. Such relationships make up a crucial part of social life, but they do not exemplify the idea that linguistic classification itself generates social fact. The linguistic labels are attached to phenomena that existed beforehand, independently of the labelling. This holds true for facts involving relational properties, too, even though their special character may create an illusion to the contrary. Since relational properties are extrinsic to things, they may somehow seem more ephemeral, as if they were not a part of the world but rather imposed upon it; yet they are as factual as non-relational properties.

LABELLING THEORY

The constructivist might attempt a final move: the claim that social classifications reflect societal relationships existing independently of the classification overlooks the fact that the classifications are often *prescriptive* as well as *descriptive*. They do not merely describe the way in which people behave towards each other, but *dictate* the manner in which they *should* behave.

The classical example of this in the literature is the concept of *deviance*, which has been examined by Howard Becker in his so-called *labelling theory*. Labelling theory holds precisely that labels do not reflect independently-existing properties and distinctions, but create them by labelling their bearers. One aspect of this creation is the prescriptive force of labelling someone a deviant: the label does not report a previously-existing social reaction to the deviant, but prescribes an attitude of censure that turns him into one.

Becker expresses these point as follows:

> *[S]ocial groups create deviance by making the rules whose infraction constitutes deviance*, and by applying those rules to particular people and labelling them as outsiders. From this point of view, deviance is *not* a quality of the act the person commits, but rather a consequence of the application by others of rules and sanctions to an 'offender'. The deviant is one to whom that label has successfully been applied, deviant behaviour is behaviour that people so label.
>
> (Becker 1973: 9, author's italics)

Some difficulties are put in the way of assessing this claim by the fact that the term 'deviance' leads a double life in Becker's account. First, it serves as a sociological term of art; thus far, Becker is at liberty to define it in any way he pleases, although a minimum of continuity with standard sociological usage would be advisable. In particular, Becker is free to define a deviant as a person who is the victim of certain segregating practices by the rest of society. Such a theory would not amount to a construction view, however, as it is not being claimed that sociologists create deviants by so labelling certain social agents. Instead, the (sociological) label 'deviant' designates an independently existing *relational property* of certain agents, namely, that of being an object of censure in the eyes of the rest of society.

But, second, it is also implied that 'deviant' is a term used by the social agents themselves in describing certain types of behaviour, for it is said that 'deviant behaviour is behaviour that people so label'. That is, behaviour is deviant when it is tagged with the term 'deviant' by the rest of society. This is a dubious doctrine, since 'deviant' is hardly a term of the vernacular; only people who have had some acquaintance with sociological jargon will use it. It is better to understand 'deviant', in this part of Becker's theory, as a proxy for the concrete and more precise labels of deviancy that ordinary people may employ, such as 'thief', 'adulterer', 'witch', 'leper', 'outlaw', and so on. The problem is that when these terms are substituted for 'deviant', there is no plausibility in a construction view. These term are partly prescriptive, partly descriptive; they prescribe a negative treatment of the individual thus labelled, but do so on the basis of certain alleged characteristics of the individual that are thought to warrant the hostility. It is obvious that application of these terms does not generate the warranting conditions; one does not make it true that somebody has caused the death of another person just by labelling him 'murderer', nor that he suffers from an infection of the bacillus *Mycobacterium leprae* simply by labelling him 'leper'.

No doubt Becker would concur with this, as we may infer from his denunciation of what he terms the common-sense view that there is something inherently (qualitatively) distinct about persons who break social rules. Deviants, including particular kinds of deviants, are not a homogeneous bunch. Common sense is wrong in assuming that such deviances as homosexuality or drug addiction are the symptoms of clearly-identifiable intrinsic states, be they genetic defects or mental diseases. By denouncing this view, Becker parts company with social constructivism as we define that position here, for, according to the latter, social agents would indeed make it a *fact* that somebody suffered from those mental diseases by so labelling him. Becker's theory contains an implicit rejection of everyday labelling practices, and his declaration that 'deviance' is a social creation does not manifest a constructivist view. The view is rather that a certain social practice makes it *appear* as if a certain group of people possess some objective feature setting them apart from the rest of society; that feature, however, is a mere projection of the discriminatory treatment to which they are subjected.

In some authors who embrace labelling theory, the critical stance to indigenous classifications is much starker and sometimes takes the form of an indignant moral protest against the social order of which those classifications are an aspect. An example is Thomas Szasz, who charges that there are no clear physiological or mental conditions associated with the general term, 'mentally ill', or its particular, special subterms, such as 'psychotic' or 'manic depressive' (Szasz 1961, 1973). These are mere labels, used to brand social misfits and set them up for various sorts of discriminative regimens, such as confinement in mental institutions or drug treatment. In declaring that madness is socially manufactured, Szasz does not mean to say that, by applying appropriate labels, society brings it about that some person is (for instance) genuinely psychotic, the subject of some clearly-definable mental malfunctioning. Such states remain fictitious and labelling cannot make them otherwise. Rather, by describing madness as 'manufactured', Szasz precisely implies that there is really no such condition as 'madness', but that a social practice is instituted which creates a collective appearance to the contrary. This is not 'social constructivism' in my sense, but is closer in import to W. I. Thomas's dictum, cited earlier, that what people define as real is real *in its consequences*. That is, as a result of 'definition', or labelling, things are *as if* mental diseases genuinely existed: certain people will find themselves confined in asylums and will be subjected to harsh regimens ostensibly designed to cure them. A somewhat similar line is adopted by Michel Foucault in *Madness and Civilization* (1965), in which he traces the shifting conceptualisations of madness in European society since the middle ages and the associated practices of confinement.

Thus, we have not managed to find a case where the mere usage of a linguistic term generates, by construction, a fact about that to which the term is applied. The use of semi-prescriptive terms to label various kinds of deviant –'murderer', 'adulterer', etc. – will indeed help generate a social fact, namely, that a certain segregating practice exists, but it does so *causally*. The introduction and dissemination of a certain normatively charged social designation will contribute to the formation of a certain attitude with respect to the people labelled, and a corresponding pattern of conduct. This may be compared to the way that social facts are generated by an explicit ordinance detailing how certain people are to be treated –

dictating, for instance, that carriers of an infectious disease should be put in quarantine. As a result of the ordinance, certain people will find themselves in confinement. This is not generation by construction, since the authorities do not make it the case that certain people are placed in quarantine *by and as of* the mere issuance of the ordinance. It takes a considerable apparatus of doctors, nurses and Ministry of Health officials to translate that ordinance into social fact through a process that is largely causal.

Summary of Part One

With the discussion of labelling theory, I conclude my examination of the Broad Arguments; it is time to recapitulate the results obtained. The Broad Arguments purport to establish the general philosophical position that socially shared cognition somehow creates its object; here, however, these arguments interest us only as they apply to social reality. Three such arguments were examined, which I called the *ethnomethodological argument*, the *cultural relativity argument* and the *linguistic relativity argument*, respectively.

The ethnomethodological argument uses ideas from Wittgenstein's later philosophy to sharpen a line of reasoning found in ethnomethodological writings. The crux is that the meaning of descriptive terms is not determinate until those terms have actually been applied, in a communally-sanctioned manner. It follows that a sentence featuring a descriptive term has no determinate truth value, either, until it has been endorsed or rejected by a community-wide consensus. Thus, communal consensus turns sentences of indeterminate truth value into determinate truths or falsehoods; putting it differently, communal agreement creates *facts*. Unfortunately, this argument leads to an infinite regress and determinate social fact never emerges. The existence of a communal consensus is itself a social fact and hence a construction, according to ethnomethodology. Thus, it presupposes the existence of a further consensus, having the former one for its object, and so on without end. The existence of even the humblest social fact presupposes an infinite hierarchy of consensus, each consensus having another as its object. Since social reality does not have room for such infinite hierarchies, we must conclude that social reality is totally indeterminate: the machinery required to render social fact determinate does not exist. Hence, there is nothing that can be determinately asserted about social reality. More succinctly put, there is no (determinate) social reality. This is a highly unwelcome result for a position that aspires to making a positive contribution to the investigation of social reality.

We next examined the cultural relativity argument. It is close kin to the ethnomethodological argument, but introduces a significant modification to avoid the regress. Instead of presenting social fact as created by a communal consensus, social fact is seen as generated by the standards of rationality valid in the community; these standards are depicted as culturally variable. The standards need not be known to the society's members and *a fortiori* need not be consensually endorsed by them; hence the consensus regress never starts. However, trouble threatens from another angle. If standards of rationality are culturally variable, and if such standards create facts, there must be a determinate answer as to which cultural stage a given society occupies at any time, even during phases of rapid social and cultural change. There cannot be allowed to exist grey zones where a society, in its historical development, is in transition between stages. During transition, there would be no canons of rationality determinately associated with that society; and since canons of rationality are alleged to be the generators of social fact, social reality would be totally indeterminate during those transitional phases. However, the existence of such transitions seems an indisputable fact. Societies sometimes undergo rapid revolutionary transformations in which they will have shed the preceding societal form and its associated rationality, without yet having reached a new stable form. Still, it is not as if social reality is completely amorphous during those transitional periods, as if absolutely nothing can be determinately asserted about a society during such times. This determinacy cannot be accounted for by the cultural relativity argument.

We briefly examined a possible way to strengthen these arguments, one inspired by Berger and Luckmann's celebrated book, *The Social Construction of Reality*. These authors combine a constructivist stance with tenets from the sociology of knowledge, declaring, with a deliberate air of paradox, both that society is a human creation and that man is a social creation. This might seem to dispose of the indeterminacy problem of social constructivism: the collective cognitive processes that generate social reality are themselves the causal product of societal conditions, operating in accordance with laws which the sociology of knowledge uncovers. Unfortunately this hybrid position fails to block the destructive regress which the constructivist argument generates. On constructivist principles, the social determinants of collective thinking must themselves issue from a process of construction; they are social creations. In consequence, they fall prey to the indeterminacy that afflicts such collective cognitions. In Berger and Luckmann's theory, constructivist processes and causal factors try in vain to borrow determinacy from one another.

Finally, we examined the linguistic relativity argument. Like the ethnomethodological argument, this one sees social fact as generated by the process of linguistic description, or classification. However, it avoids the by-now familiar regress by claiming that the mere existence of a classificatory term in the vocabulary suffices to generate reality, or facts; it is no longer claimed that linguistic terms only create reality when and in so far as they are actually applied. The view is based on the observation that things can be classified in indefinitely many ways; hence, their generic (classifying) properties are indeterminate, too. Once a generic term is introduced into language, however, the thing achieves determinacy, namely as either belonging or not belonging to the extension of this term; in this way a determinate fact about the thing is generated. But this argument overlooks the way that classifying terms reflect similarities among things, existing prior to the process of classification. These similarities need not be intrinsic to the things classified, but may pertain to people's reactions to them or to their societal function. Of whichever kind, they are not generated by the very introduction of a classifying term into language; on the contrary, the employment of a classifying term presupposes their existence. Hence the linguistic relativity argument, like its predecessors, fails to establish a constructivist position.

We conclude that social constructivism cannot be demonstrated on the basis of the general philosophical premises invoked in the Broad Arguments. The snag to those arguments is that the modification they introduce to our ordinary picture of social reality turns out to be uncontrollable. Once the constructivist premise is adopted, there is no way we can sustain something remotely resembling our customary picture of the social world. As a matter of fact, social reality disappears altogether. In Part Two, we shall see that a more moderate constructivist position can be established on the basis of arguments that take their point of departure in the specific properties of human action.

Part Two

The Narrow Arguments

In Part Two, we shall be considering arguments in favour of the construction thesis that reflect the special features of human action, and thereby of social action; they are not arguments that can be generalised to cover every type of fact. The general strategy of the arguments is to show that individual human actions are somehow constituted by the descriptions applied to them by the agent. From this it follows that social reality is similarly constituted. As I argued in the Introduction, social facts rest upon a stratum of facts pertaining to the actions of individual human beings. Social facts are essentially collective facts; that is, they are facts about a plurality of human individuals and their mutual relationships. If you have individual facts plus a suitable setting, you have social facts; and where there are no facts about individual human beings, neither are there social facts. The connection between the two kinds of facts is so tight that if a constructivist thesis can be shown to hold true for individual human facts, it will hold for social facts as well.

This is not to say that social facts can be *defined* in terms of individual facts, except in trivial cases: the tie between the two kinds is ontological, not semantic. What blocks definability is that a particular setting is typically required for individual facts, even when taken collectively, to constitute social facts (in a non-trivial way); this setting is not definable in terms of individual facts. This is an important point, to which we shall return in Part Three.

CHAPTER V

The Arguments from the 'Meaningfulness' of Action

The Phenomenological Argument

A number of arguments in favour of a social constructivist position are based upon the observation that action is imbued with subjective 'meaning'. Action is not just behaviour, mere bodily motion, but also has an 'inside' comprising the agents' concomitant mental processes. This 'inside' is not merely an epiphenomenon and, hence, irrelevant to the nature of the action, but is precisely that which bestows upon action its nature *as* action; moreover, it gives each particular action its individual essence. In this way, the doctrine of the 'meaningfulness' of action assumes the character of a social constructivist thesis. If we equate (if only tentatively, so far) these 'meanings' with thoughts and judgements, or at least grant that thoughts and judgements are *instances* of meaning, we must conclude that human thought brings social reality into being by bestowing upon human action a determinate essence. Later, we shall see that this equation is indeed legitimate; this serves to tie the thesis of the 'meaningfulness' of action firmly to the construction issue and also gives a precise content to the somewhat obscure notion of 'meaning'.

It is important to appreciate the difference between the positions we are about to examine here in Part Two and those discussed in Part One. An adequate grasp of the difference will be achieved only through an examination of the various versions of the Narrow Argument, but a simple preliminary statement may be useful. The Broad Arguments all claimed that social facts were generated by agents giving them credence, classifying them, reaching a consensus about them, or otherwise making them topics of their thinking. The facts created were the *objects* of collective processes of belief or consensus formation, classification, explanation or conceptualisation. Here, on the other hand, we shall be examining positions maintaining that social facts are generated by the way that such cognitive states form a *part* or *aspect* of those facts. As we shall see, this way of putting it may slightly overstate the difference. Still, there is a difference; there had better be, lest the present position immediately succumb to the objections which disposed of the previous interpretation. We may refer to the position previously discussed as *construction by objectification*, the one to be examined here as *construction by composition*.

THE MEANINGFULNESS OF ACTION ACCORDING TO WILHELM DILTHEY

The doctrine that human action displays a distinct type of 'meaningfulness' was pivotal to the writings of Wilhelm Dilthey and other seminal figures of nineteenth-century German thought. In its historical context this ontological doctrine was primarily advanced to buttress a specific methodological stance. Dilthey and kindred thinkers were concerned to demonstrate that the *Geisteswissenschaften* – the sciences of man and culture – should not be modelled on the natural sciences. In pressing this position, these authors put themselves in opposition to the prevailing tendency to see the sciences of man as susceptible of the same approach as that characteristic of the natural sciences; this methodological assumption had been imported into German thinking from abroad, through the writings of Auguste Comte and John Stuart Mill.

Comte and Mill sought to institute a science of man capable of producing general laws of human action and explaining individual actions by subsuming them under such laws. By contrast, Dilthey insisted that the *Geisteswissenschaften* have a method uniquely their own, a claim encapsulated in his celebrated dictum, 'We explain nature, but we understand mental life' (Dilthey 1894: 144). This is not to say that Dilthey rejected the possibility or usefulness of general truths and causal explanation in the 'moral sciences', but merely that he insisted that these disciplines employ other and more specialised techniques as well.

The distinction between two ways of grasping an object introduced by Dilthey in the dictum cited above is familiar from our everyday ways of thinking. We *understand* what people are about when, on a baking hot day, they go to the beach and plunge headlong into the sea; but we cannot *understand*, in the same sense, what propels a raindrop when it trickles down a rock, merges with others to form a stream, ultimately to flow into the sea. In the first case, we appeal to wishes, desires and motives, whereas in the latter case, we can only cite the law of gravitation: water will tend to move towards the centre of gravity of the system of which it is a part, unless obstructed. Not since the Middle Ages have we attributed to water any desire to move to the centre of gravity, and even less to plunge into the sea.

This familiar everyday contrast, however, is recast in highly theoretical terms in the context of Dilthey's philosophy, where it becomes clear how, in his view, it builds upon an ontological foundation. Underlying our everyday practices of explaining events and actions, and underlying, too, their sophisticated counterparts in the projected Science of Man, is the triad of *Experience, Expression* and *Understanding*.[1] 'Experience' is the ground and source of human action. It constitutes the subjective, mental life of man from which his actions flow as its manifestations. The critical thrust of the doctrine of experience was targeted at two widely divergent, contemporaneous conceptions of man which nonetheless share a strongly rationalist or intellectualist bias. One is the model of man that emerged in eighteenth century empiricist and enlightenment thought, and that lived on in the methodological writings of John Stuart Mill. This conception views human action as springing from two neatly separated mental sources, viz. beliefs and desires, while a third element, reason, serves to compute the proper way for these two to issue in action. The paradigm example of this kind of model is the economists' *homo economicus*. The other conception finds expression in Hegel's view of history, which does not attribute reason primarily to individual human beings but instead ascribes it to a hidden agent of world history, *Reason* writ large. This quasi-agent cunningly steers individual action towards the goal of world history.

As against this, Dilthey's notions of 'experience' has a distinctive romantic tinge to it: experience is the undivided source of action in which thought, desire and will are indissolubly fused, not neatly segregated as the empiricist conception holds. Dilthey often refers to this holistic unity simply as 'life'. This conception is also intended to mark a contrast to Hegel's Reason, 'life' being a more empirical and contingent, less metaphysical, source of human history. History and society are formed through the aggregation of countless anonymous individual lives, not by the guiding power of a transcendent entity directing human action towards world-historical goals.

Experience, in short, is man's subjectivity through which his ordinary, unreflectively lived existence is realised and mediated. It is in the nature of experience never to remain merely subjective, however, but to exteriorise itself in actions and in the permanent artefacts that actions leave behind: buildings, monuments, works of art, and written documents. In such artefacts, human experience is crystallised, perhaps to be extracted at a later point through the activities of the third member of Dilthey's triad of basic concepts, *understanding*.

In characterising understanding, Dilthey uses such terms as 'reexperiencing', 'recreating', and 'empathising'. Understanding is seen as somehow replicating the state of 'experience' that the agent was in when he performed the act, produced the work of art or built the monument. This is not to say, however, that Dilthey considered understanding to be a simple, intuitive act. On the contrary, the interpretative enterprise will often expand into a general discursive process where the object of understanding, for instance, an individual human action, is situated in a larger context of comparable actions, either those performed by the agent in the course of a lifetime, or more broadly, those actions figuring in the context of an entire epoch or society. This is often apt when we seek to understand a historical figure as a 'child of his times', as it is often put. Understanding proceeds through a tacking back and forth between the individual act and its wider setting, gradually reaching to deeper levels through so doing; this is the celebrated hermeneutical circle. Nonetheless, the unit operation in this entire process of interpretation remains the simple experiential state of empathy.

Such, then, were the ideas that Dilthey bequeathed to his successors: in the first place, a strict division between the methodological procedures used in the two realms of natural science and the *Geisteswissenschaften*, the sciences of man. Secondly, this division is represented as reflecting an ontological difference: natural phenomena are ontologically monistic, whereas phenomena involving man have a composite nature. They have an 'outside', which may actually be made the object of naturalistic investigation, but also an 'inside', consisting of that primordial stratum of human existence, 'experience'. For Dilthey and his followers, this doctrine was seen primarily as an argument in favour of a specific methodology, a move in the *Methodenstreit* between positivists and anti-positivists in German social science around the turn of the century. But the doctrine in question can be put to immediate effect with respect to the themes that concern us here, viz., as an argument in support of a viable version of social constructivism. We shall look at the methodological aspect in greater detail, however, before returning to ontology and the issue of constructivism.

THE METHODOLOGY OF SOCIAL SCIENCE ACCORDING TO MAX WEBER

Dilthey was primarily a philosopher, and his work on the methodology of the human sciences remained highly programmatic, a prolegomenon to any future science of man, as it were. To see these ideas turned into concrete methodological recommendations, and indeed to see actual scientific research undertaken under their aegis, we have to turn to Max Weber.

A classic, immensely influential statement of the meaningfulness of human action and its methodological implications is to be found in Weber's main work, *The Theory of Social and Economic Organization* (Weber 1947). Following Dilthey, Weber points out that we may distinguish, within the overall phenomenon of human conduct, between purely outward behaviour (*Verhalten*) – bodily movement – and its 'inside' in the form of subjective meaning (*Sinn*). If, to take Weber's oft-repeated example, we observe somebody swinging an axe at some logs (and, strictly speaking, we should be even more behaviouristic in our description of what is happening, since even this pared-down description presupposes certain 'inner' occurrences), we do not yet know what action is being performed, until we penetrate to the subjective intentions of the agent. Is his intention to produce firewood, so that his behaviour counts as the action of chopping firewood? Or is it to earn a wage, making his action that of working for a livelihood? Or is the man just working off a fit of anger? Only a grasp of the agent's subjective meaning will decide the issue.

The contribution of the internal aspect is marked by variations in degree of clarity and explicitness. In the paradigm case of human action, a clear and determinate meaning is associated with the behaviour. But, according to Weber, this exemplary case shades imperceptibly into less distinct forms. Thus, *traditional* conduct represents a less central case of action since the meaningful aspect is less prominent. A person who 'acts traditionally' may not, on being asked, be able to cite any clearly defined 'meaning' in his action, or, at least, not any individual purpose. He will simply say that he did what 'we have always done', or what 'one is supposed to do'. 'Traditional' action is semi-automatic, hence less fully a human action. Other cases that are far removed from the paradigm are those of *reactive* behaviour, such as the behaviour displayed in a fit of rage. Diametrically opposed to the paradigm case is pure reflex behaviour, as in a man abruptly withdrawing his hand from a hot stove.

Weber is none too clear as to the nature of the 'meanings' that he imputes to action. As the examples illustrate, however, he uses the term in a broad sense to include both what we would call purely cognitive and purely conative elements (wishes and desires, but also emotions). Weber's presentation is obfuscated by his tendency to characterise the various kinds of 'meanings' in terms of the types of understanding to which they are related. Weber distinguishes between a rational kind of understanding and that possessed of an 'emotionally empathic or artistically appreciative quality'. Thus, we have a rational understanding of the purely intellectual content of somebody's utterance, or the content of the accompanying thought, when (for instance) we hear a person uttering the sentence, '$2 \times 2 = 4$'. Likewise, we have a rational understanding of somebody's motives, in the sense that we intellectually identify the values and goals underlying his conduct. On the other hand, the 'empathic or appreciative' type of understanding is involved when we try to understand the emotional context in which an action was performed. Weber describes it as consisting of some sort of 'sympathetic participation' in the emotional life of the other person. It is a matter of re-creating in one's own mind what goes on in the other person's mind; to savour the flavour of his emotional life, as it were. And, although he states explicitly that 'one need not have been Caesar in order to understand Caesar' (Weber 1947: 90), he still seems to hold that such 'participation' represents the highest level of understanding.

The distinction between rational and empathic understanding intersects with that obtaining between *observational* and *explanatory* understanding. After we have identified a person's thoughts or motives correctly, thus attaining observational understanding, there remains the further task of explaining why the person would think like this or act from those motives. Weber seems to construe the difference between the two kinds of understanding as one of scope –

in seeking explanatory understanding, we place an action already correctly identified at the observational level in a larger context of meaning. The item is explained by the way it fits into this broader context.

In the case of social action, this subjective 'meaning' takes cognisance of the action of others; this is precisely what makes the action social. Weber's famous definition of social action states that 'action is social in so far as, by virtue of the subjective meaning attached to it by the acting individual (or individuals), it takes account of the behaviour of others and is thereby oriented in its course' (Weber 1947: 88). Hence, to the extent that social action is precisely that with which social science is concerned, social science must determine the subjective side of human action.

In the light of this duality of action, Weber called for a duality in the methods used in social science. Social explanation must strive for 'adequacy' both at the causal and the meaningful level. Adequacy at the meaningful level implies that the connection between the action and the motives imputed to the agent must be understandable, either in terms of rational understanding or in terms of understanding of the 'empathic, appreciative' kind. Adequacy at the causal level requires the demonstration that the postulated motivational states were actually present and did indeed originate the action. The mere meaningfulness of the connection does not guarantee this. Such a guarantee can only be provided on the basis of experiment or, failing that, an investigation of comparable situations in which the alleged motivational factors are present and the same action, therefore, should occur.

The showpiece of this methodological conception at work is Weber's famous study of the origins of capitalism in *The Protestant Ethic and the Spirit of Capitalism* (Weber 1930). Here, Weber tries to show us the meaningful 'inside' of a particular historical phenomenon, the birth of capitalism – the thoughts and concerns propelling forward those who first engaged in the kind of accumulation of wealth characteristic of capitalism. Weber conceives more narrowly than others the connection between protestantism and economical activity which had been noted and commented upon by earlier social scientists, construing it as a connection between Calvinism and industry. According to Calvinism, strict determinism rules in the world of human action; God has preordained everything in human affairs, including the question of who will be saved and who will be damned. But, Weber claims, this state of affairs is intolerable to man, rendering him helpless with respect to the most important issue he is ever to face. Thus, in order to provide deliverance from this plight, a doctrine is introduced, according to which Good Works are an indication that a person will be saved: constituting the signs by which God shows that the given individual is among the chosen few. There is, then, something a person can do to ascertain what is in store for him – not by changing his fate, but by producing an omen of what that fate will be. This religious doctrine engendered a general pattern of behaviour marked by emphasis on industry and the accumulation of wealth, thus creating ideal preconditions for the emergence of capitalism.

ALFRED SCHUTZ AND PHENOMENOLOGY

Weber's dual-aspect theory of action and of subjective interpretation was further developed by members of the phenomenological school, and given its most systematic elaboration by Alfred Schutz. Schutz accepted Weber's insight that action has a subjective, 'meaningful' side, which invests social action with its peculiarly social aspect and, indeed, makes it truly action. The social sciences call for a special methodology, one combining causal explanation of action with understanding of its subjective meaning. Schutz held, however, that Weber had left a crucial gap in his account by treating 'meaning' and understanding as unanalysed notions, supposedly sufficiently well understood from everyday use to serve as scientific concepts as well. According to Schutz, this was a mistake; indeed, it is one of the prime tasks of social science to analyse these notions. To supply the requisite analysis he had recourse to Husserlian phenomenology.

Phenomenology represents a grandiose attempt to revive the ancient idea of philosophy as a science that discloses the essence of things. For Edmund Husserl, the route to an understanding of essences runs through an examination of the mental acts by which we grasp reality in intentional acts. A detailed analysis of the structure of cognitive acts through which external reality is presented to us will tell us something about the structure of reality itself; indeed, it will reveal the essence of the objects towards which consciousness is directed. The procedure leading to this result consists first, of engaging in a distinctive type of introspection in which attention is shifted from the external object to the internal states of consciousness through which it is grasped; Husserl calls this 'bracketing' or *epoché*. *Epoché is contrived through the suspension of belief in the objective, external existence of the objects of one's perceptual or other cognitive acts, and in fixing one's attention instead on the very act through which that object is represented. One will then be able to separate out the strands of the complicated structure of mental processes through which the object is grasped. One then puts the object so conceived through a complex thought experiment, comprising a series of systematic hypothetical modifications designed to establish which changes will transform that object (i.e. that kind of object) into another kind, and which will allow it to retain its identity. In this way, the contours of that kind of thing will eventually be made out, and the thing's essence thereby determined. Husserl calls this process Wesensschau ('the intuiting of essences').*

Now, there may be doubts about the credentials of this procedure as a general philosophical methodology. It would seem that it is predicated on the premise that the object itself is constituted by the mental processes by which it is conceived; otherwise, an analysis of the cognitive processes will tell us little about the object. Indeed, Husserl apparently came to accept some such premise in a later stage of his thinking when he developed his so-called 'transcendental phenomenology'. Here, reality seems to be conceived as the creation of a special metaphysical agency, the 'transcendental ego'; phenomenology thus seems to have taken the fateful step from being a subjectivist method of philosophical enquiry to being a substantive idealist view.

The question whether or not Husserl's thought actually took this idealist turn is still debated among scholars; the textual evidence seems to be systematically ambiguous. However, we may bypass this contentious issue here, since we are interested in phenomenology only as it was applied to human reality by Schutz. Now, in his early work, *Phenomenology of the Social World* (Schutz 1967), Schutz touches upon the problems of transcendental phenomenology, in particular the problem of how the Other is constituted by the transcendental ego. He stresses the importance of these problems and refers with approval to Husserl's efforts to solve them; however, he goes on to declare that these issues are of no import for his own undertaking. We might mention in passing that in so doing, Schutz forgoes the use of a very direct but treacherous route to a constructivist conclusion. If he were to adopt the position of transcendental phenomenology it would, under a strong idealist reading, allow Schutz simply to argue that social reality is a creation of this metaphysical subject and, hence, a construction. But by the same token, so would everything else be, and we should be saddled with a general idealism of the kind that we found ample reason to shun in the previous chapters. In fact, later in life, Schutz grew increasingly sceptical of this part of Husserl's system and ended by dismissing the possibility of a truly transcendental phenomenology.

Rather than an exercise in transcendental phenomenology then, what we get in *Phenomenology of the Social World* is the Husserlian method deployed to give detailed descriptions of what goes on in an agent's mind when he acts, which is to say, an analysis of the 'meaningful' aspect of those acts. We also get an account of the corresponding processes that must take place in an observer's mind when he tries to understand another person's actions. Now, when applied in this field, the phenomenological approach seems to come into its own. Here, the claim that we exhibit the essence of a phenomenon by tracing the mental processes through which it is grasped is actually quite plausible, since it amounts to the claim that the way to exhibit the essence of an action is to specify what goes on in the agent's mind concomitantly with the outward behaviour. The purely behavioural aspect of an action does not suffice to fix its essence. This seems quite plausible; as Schutz pointed out, one and the same routine of native behaviour, as recorded by a social anthropologist on film, may amount to entirely different actions depending on what goes on in the minds of those engaged in it: it may be a war dance, the ceremony surrounding a barter trade between two tribes, or the reception of an ambassador (Schutz 1962: 54). The social world is interpreted and categorised by the subjects inhabiting it; more specifically, social actions are interpreted and individuated by the thoughts of the actors. Such thoughts section the continuous flow of external motion into proper units, individual acts, and thus determine when one act stops and the next begins. Only the mental 'inside' of the act establishes its identity *as* an act, and thereby defines its essence. The actor imposes a means–end structure upon the continuum of bodily motion, thereby segmenting it and converting it into a sequence of actions. Only the actor knows precisely where one action ends and another begins and, hence, their true identity. In brief, the actor *constructs* social reality through his interpretation of his own outward behaviour.

Yet there are serious weaknesses in Schutz's account and, hence, doubts about its usefulness in supporting a moderate constructivist position. Schutz's reports from the inner world of meaning and understanding are rife with examples of what Ryle was later to ridicule as the 'paramechanic conception of the mind' (Ryle 1949). Logical and epistemological features of psychological processes are crudely transformed into stories about how the mind goes about its work; attention is depicted rather as a ray of mental energy with which the mind illuminates, dissects and welds together its contents into larger units. The overall impression is that of a somewhat naive literalism which takes the mechanical or manufacturing metaphors we use to describe our mental faculties at face value.

It might be said with some justification that we are flogging a dead horse here since, later in his career, Schutz greatly downplayed his Husserlian heritage and thus the aspects of his thought that we are currently criticising. This formed part of a general reorientation of his interests away from metaphysics and towards methodological issues. To some extent, the thought of George Herbert Mead came to replace that of Husserl as providing the theoretical under-pinnings of his thinking in social science. But even if we disregard the metaphysical aspect of Schutz's system and confine ourselves to his methodological views, the charge of psychologism still sticks. In his reflections upon the nature of interpretation of human action, for instance, Schutz insisted that the most adequate understanding of another person resides in that immediate participation in his ongoing thought that occurs only in face-to-face contact, which Schutz termed the 'We-relationship'. True, this is not a case of participation in the sense that the observer reduplicates in himself the very same kinds of mental states as those occurring in the other person; Schutz repudiates the idea that two human beings could ever come to have exactly the same kinds of mental experience. Still, it is participation in the sense of constituting an intuitive and unmediated way of cognitive access to the other person's mental states. It is achieved through unreflectively entering into and sustaining a stretch of social interaction with that person.

In fairness to Schutz, it must be stressed that he considers face-to-face interaction a limiting case of understanding, even in everyday affairs. In the general run of things we do not have this kind of direct access when seeking to understand action – if only because the agents are not with us. Instead, we must make do with a less direct mode of understanding, namely, grasping action in discursive categories that are of our (the understanders') devising, not the agents' own. Moreover, Schutz is emphatic that this more abstract kind of understanding is the only one that has any legitimate role in science. For, as Schutz sees it, the social scientist never *participates* in social encounters when doing science, but observes them rather, from a detached stance. Still, the charge of psychologism against Schutz is clearly warranted.[2]

Thus, both Schutz and Weber commit what has been termed 'the reproductive fallacy' (Rudner 1966), taking the understanding of a human phenomenon to consist of rehearsing or re-creating it in thought, rather than describing it. In Schutz, the roots of the fallacy reside in his initial commitment to Husserlian phenomenology, which he applied, in a rather rigorous and literal-minded way, to the phenomenon of social action. As for Weber, it would seem that he was too impressed with the fact that emotions, unlike pure thoughts, have a phenomenal 'feel' to them, and compounded this with a failure to appreciate that emotions have a cognitive content as well, and are relevant to the understanding of action only in virtue of the latter. These related errors easily lead to the idea that the understanding of action springing from such phenomenally full-bodied emotions consists in re-experiencing the emotion. In actual fact, the purely phenomenal 'tone' of emotions is irrelevant to action explanation, however.

I have offered a brief sketch of the historical lineage of the doctrine that action is imbued with meaning, where meaning is construed as something 'inner' and experiential. We have seen that this doctrine was originally set forth as a contribution to a methodological debate, buttressing attempts to defend the distinctiveness of the sciences of human action against various positivist challenges. We have also seen that this methodological claim is based upon certain ontological assumptions. These assumptions can be extricated from their context and used to support a moderate constructivist position with respect to social facts. This is the move I have named 'the phenomenological argument', and it is time to spell it out in detail. Our enquiry also showed that the phenomenological view in the traditional version is vitiated by a fatal psychologism. If the view is to be of any use in the support of a constructivist position, we need to recast it to rid it of this weakness. Thus, there is a dual task ahead of us: we must first show how the phenomenological approach supports a constructivist position, and then indicate how it can shed its excess of metaphysical weight.

THE PHENOMENOLOGICAL ARGUMENT EXPLICATED

The phenomenological argument in support of constructivism is really made all but explicit in the above sections, and it takes very little work to bring it fully out into the open.

The argument simply asserts that human and social facts are generated when human behaviour is conjoined with the 'meaning' with which the agent invests it. This meaning generates a fact over and above the purely behavioural facts, viz. a fact about the *action* performed by him in evincing that behaviour. In this way, the constructivist formula is satisfied. That formula, you will recall (cf. pp. 2–3), defines constructivism as the position that human thoughts, beliefs, explanations or concepts create the social facts they are about. The phenomenological formula clearly satisfies this form of words, since the meanings with which a person accompanies his behaviour may plausibly be described as thoughts about that behaviour. (There will be more about this later.)

So far, the formula merely describes the generation of facts about individual human actions. Strictly speaking, a *social* fact is generated only when we have a plurality of agents whose 'meanings' are somehow interrelated and mutually refer to each other. (See our initial definition of social facts on pp. 6–7. Notice the affinity of this definition with Weber's definition of social action above). This is not to say that social facts are reducible to a set of individual facts. As we shall see later in this part, as well as in Part Three, social facts extend beyond purely individual facts. The truth remains that all social facts have facts about individual action and thought as their necessary condition.

The phenomenological argument is immune to the criticisms directed against the Broad Arguments in Part One. According to those arguments, thought generates action (and other social phenomena) by having action (etc.) as its *object*, an object that is created by the very process in which it is grasped. On the present conception, meanings create action by being a *component* or *aspect* thereof. Meaning is the 'inner' aspect of action that combines with the 'external' aspect – bodily movement – to constitute the unity that is action. In their several ways, both aspects of action enjoy an autonomous existence; they are not constructions. Behaviour is not constructed by the meanings accompanying it, or any other meanings, nor are the accompanying meanings constructed by further, higher-level meanings that are turned upon them in reflection. Thus, there is no threat of regress here, no threat of an infinite hierarchy of meanings each having another as its respective object. To repeat an expression used above, we are dealing with generation by *composition*, not by *objectification*.[3]

The remarks made above might seem to represent the 'inside' and 'outside' of human action as running on parallel but separate tracks, synchronised yet otherwise oblivious of each other. This would, of course, be a serious misrepresentation of action, and might also raise a suspicion that this account actually fails to satisfy the constructivist formula. For it would not be obvious, on this picture, that the 'meaning' accompanying a sequence of behaviour could really be said to be *about* that behaviour. Fortunately, the dual-aspect account can do justice to the formula and accommodate all the familiar facts about action. The 'meaning' accompanying behaviour has a complexity that makes it correct to say that it is *about* the behaviour. The 'meaning' consists, at ground level, of the agent's anticipations of the goal that he seeks to realise. At a higher level, it comprises the agent's awareness of his ongoing behaviour through which he constantly monitors its progress, making sure that it is taking him towards the realisation of his end.

Hence, as a manifestation of mind, action is different from the way in which teeth chattering manifests a person's fear. That his teeth are chattering may be unmonitored by the frightened person and, indeed, he may not be aware of it at all. Action, at least high-level action, is different. The agent constantly checks his ongoing behaviour to estimate whether or not it brings him closer to his goal. His motivational states do not erupt into action in a brute mechanical way; rather, they have the status of a plan that the agent keeps consulting to see if his action is realising his goals in an appropriate way. Behaviour is not like a rocket that is beyond control once it blasts off, but is more like a missile that is constantly monitored and kept on course. In other words, in typical high-level action, the agent conceives of his current outward movements as the realisation of his intentions; it is this thought that transforms those movements into action. (Consider the puzzling experience of suddenly forgetting, in the middle of some action, what you are doing. With the 'meaning' gone, the action immediately becomes mere bodily movement that may run on briefly before coming to a halt.) Hence, it is entirely appropriate to apply the constructivist formula to human action: it is the agent's *thought* of his concurrent movement that makes that movement the action it is. It is this monitoring consciousness, constantly comparing outward movement with some inner plan, that bestows upon that movement the status of an action, aimed at achieving some particular goal.[4]

THE PHENOMENOLOGICAL ARGUMENT RECONSTRUCTED

Next, we have to address the psychologism that the phenomenological argument would seem to inherit from Weber and Schutz. We saw that there are really two worries here. One concerns the theory of explanation espoused by Weber and Schutz, which maintains that explanation, at least in certain privileged cases, is achieved by subjective identification or re-enactment. The other, more serious worry pertains to the ontological implications of the phenomenological argument as construed by Schutz. This argument seems to saddle us with a crude dualism, since it presents the mental as a separate realm of being, alongside the physical world.

I believe we can solve both problems at once. I shall proceed in the same manner as the authors we have examined above, which is by way of reflecting on the nature of explanation of human action. First, I shall present a theory of explanation that embodies the insights gained by Dilthey, Weber and Schutz while staying clear of the 'reproductive fallacy'; the analysis is by no means new or original.[5] Second, we will look at the ontological presuppositions of this theory only to find that they support a constructivist stance. But those presuppositions are not dualist in any substantive sense; hence, the fundamental thrust of the phenomenological argument does not hinge upon any particular construal of the 'meaningful' aspect of action. In particular, it does not compel us to underwrite Dilthey's, Weber's, Husserl's or Schutz's dualist understanding of this notion. It is possible to produce a sanitised version of the phenomenological argument, stripped of the particular trappings with which it is invested in the writings of these authors.

Suppose we say that Mrs NN went on a low-cholesterol diet in order to reduce the risk of a heart attack. When we examine this purposive explanation more closely, we find that it may be unpacked into certain characteristic structural components. There is, first, the *desire* to live to ripe old age. There is, second, the *belief* that a high cholesterol level in the bloodstream lowers life expectancy, by increasing, for instance, the risk of arterial sclerosis and heart failure. There is, third, the *belief* that a reduced intake of cholesterol will lower the cholesterol level in the body.

This kind of account evinces explanatory power by showing, *inter alia*, that the action done was a (good or at least satisfactory) means towards achieving the agent's goals, given the agent's beliefs about the world. We can bring out this feature by recasting the explanation as an example of practical reasoning. Supplemented with various implicit additional premises, the reasoning will run somewhat as follows:

- Mrs NN desires that she live to ripe old age.
- Mrs NN believes that if she is to live to ripe old age, she must reduce the risk of heart failure.
- Mrs NN believes that the risk of heart failure can be reduced if she lowers the level of cholesterol in her bloodstream.
- Mrs NN believes that she can lower the cholesterol level in her bloodstream by reducing her intake of cholesterol.

- Therefore, Mrs NN should go on a low-cholesterol diet.

Yet further supplementation is needed to make this practical argument logically valid. Even with such supplementation, what we have here is only an argument to support the conclusion that dieting was *the right thing* for Mrs NN to do. To get an *explanation* of the action itself, we need to add that it was the agent's grasp of this practical argument that actually *caused her* to start dieting. The necessity of this clause was demonstrated in a celebrated paper by Donald Davidson (Davidson 1963); but in fact this is simply Weber's now familiar point that the 'meaning-adequacy' of an explanation must be supplemented with causal adequacy as well. We need not delve any further into this issue here.

The crucial feature of this analysis is the role it assigns to *propositions* as embedded in sentences that describe the agent's motivational states. These propositions form a logical structure that amounts in effect to a practical argument, as we saw above. The motivational states that explain action – the 'meanings' that form the 'inside' of action – enter into action explanations only in the abstract form of so-called *propositional attitudes* that collectively have that argument as their object. A 'propositional attitude' is a standardised format for describing mental states, in which only their cognitive content is exhibited. This content is rendered in the form of propositions, which we may, without too much distortion, construe as the meanings of sentences. Thus, in so far as they appear in purposive explanations, mental states are reconstrued as relations to propositions.

On such a construal, the purely intellectual content of motivational states is sequestered out and the phenomenal aspect of the mental acts in question falls away as irrelevant to understanding. To understand the actions of someone who desires-true the proposition that he quit smoking, who believes-true the proposition that he can only succeed in this if he can suppress the withdrawal symptoms, and who believes-true the proposition that chewing nicotine gum is the best way to achieve the latter, we need not ever have shared the special phenomenal feel of craving a cigarette: even nonsmokers can do it. All we need is to compare the three stated propositions and recognise the rational means–end connection between them. Understanding action becomes a matter of grasping the logical connections between propositions. Note that even emotional states have a propositional content, which alone is relevant to an understanding of the actions to which they give rise. Emotions such as love, hatred, patriotism, etc. may all be construed as propositional attitudes: 'I will do anything to make NN happy', 'I believe NN to be an odious creature', 'I accept that I owe everything to my country, right or wrong', and so on.

However, our present interest is not in action explanation, but rather in a particular argument in favour of constructivism: there was a worry that adoption of this argument would carry a heavy ontological penalty. The propositional attitude analysis delivers us from this predicament by showing, first, that it must be acknowledged that action is indeed possessed of a further aspect beyond the purely behavioural one, and, second, that this aspect does not saddle us with unacceptable ontological burdens. The propositional attitude analysis achieves this by yielding a purely relational account of the mental: it characterises the mental via its relationship to a certain kind of item, viz. a proposition. But it refuses to be drawn into speculations as to the intrinsic nature of mental states.[6]

Thus, the 'double-aspect' conception of action that I have sketched out, as part of an account of social facts, is not meant to provide a complete philosophical analysis of this concept, but simply to indicate elements that I believe must figure minimally in any adequate analysis. The proposal is studiedly neutral with regard to the classical points of contention in the philosophy of mind; quite specifically, it is designed to avoid any commitment to traditional dualism. Any philosophical analysis must somehow accommodate the fact that human conduct involves physical movement plus another component or aspect, which competing schools construe differently. It may be conceived as consisting of brain processes, or of some kind of unique mind-stuff, or perhaps just a more comprehensive set of behaviours, actual or hypothetical, in which the agent's current behaviour is embedded; or perhaps a wider social setting, involving other people's actions as well. No matter how it is construed, it is the conjunction of occurrent behaviour (bodily motion) with this component that transforms the former into action.

The minimalist account of the mental presented above shows that the expression 'construction by composition, not objectification' should not be taken too literally in talking about *composition*; this is merely a convenient way of labelling the position. I have just stressed that the account of propositional attitudes is consistent with a broad range of different views concerning the substantive nature of the mental; and among these are theories that are incompatible with a compositional theory of the mental in a strict sense. For instance, those theorists who see the meaning of an action as residing in the wider setting of that action (neo-Wittgensteinians such as G. E. M. Anscombe and A. I. Melden) would certainly hold that it makes dubious sense to describe action as *composed* of pure behaviour and its setting. The canonical way of expressing 'construction by composition' would be to say that social facts may be analysed into the conjunction of two sets of more basic facts, namely, (1) facts about behaviour and (2) facts about mind-stuff, if such there be; or about brains; or about a wider setting of the aforementioned behaviour which may include further behaviour, actual as well as potential, possibly involving other people; or perhaps even some further alternative. Still, we may stick to the term 'construction by composition' as a convenient label.

After all this work of clarification, it is finally time to assess the phenomenological argument, as reconstructed in terms of propositional attitudes. I believe that this argument defines and supports a defensible version of the social construction view. The propositional attitude interpretation yields a precise and non-metaphorical reading of the claim that human action has a meaningful 'inside', and one moreover that serves to place that claim beyond serious dispute. Barring philosophical niceties that need not detain us here, there is no doubt that action has an intentional aspect; no purely behavioural conception will do. It is true that philosophers argue endlessly over the nature of the intentional aspect and its relation to behaviour. But I believe that, whatever position is ultimately correct will have to accommodate those features of action that serve to give the argument from 'meaning' a foothold. Furthermore, our initial subsumption of thoughts and judgements (about social reality) under the headings of 'meanings' has been vindicated. Thoughts and judgements are prime examples of propositional attitudes. This means, ultimately, that the doctrine of the meaningfulness of action implies a version of the social construction view: this doctrine leads to the conclusion that social facts are constituted by human thought and judgement, in so far as social facts include, *inter alia*, human actions as their elements.

Having established that the concept of 'meaning' can be given a legitimate and precise content, I shall henceforth drop the quotation marks around the word. However, the fact remains that this term is often too broad to serve as an efficient tool of analysis, and may profitably be replaced by the more precise terms falling under it – 'thought', 'belief', or 'intention' – wherever possible.

MAY SOCIAL FACTS BE WHOLLY CONSTITUTED BY MEANINGS?

The position established by the argument from meaningfulness is less ambitious than that which the Broad Arguments were designed (but failed) to support. The argument just examined only shows that meanings are a *necessary* condition for social fact, not a sufficient condition. Human meanings are an aspect of social fact and, hence, generate social fact only in conjunction with the other aspects. Putting it differently, human meanings generate social fact, but only provided other conditions are already satisfied. The other aspects needed include, typically, the purely external, behavioural side of action and the physical and other items that constitute the setting and the props for that behaviour.

However, while this is all the argument establishes *per se*, it raises an interesting possibility. The two aspects of social facts may presumably be present in varying degrees; specifically, there may be cases where the behavioural side of a social fact is negligible. Is it possible to imagine a limiting case in which only the subjective side is present, but in which we would still be justified in saying that a social fact is thereby created? In other words, could there, according to the argument from meaningfulness, be social facts that are wholly comprised of meanings?

We must hasten to add a proviso: such generation must be of a non-trivial sort. Without it, the question could immediately be answered in the affirmative, but in a manner that would completely rob it of interest. If an opinion poll shows that 35 per cent of the population believes that the economy will pick up over the next six months, what is recorded is evidently a social fact, incontestably constituted by meanings, *in casu* the beliefs of the population. But this social fact wears its belief-constitution on its sleeve. What we want are facts that are not at first glance comprised of people's meanings, but which still, on reflection, are seen to be so.

As it happens, ideas that would imply a positive answer to this question were suggested by Max Weber (Weber 1947: 136), but found their most striking articulation in the work of Weber's younger compatriot, Georg Simmel. Simmel was preoccupied with the same fundamental problems of social life as Weber, which is to say, the nature of that communality among a multitude of human individuals that transforms them into a society. A philosopher by training, Simmel looked to the great philosophers for a model which would enable him to get to grips with this issue, and found it in the teachings of Immanuel Kant. Kant may be described as a constructivist with regard to physical nature: the phenomenal, physical world with which we are confronted is our own creation as observers, albeit not as empirical, biological beings, but rather as transcendental egos. The world as we experience it is generated by the content of experience being moulded by the structural forms of the transcendental ego. The partly transcendental origins of phenomenal reality are evidenced by its displaying certain features that it possesses by necessity. Among these features are time, space and causality. These structural features produce the unity of experience, which is at the same time the unity of the world-as-experienced.

Transferring this philosophical framework to the problems of social reality prompts the question of what it is that creates unity and thus reality in the social sphere. The answer, according to Simmel, is that society exists in virtue of a particular mode of consciousness shared by its members. He says:

Societal unification needs no factors outside its own

component elements, the individuals. Each of them exercises
the function which the psychic energy of the observer exercises
in regard to external nature: the consciousness of constituting
with the others a unity is actually all there is to this unity.

(Simmel 1959: 338)

That is: in the physical sphere it is the powers of the observer (or
more correctly: the transcendental ego) that simultaneously
generate the unity of experience and constitute the object. Unity
is imposed from the outside, as it were. In the social sphere, on the
other hand, there is no need for an outside agency, an external
consciousness, to form society. That task is discharged by the
members of society themselves in virtue of their subscribing to a
particular idea, namely that of forming a unity together with the
others.

Later the point is put with great succinctness:

The consciousness of sociation is...the immediate agent, the
inner significance, of sociation itself.

(Ibid.: 342)

But let us forget about the roots of Simmel's theorising in Kantian
idealism in order to consider the above claims on their own merits,
as a possible source of support for a constructivist view. It is
obvious that, as it stands, Simmel's proposal is very vague and in
need of further specification. To begin with, it is even open to a
suspicion of regress. How can we spell out the content of A, B and
C's consciousness, or their shared belief, that they form a unity? To
say that they are conscious of forming a unity is only to say that
they are conscious of having some property or feature in common.
What could this common feature be? On pain of driving in a wedge
between the laymen's (A, B and C's) and the sociologist's (Simmel's)
notions of society, and of throwing doubt upon the everyday notion
and thereby the scientific one (which is predicated upon the former),
our reply must needs be: the common feature is the fact that A, B
and C are *conscious* that they form a unity. Now, however, it is
evident that this analysis leads to a regress. We say that society is
constituted by A, B, and C being conscious that A, B, and C are
conscious that A, B, and C ... so on without end. We never get to
the real substance of this belief.

However, it is clear from the way that Simmel continues the first of the above passages that he has something different in mind. He says,

> This does not mean, of course, that each member of a society is conscious of such an abstract notion of unity. It means that he is absorbed in innumerable, specific relations and in the feeling and the knowledge of determining others and of being determined by them.
>
> (1959: 338)

The final part of this quotation actually seems to reintroduce interaction between the members of society, thereby blunting the controversial nature of Simmel's theory. So, since our aim here is not Simmelian exegesis, but rather to examine the viability of a general position, let us concentrate on the first part, according to which society is constituted by the members' consciousness of a unity of a less abstract kind.

What kind of (consciousness of) unity, if any, would suffice to generate society? Certainly not any old property shared by the members of society, or the consciousness of that property, will do. For example, my recognition that I form an identity class with all other people born under some particular stellar sign does not forge us into a social unit. Somehow, social unity demands a more intimate relationship. It might be suggested that, among a set of people, only the recognition that they *interact* in certain ways will make them a social unit. But, in that case, it is no longer the mere consciousness of unity, but also some 'real', external nexus, that makes them a social unit.

Margaret Gilbert has penetratingly analysed this question. Gilbert (1989) sets out to develop a theory, which she herself describes as Simmelian, that a social unit is said to be formed by some 'inner', psychological state in its members. (Gilbert conducts her discussion in term of groups rather than societies, but the general point remains the same.) Gilbert eventually manages to construct a rather plausible theory, according to which the psychological state required is not the mere passive feeling of togetherness among the members of the group. Instead, the social glue has to do with the will, a willingness to engage in common undertakings. This willingness, moreover, has to be somehow made public in the group; indeed, it has to be the object of *common knowledge*, in the technical sense we introduced on p. 39. This means that any member of the group must know of any other member that this member has declared such willingness; this knowledge, on the part of every member, must again be known to every member of the group, and so on. There are many technical trappings to this analysis, but the core idea is simple: for certain people to form a group, there must be some element of declared and mutually recognised common will to participate in common undertakings.

Armed with this theory, let us return to the issue of whether groups or societies may exist merely by virtue of meanings. I believe that Gilbert's theory gives a plausible reading to the claim that a group can exist, even though there is no interaction between its members. As long as the preparedness to participate in common projects is present, we would not deny that the group still exists, although there are no joint activities between its members at the moment. It must be granted that groups are not always active; there will inevitably be periods during which the members are in the company of persons outside the group, or are alone. Saying that the group ceases to exist during those periods would be counter-intuitive. There is a perfectly gradual transition from this case to the one in which a group lies dormant for long periods of time. Even in such situations, we will want to distinguish between the case in which the group still exists as a mere potential for joint action and the situation in which such a potential is no longer present. Gilbert's analysis provides a natural way to construe this distinction: we will say that the group still exists if the members maintain a readiness for mutual action and that it has ceased to exist when the members have given up this commitment. In the former case, the mental set of the members of the group generates, in a non-trivial way, a social fact: the fact that this group is still in existence.

We may strengthen this conclusion by looking at the way the notion of a group has been put to use in current social psychology. It has become customary to draw a distinction highly relevant for our concerns, namely that between *membership groups* and *reference groups*. (We may mention in passing that Simmel was one of the founders of the specialty of social psychology called group theory.)

The membership group consists of people who have frequent interaction with one another. The high level of interaction is accompanied by a strong feeling of identification among the group members; this is the 'in-group'/'out-group' sentiment typically invoked in explaining the relationship of one group to other groups. I believe that the intuitive plausibility of Gilbert's definition of a group springs from the way that it captures the essence of this 'in-group' feeling. It is really a condition of the will, a commitment to the common projects of the group. Sometimes, definitions of 'group' may feature further elements, such as the stipulation that group members form a social hierarchy or share important norms or values. Here, however, we may stay with the minimal definition in terms of interaction and identification.

The reference group is often defined simply by the presence of a feeling of identity among a set of people, in the absence of actual interaction; it is, as it were, the membership group with the interaction subtracted. (No doubt, this kind of definition would gain strength if Gilbert's analysis were substituted for the vague reference to 'feeling'.) However, some definitions are richer. Often, the reference group is defined as the set of people that a person tries to emulate, or whose standards he uses to evaluate himself. (For a discussion of the two concepts of groups, see Sherif and Sherif 1969.)

It follows that reference groups are not totally devoid of behavioural manifestations; it is just the *interaction* between group members that is absent. Still, the fact remains that reference groups are not defined in terms of the presence of such manifestations, but by the presence of an attitude towards the other group members (such as a desire to be a member of the group). The notion of reference groups was introduced into social psychology to do justice to the idea that there may be important societal entities that do not at any given moment (and, indeed, for prolonged periods) issue observable actions, but instead lie behind such action, ready to generate it under appropriate circumstances. The reference group represents a social energy potential, as it were, waiting to exert itself in action, whether at the voting polls, in strikes, or in street riots. This is why the claim that a group is in existence, although dormantly, is a substantial and important one from the point of view of social science. The reference group does not exist merely when it manifests itself – no more than a magnetic field exists only when some object is affected by it.

Notice, finally, that we are not discussing whether the circumstance of a number of people sharing a certain set of attitudes towards each other constitutes a social fact; this it does, trivially. We are discussing whether it also constitutes a fact in a non-trivial way, by showing enough positive analogies with membership groups to deserve the name. I have argued that this is so. Social agents generate social fact by the subjective meaning with which they collectively accompany their behaviour; occasionally, this subjective side alone is enough to constitute, non-trivially, a social fact.

THE CONSTRUCTION THESIS MODIFIED

We have adopted a version of the construction view, based upon the phenomenological argument. Now, however, there is the threat that this result ushers in an unwelcome proliferation of facts. Suppose a native accompanies some external movement with the thought, 'This will achieve the goal of chasing away the evil spirits that have possessed my cattle', thereby converting his bodily movements into an act of exorcism. We seem to be encumbered with a highly undesirable enlargement of our ontology. Not only does it include a certain action, it also seems to include evil spirits, since the existence of an action to chase away evil spirits would seem to imply the existence of spirits to be chased away. Thus, it seems that our social ontology will be enriched with every kind of item that any community has ever believed to exist, such as spirits, gods, demons, magical elixirs or mana.

This permissive attitude towards ontology would seem to have been adopted, we may recall, by Berger and Luckmann in *The Social Construction of Reality*, at least on the strongest reading of that text. In the passage quoted on p. 68, these authors seem to be saying that, if we accept a Haitian's claim that he is engaged in acts directed at the demons that are possessing him, we are committed to the actual existence of those demons. Their existence, the authors concede, may only be a fact according to Haitian ontology; this does not amount to a withdrawal of the existence claim, however, since towards the end of their book Berger and Luckmann seem to imply that all reality is relative to some culturally-determined criterion of existence. There is no absolute frame of reference in terms of which culturally-relative world views may be assessed. Thus, voodoo demons are as real as things ever can be – certainly as real as the New Yorker's neuroses and 'libidinal energy' (Berger and Luckmann 1967: 197–8).

Here, however, I assume that we will want to adopt a less permissive ontological policy. We need to introduce a distinction between two ways in which a specification of the meaning of an action may be taken, diverging in the extent to which they underwrite existential and other claims made in any such specification. One version embraces only what I shall call the *internal implications*. Intuitively, internal implications are those parts of the action specification that detail the properties of the associated meanings *qua* mental states (that is, as purely subjective phenomena). The other version endorses all implications, including the *external implications*. Once again speaking intuitively, the external implications of action descriptions concern items that are not in themselves thoughts or constituents of the agent's mind but parts of the world outside it, towards which the action and the meanings inherent in it are directed.

Utilising the format of propositional attitudes (cf. p. 118), we can express this distinction in a more precise and adequate manner. All the meanings implicit in an action can be expressed as propositional attitudes. Sentences ascribing a propositional attitude have the general form, 'NN thinks that p', 'NN hopes that p', 'NN believes that p', 'NN intends that p', etc. The content component p specifies the proposition (or sentence) which the agent is said to have an attitude towards; content components are sentences such as 'It is going to rain soon', 'NN is about to get a promotion', 'NN has stopped smoking', etc.

Now we can define the external implications of an action description as those that follow from the *content sentence alone*, when that sentence is considered in isolation. The internal implications, on the other hand, are those that follow from the entire propositional attitude sentence, of the form 'NN believes that p'. Notice that this definition does not make the external implications a subset of the internal implications, since the implications of p (the external implications) are neutralised when p is embedded in the sentential context of 'NN believes that ...'.

Let us illustrate with an example. If a native declares that he has cast a spell in order to chase away evil spirits which possess his cattle, we may construe this description in such a way that, by accepting it, we admit that there are evil spirits around to be exorcised; we would thereby have accepted an external implication. Alternatively, we may interpret the specification in such a way that we are not committed to the existence of evil spirits, but only to the agent's *belief* that such spirits exist and to a *desire* on his part to chase them away. We are committed to the existence of his mental states, but not to the existence of real, external items as the objects of those mental states.

Armed with this distinction, we may reformulate the phenomenological version of constructivism as follows: the meanings with which social agents inform their behaviour generate social facts in so far as those facts comprise (the behaviour in conjunction with) the *internal* implications of the agents' meanings; sometimes meanings generate facts even when unaccompanied by behaviour. The phenomenological argument does not commit us to the *external* implications of agents' descriptions and thus to the claim that these, too, generate facts. The only way one might defend a more liberal policy would be by invoking some of the arguments of Part One, to the effect that human agreement creates social fact in a more wide-ranging sense. We have found reason to reject those arguments.

Thus, we adopt the thesis that subjective meanings suffice to constitute social facts (alone or together with accompanying behaviour), as long as those facts involve only the internal implications of the action descriptions (and, maybe, behaviour). When social facts presuppose the truth of the external implications of action descriptions, such as claims about real material or spiritual beings, the agents' meanings do not guarantee their reality; hence, the meanings do not generate social facts of this kind.

Alfred Schutz and subsequent phenomenologically-oriented social scientists have given currency to a terminology that blurs the distinction between the external and internal implications of meanings, occasionally leading to a mistaken endorsement of the external implications. This is the terminology of *Lebenswelt*, or 'life-world' (the terminology was originally coined by Husserl). The *Lebenswelt* is defined as the world-as-the-agent-views-it, a mode of description that easily leads (as I believe it occasionally did for Schutz) to the misconception that the *Lebenswelt* is indeed a particular world, or sector of the world existing alongside other such sectors. This is the doctrine of 'multiple realities', a profusion of worlds in which the agent lives and among which he may move by means of shifts in his attentional focus (Schutz 1945). Moreover, different cultures produce different *Lebenswelten*. The native *Lebenswelt* is populated by witches, gods and demons, whereas the *Lebenswelt* of the modern Westerner includes neuroses and suppressed desires. The service that is rendered by the term *Lebenswelt* in phenomenological social science is better delivered by the straightforward notion of the (sum total of the) agent's *beliefs* about the world. This mode of expression is proof against ontological extravagance.

We have imposed a restriction upon the constructivist position based upon the phenomenological argument, to the effect that meanings only generate social facts as far as their internal implications go; we are never committed to any extrinsic implications. It is tempting at this point to raise a further question: are we invariably committed even to the *intrinsic* implications of agents' meanings? We must reformulate this question, however; as it stands, it can only be answered, trivially, with a 'yes'. Meanings coincide perfectly with their internal implications; no wedge can be driven in between the assumption that a person has (for instance) a belief to this or that effect, and the internal implications of that mental state, to the effect that such-and-such is believed by him to be the case. This follows from the way we defined internal implications as the logical consequences of such forms of words as 'NN believes that ...' or 'NN intends that ...'. A logical wedge may be driven in, however, between an agent's meanings and his verbal *avowals* of those meanings, even when sincere; the two are not the same by definition. So, the question we want to ask is, 'Could we ever have reason for not accepting agents' explications of their own meanings?' That is, could we ever have reason to judge that a group of persons were misguided as to the very subjective meaning of their own actions, suffering from some collective illusion about the intentions and motives behind their own conduct?

I believe the answer is yes. Certain customs in both Western and native societies force us to reject the (sincere) self-descriptions of the interactants, at least is so far as they claim to express the whole truth. (The point about sincerity is crucial: the existence of false or embellished descriptions of motives is a trivial fact.) In other words, we are forced to draw a distinction between the meanings inherent in an action and the agent's honest verbal explication of those meanings. An example is demon possession. In tribal societies, weird and socially disruptive behaviour in an individual may be attributed to possession by demons, a diagnosis that is occasionally accepted even by the supposed victim. To a Westerner, this is a case of a neurotic or psychotic personality; aberrant patterns of conduct are seen as subconscious attempts to satisfy suppressed urges. That is, not only will a Westerner reject the external implication of the action description (the objective existence of demons); he will also reject (at least as an expression of the whole truth) the native's sincere statement that it is not he who is acting, but some alien being that controls him. It is really the agent himself who is acting out subconscious motives; to this extent, the agent will know his actions and will know that they are his, albeit subconsciously. Hence, the action to the agent has a meaning of which he is not consciously aware.

One might refuse to parallel the case of the neurotic in our culture and the individual possessed by spirits in a tribal community, on the grounds that the former stands alone with his interpretation, whereas the native's interpretation is accepted by the whole community – indeed, it is the standard, socially endorsed interpretation. But I do not believe that this makes for a crucial difference. The claim that it does would have to appeal to some of the arguments we discussed (and rejected) in Part One.

How can we modify the constructivist position as based on the phenomenological argument to avoid the implication that social subjects have authority concerning the nature of their actions? The simplest way is to stipulate that it is not the agents' verbal explications of their meanings that determine the nature of an action, but only the *true* account of those subjective states. This, of course, will leave us with very difficult problems concerning how to get at the true account and, indeed, how to define what to take as the true account; these are issues that we cannot go into here. We shall restrict ourselves to the observation that it is sometimes permissible, or even mandatory, to reject a community's standard self-interpretation, even as far as its intrinsic implications are concerned.

THE SCOPE OF THE PHENOMENOLOGICAL ARGUMENT

We have endorsed a reconstructed version of the phenomenological argument and concluded that certain social facts are constituted by agents' meanings. It is now time to explore the scope of this mode of construction. We shall learn that strict limits are set to it by the fact that most social concepts imply the objective existence of things over and above the agents' subjective states; that is, those concepts have *external* implications. The investigation may be carried out with the analysis of social classes proposed by I. C. Jarvie in *Concepts and Society* as an example (Jarvie 1972).

Naively, we might describe a *class* as a group of people sharing some set of objective characteristics – progeny, abilities, religion, and so on – that determine social status and opportunities with respect to jobs and income. However, Jarvie demonstrates that this notion will not stand up under scrutiny. These grounds for inclusion in a class are neither sufficient nor necessary, whether singly or jointly, for actual membership in a class – 'actual membership' meaning that everybody in the society recognises the person in question as a member. In any society, one will meet people who satisfy the criteria that conventional wisdom holds sufficient for inclusion in some preferred class, but who are still not regarded as members of 'good society'; instead, they are rejected as imposters. On the other hand, there will be people who lack all the properties of the rest of the class members, but are still accepted as belonging to it. This might motivate social scientists to formulate a sophisticated concept, along clearly Simmelian lines, according to which membership of a class is simply a matter of *peer recognition*: the recognition of somebody as belonging to a class is not the honouring of an objective fact, namely, that the person in question has this or that combination of properties qualifying him for membership; it is the very *recognition* itself that makes him a member. Hence, a class is a group of people who recognise each other as belonging to the same class, or, in a non-circular formulation, a group of people who recognise each other as social equals. In other words, mere recognition constitutes the class, which marks this theory of classes as a social construction view.

Although this is, according to Jarvie, the sum of what we refer to as 'class phenomena', he prefers to express the conclusion in a different way. The proposed analysis is so far removed from the naive notion of a class that the proper conclusion can only be *that classes do not exist*. It is a crucial part of the pre-analytical concept of a class that class membership is based upon objective characteristics. The concept of class is meant to *explain*, and thereby *justify*, the differences in people's fortunes in life, by pointing to some objective ground for that difference. The recognition theory fails to do this, as we obviously cannot justify the recognition by the recognition itself.

Thus, Jarvie's conclusion is that people who believe in the existence of classes – that is, more or less all of us – are simply mistaken. We are mistaken, even though we all act on the basis of the belief that there are classes and, hence, according to a simplistic version of the social constructivist position, would actually generate the reality believed in by our actions, thereby making those beliefs true. The conduct motivated by a belief in classes consists in various discriminatory practices, such as refusing to hire people for certain jobs because of their unfortunate 'class background', or avoiding to mingle with people with such undesirable pedigree. To accept the idea that such social practices actually generate a class system would overlook that the concept of a class comprises the idea of an objective basis for these discriminatory practices; however, such a basis is not generated by those practices. Thus, what Jarvie claims, as paraphrased in my terminology, is that classes have certain features that belong among the *external implications* of the belief that classes exist and, hence, are not guaranteed to exist by the mere occurrence of that belief, nor by a social practice springing from it.

Another illustration is provided by Ernest Gellner's methodological reflections on his research among the Moroccan Berbers, in particular upon the notion of an *agurram* (plural *igurramen*) (Gellner 1962). The *igurramen* are a privileged and influential class who fulfil an essential role in Berber society as arbitrators in the perennial feuds characteristic of a tribal society. According to certain social anthropologists who have studied the Berbers, individuals are made *igurramen* by the fact that people recognise them as such and conduct themselves accordingly, submitting to their verdicts. Moreover, people honour them with donations, thus enabling the *igurramen* to display the prosperity and generosity that is a part of their status. In other words, the status of being an *agurram* is a case of recognition and, hence, social construction, according to these anthropologists. As Gellner points out, however, to describe the case this way is to overlook the meanings that the Berbers associate with the status of *agurram*. They hold that the *igurramen* are selected by God, who bestows upon them their powers and their riches; the social eminence they enjoy is viewed as a mere recognition of this independent status. To be an *agurram* is to have an independent source of income and to be blessed by God – but these fortunate circumstances are not brought about by social recognition. Hence *agurram*-hood is not a social construction.

The two examples we have just examined show two things. First, the social facts that are generated by meanings alone form a strictly limited set; most social phenomena comprise various external, objective features and are not guaranteed to exist by the internal implications of the agents' meanings. This holds in particular for meanings consisting of the recognition that someone possesses a particular status. The constructivist overlooks the fact that, in the agents' view, such a status rests on the basis of a certain warrant, reflecting certain qualities believed to be possessed by the occupant of the status. This warrant does not prevail just because people believe so. A status consists of the linking of a particular set of putative objective properties of certain persons with a cluster of obligations and rights on the parts of those persons, reflected in the conduct that other people display towards them. The objective properties are thought to warrant the privileges and rights in question and to justify the obligations. But the conduct does not suffice to generate those objective warranting conditions, nor does the belief that they are satisfied.

Second, the investigation demonstrated a tendency among social scientists to neglect those external implications, redefining status concepts so as to exhaust them by the obligations-and-rights part, which allows the scientists to adopt a constructivist position with respect to those concepts after all. Jarvie criticised this tendency in his rejection of a Simmellian construal of 'class', while Gellner did the same for a purely recognitional concept of *igurramen* and other Berber concepts. I believe we can see the motivation for this reconstructivist tendency: for many social-science concerns, it is immaterial whether a person genuinely qualifies for a status, as long as everybody believes that he does and acts accordingly. As long as everyone believes that the person apprehended is the murderer, the public sentiment of outrage will be appeased, the preventive effect on prospective wrong-doers will be achieved, and the victim's dependants will feel that he has been avenged. (This is the thrust of W. I. Thomas's dictum, as quoted on p. 16.) Thus, there will be a temptation in social science to associate the status, and the label, with the obligations-and-rights part only and, hence, with the behaviour consequent upon the status, and to forget about the conditions that are needed for someone to qualify for that status.

It is especially tempting to accept that facts about social status are constituted solely by the societal reaction in cases where the qualifying conditions are, by the social scientist's lights, entirely fictitious. Since, in such cases, the warranting conditions have never in fact prevailed, it is tempting to see the whole pattern of conduct, revolving around the putative status, as having nothing to do with those conditions, but having some extrinsic rationale instead. A case in point may be the practice in native societies of identifying certain people as witches. Ostensibly, this identifies some people as having magical powers, sometimes thought to reside in certain parts of their bodies, and detectable through autopsy. This seems like a case of systematically mistaken diagnosis. There is a tendency among social anthropologists, however, to construe the phenomenon differently, granting that the people in question are indeed witches, but adding that being a witch is just a socially-defined status, say, that of a ritually-defined scapegoat. The status of a witch is totally defined by the communal reaction. The anthropologists criticised by Gellner make similar claims for the Berbers' *igurramen*. Since there are no such things as people being selected by God to serve in a judicial function, and since their riches never derive from God, we cannot take the religious aspect of the concept of an *agurram* at face value: rather, this is just a metaphorical way of describing the entirely secular process of electing an official to arbitrate tribal conflicts.

There is a deeper motive for the policy of reinterpreting native notions. Many anthropologists want to combine a charitable attitude towards the native world view, including its ontology, with the realisation that there are no evil spirits, witches or magical potions. This leads to the position that the native point of view does not really imply the existence of such entities. We can accept the native magical or religious 'language game' of oracles, shamans or witches, without at any stage accepting such entities as truly supernatural. This general strategy of interpretation may take the form of a symbolist reading of native magic or religion, seeing it as making indirect, metaphorical statements about the social order. Alternatively, it may focus on ritual, insisting that the essence of religion is the communal activity of ritual ceremony and that the supernatural ontology put on top of this practice is purely ornamental. This is basically Durkheim's view, as presented in *The Elementary Forms of the Religious Life* (Durkheim 1915).

However, this position is as misguided as the one that accepts the existence of the native spirits and gods in the literal sense. It is a misrepresentation of the native world view to deny that it has extrinsic, supernatural implications, and is no less so for all that it reflects an honourable, anti-ethnocentric motive. Spirits and gods are theoretical entities, postulated in order to account for the diverse and strange events of social and natural existence. The natives attribute existence to them, just as Western man attributes existence to the atoms and molecules he invokes to account for the facts of nature.

CHAPTER VI

The Arguments from the 'Meaningfulness' of Action

The Hermeneutic Argument

Like the phenomenological argument, the hermeneutic argument draws out the implications of various views not originally intended as contributions to the social construction debate; they were put forward, rather, in the context of a general discussion about the methodology of social science. I shall refer to these methodological views as *hermeneutic positions*, using this term in a sense that is at once narrower and broader than its standard meaning. It is narrower, because it is intended to mark a contrast to the views of Dilthey and Weber, whose positions are customarily termed 'hermeneutic'. It is broader, because it is designed to cover certain positions in Anglo-American philosophy that are normally not so labelled.

In our specifically appropriated sense of the term, 'hermeneutic positions' are positions that agree that action is meaningful and that the meaning in question is to be assimilated to linguistic meaning. Important contemporary hermeneuticians include thinkers such as Jürgen Habermas, Karl-Otto Apel and other practitioners of what might be termed 'critical hermeneutics'; this approach to social science is associated with the Frankfurt School.[7] A similar position was evolved in Anglo-American philosophy and social science, chiefly as a result of the influence of the later Wittgenstein; important figures here include Peter Winch (Winch 1958), Elizabeth Anscombe (Anscombe 1957), and A. I. Melden (Melden 1961). In what follows I shall also endeavour to show how more recent results from Anglo-American philosophy can be used to support the construction claim, all of this under the heading of the relationship between meaning and language.

The hermeneutic position, as advanced by such thinkers as Habermas and Apel, is closely linked to the phenomenological point of view; and, as regards the versions that evolved in German soil, the two traditions have significant stretches of history in common. Latter-day Continental hermeneuticians hail Dilthey as a philosophical forebear, tracing, through him, an ancestry going back to Friedrich Wolf, Friedrich Ast and Friedrich Schleiermacher, all of them important representatives of the German hermeneutic tradition. Still, it conduces to clarity to draw an analytic distinction between the two traditions, especially since modern hermeneuticians, even those of the Continental schools, stress the differences between the two and disown many aspects of the phenomenological approach. Both the critical hermeneutics of Habermas and Apel and the conservative hermeneutics of Hans-Georg Gadamer manifest this attitude.

The history of hermeneutics is the story of how a distinctive scientific approach to human action in general evolved from reflection on the nature of textual interpretation; it is here that we find the origins of the commitment of hermeneutics to a linguistic model for understanding human beings. When first introduced into the German-speaking world in the seventeenth century, the term 'hermeneutics' referred to the techniques of biblical interpretation. This art had gained in prominence when, after the reformation, recourse to the authority of the church to settle issues of scriptural exegesis was no longer available to ministers of religion. Later, the use of the term was broadened to encompass the exegesis of other authoritative texts such as legal documents. With the advent of the enlightenment and the Age of Reason, all textual exegesis was made subject to general standards of rational criticism; sacred scripture was exposed to the same historical–critical method of interpretation as secular documents. In consequence, the designation of the narrower enterprise came to serve as a blanket term for all textual interpretation. In nineteenth-century hermeneutics there was a shift in focus from the text as an object in its own right to its potential as a source of insight into the *Geist* of the epoch in which it was written. To the great philologists of the German romantic movement, textual interpretation came to mean the endeavour to penetrate the spiritual unity of the classical cultures. An important name here was that of Friedrich Ast. His pupil, Friedrich Schleiermacher, gave an individualist twist to this development by extending the hermeneutic enterprise to one encompassing the mind of the individual author as well. Thus a significant step was taken towards making hermeneutics a general theory of the understanding of human thought and action. This movement reached its fulfilment in Dilthey. As we saw above, however, he built his doctrine of interpretation upon a metaphysics of 'experience' which makes it just as natural to class him as an adherent of the phenomenological argument, as I did above.

Both phenomenologists and hermeneuticians hold that action possesses a meaning that defines its nature, both generically and individually. The hermeneuticians, however, object to certain features of the phenomenological position – above all, to its psychologistic and subjectivistic tendencies. I raised a similar criticism in the previous chapter and showed how the phenomenological position can be amended so as to remedy these defects. Hermeneuticians make the further point that once the interpretation of action is freed from the subjectivist straitjacket, more will be gained than a mere improved epistemology of interpretation: the scope of the interpretive enterprise will be enlarged, since the social meaning of an act will now rest upon a much broader base of data than that residing in the individual agent's consciousness. Interpretation will refer to meanings located in the minds of other people, or perhaps even in non-human repositories such as books and computer files. (We saw above that Dilthey included such items as buildings, monuments and works of art to figure as objects of interpretation. This serves once again to demonstrate how he straddles the divide between the hermeneutic and the phenomenological argument.)[8]

To interpret, for instance, the actions of those actively serving in the Crusades, it is necessary to take account of the intellectual content of this struggle between Europeans and Middle East peoples. One needs to see one party to the conflict as representing a religion, Christianity, which depicts the relationship between God and man as mediated by a person who is at once divine and human, Jesus Christ; to the opposing religious group, the Muslims, Jesus is merely one holy man among others, such as Moses and Muhammad. There is also a difference between the understanding of the religious way of life in the two groups. In Christianity, there is a strict separation between the sacred and the profane; an entire sphere of human existence is marked off in which religion plays no part. This is the idea expressed in the famous saying about giving to Caesar what is Caesar's and to God what is God's. In orthodox Muslim societies, on the other hand, the affairs of life, including business dealings and politics, are all conducted in accordance with the dictates of the Koran. Thus, to each religion, Christianity and

Islam, the other represents a grave heresy. The point is that such niceties of theology were not likely to have been uppermost in the minds of the individuals taking part in the Crusades. Many of them, we may assume, simply had no inkling of them. Still, no adequate understanding of the Crusades is possible without taking these issues into consideration.[9]

We may here enter a caveat similar to that articulated in connection with the phenomenological argument. The hermeneutic position need not (and should not) be taken to say that the descriptions that a community applies to its actions are sacrosanct. Such descriptions may be overruled, even with respect to their internal implications, by descriptions offered by outsiders if they have sufficient evidential support. Thus, many historians would claim that theological issues played a very limited role in the genesis of the Crusades. What we have instead is a somewhat banal conflict between worldly powers over spheres of economic influence. Such historians point to the crusaders' sacking of Byzantium as evidence for this interpretation.

This is not the place, of course, to discuss the merits of rival interpretations of the Crusades. I introduced that example simply in order to illustrate the fact that we sometimes have compelling reasons for not accepting agents' own description of their actions, even when they are sincere. One additional comment might be made: even when the agents' own understanding of their action is invalid, or expresses only a partial truth, it still has a place in the full picture. For instance, even if one subscribes to a more 'materialist' interpretation of the Crusades, seeing it in terms of rivalry over power and markets, one will fail to appreciate the particular ways in which these interests were given ideological expression unless one understands the ideational contents of the Christian and Muslim religions.

Let us return to the criticism that hermeneuticians level at the phenomenological position. Hermeneuticians assign an objective status to the interpretation of action, rejecting the psychological re-enactment construal found in Weber and Schutz. This is where the positive methodological doctrine of hermeneutics, viz. the assimilation of understanding of action to linguistic interpretation, enters in. Hermeneuticians use the assimilation of the understanding of action to linguistic understanding to break the hold of the re-enactment model, drawing our attention to the utter implausibility of that model as applied to speech. It is highly implausible to hold that in understanding the meaning of a speaker's utterance, 'I believe it is soon going to rain', I attempt to figure out what I would mean by uttering that sentence, and then impute the same meaning to the speaker. The problem is, of course, that I can only accomplish the former by determining what the sentence means in itself, independently of what I might use it to mean on any concrete occasion. Similarly, I can only determine what I would be doing in displaying a certain behaviour by asking myself to what end that action would be a rational means. If I am to ask that question at all, however, I may just as well ask it as it relates to the person concerned, not myself.

While the hermeneuticians' criticism of psychologism is salutary, there are dangers in assimilating the meaning of actions to the meaning of linguistic items, however. In particular, such a move may lead to a neglect of the difference between language, which is conventional (we shall return to this concept below) and the meaning of action, which is only partly so; many acts are not conventional at all. There is a world of difference between the way that the statement, 'I like the food', means that I like the food, and the way that my wolfing down the meal 'means' the same. Whereas the meaning of the sentence is dependent upon an entire social context, involving other speakers, the non-linguistic action is not so dependent. It would have the same meaning even if I were the only human being in the universe.

This is not to deny, of course, that much action is indeed conventional and that the hermeneuticians do us a service by pointing out that in determining its meaning, we do better to appeal to the general code than to examine what went on in the individual actor's mind. There may be little going on there of relevance to the conventional meaning of that act. Still, we must beware of overstating this insight.

Above, I have focused upon the criticism levelled by the hermeneuticians against the phenomenologists, in order to distinguish these two closely affiliated schools. In recent debates concerning the methodology of the social sciences, however, hermeneuticians and phenomenologists have closed ranks against a common foe, namely the neo-positivist philosophy of science as represented by such writers as Ernest Nagel and Carl G. Hempel. The primary criticisms directed against this opponent are twofold: first, according to the positivist theory of explanation, the logical form of all explanation, including explanation of human action, is the deductive or probabilistic inference of the explanandum from general laws. This kind of account can be seen as a refinement on the common-sense idea of a causal account, and is opposed by hermeneuticians and phenomenologists on the grounds that accounts of human action are not causal in nature, but teleological. Secondly, exception is taken to the empiricist commitments of neo-positivism which are held to lead to an epistemology far too crude to do justice to the subtleties of action interpretation. Positivists are drawn towards materialism or physicalism, either in the form of behaviourism or of neurophysiological reductionism. Against this, the hermeneuticians insists that human action is informed by language in a manner that makes it resistant to either kind of reduction.

The thesis articulating the language-impregnated nature of action constitutes the locus of the similarity between the hermeneuticians of German extraction and the British and American neo-Wittgensteinians. I shall begin by offering a brief sketch of how the analytical philosophers argue this thesis, and then provide a somewhat fuller account of the way the doctrine is construed by the most prominent of the German hermeneuticians, Jürgen Habermas.

THE HERMENEUTIC POSITION ACCORDING TO PETER WINCH

In analytical philosophy, the hermeneutic position serves to illustrate the general emphasis upon language so characteristic of this tradition. Quite specifically, language and action are seen as inextricably intertwined; Wittgenstein coined the term 'language game' to capture the intimate relationship between language and the context of action in which it is embedded.

For Winch and other neo-Wittgensteinians, the key to this relationship resides in the celebrated doctrine of *rule-following* in the *Philosophical Investigations*. Let us recapitulate the crucial points of this doctrine, as set out in Chapter I, all the while bearing in mind that the thesis which the hermeneuticians use this argument to prove is much less extreme than the ethnomethodologist position.

According to Wittgenstein, there is no absolute or objective notion of 'sameness' that can be used to answer the question whether behaviour displayed on two separate occasions amounts to performances of *the same kind* of action or not. The correct answer is determined solely by whether or not the behaviour counts as 'the same' according to the rules under which the agents subsume their actions. Hence, in order to identify the nature of any particular social action, we have to grasp the rules which the agents apply to it. These rules are typically semantic rules, definitive of the linguistic terms with which agents label their actions. This means that we have to grasp the description or label that the agents impose upon their conduct. In this way, the linguistically embodied concepts used by the agents determine the nature of the actions they engage in. Social actions are constituted by the linguistic categories in terms of which agents conceive them; or so Winch argues (Winch 1958: 85).

So far, this argument looks suspiciously like the one from Linguistic Relativity, which was discussed in Chapter IV, and it would be vulnerable to the same objection. That objection was to the effect that the mere imposition of a linguistic label is not enough to bestow a determinate essence on a human action; for this to be achieved, the labelling needs to be associated with behavioural differences, i.e. the behavioural sequences variously labelled must subsequently diverge. But to concede this is to acknowledge that the mere act of labelling has no intrinsic significance. Now this criticism embodies an insight which is very much of a piece with one of the central tenets in the *Philosophical Investigations*, viz. that meaning is use. Wittgenstein's point is precisely that it is action that bestows meaning upon the signs that human beings use to describe the world and their own actions in it. Hence, Winch's argument seems in a curious way to run directly contrary to a crucial principle of Wittgenstein's philosophy here and to stand the notion of 'language-games' on its head. He appears to use linguistic labelling to impose a determinate meaning upon action while, on Wittgensteinian principles, it has to be the other way around. Winch does actually seem to sense this problem and, elsewhere in his presentation of the argument, downgrades the role of explicit self-description and upgrades the role of (non-verbal) behaviour. The final impression is one of an unresolved tension in Winch's position.

We can recast Winch's argument so as to save it from this embarrassment, however. The argument should be understood as making the point that in order to grasp the meaning of an action, we need always to look beyond the specific time and place at which the action takes place (putting it intuitively and crudely). The meaning of any current action is contingent on what the agent will go on to do in the future. To take Wittgenstein's favourite example, the nature of the action performed by the pupil in response to the teacher's instruction to 'add two', is not fixed by his writing down the first four numbers, or even the first four hundred. For there may be a quirk in the pupil's understanding of the instruction that will only show once he is up into the thousands and starts writing 1004, 1008, etc.

Thus the rule-following considerations offer a dramatisation of the insight of there being more to action than what appears from the local, concrete occasion of its performance. It is this 'something more', which may plausibly be called 'the agent's interpretation of his own action', that the hermeneutic argument insists must be captured by the social scientist. This additional element would include the agent's subsequent conduct; but it would not, on this construal of the argument, be essentially tied to the agent's performance of speech acts in which he described his own action. This argument would link action with language, and hence earn the epithet 'hermeneutic', only in virtue of the fact that the behavioural repertoire manifested in the action would have been acquired through verbal drill. The act of writing down numbers would thus have been learnt as a response to the instruction, 'Add two'. The rules that govern human actions are essentially rules couched in terms of a shared language, inculcated through social practice. It also remains true, of course, that the most direct way to establish what rule an agent seeks to conform to in his actions is to ask him to state that rule.

As was mentioned at the beginning of this section, Winch and the other neo-Wittgensteinians advanced these arguments primarily in order to make a methodological point, to the effect that positivist methods should be eschewed in social science in favour of a hermeneutic approach which aims at 'understanding' action in terms of the agents' own categories. But methodology and ontology are intimately fused in Winch's argument; indeed, we might say that the argument infers a methodological conclusion from ontological premises. The overall form of the argument is that since social reality is constituted by the rules (or concepts) the agents apply to it, to miss the rules would be to miss social reality. Thus, a constructivist position is all but explicit in the Winchean argument; it is really only the terminology that is lacking.

We may reproduce the implicit constructivist argument in the following succinct form: ultimately, social facts consist of some sequence of (communal) human behaviour, set against a broader context of patterns of social practices; this wider context invests the behaviour with a meaning, thereby subsuming it under richer descriptions. The adhesive that binds the action to its context is the agents' sense of doing 'the same' on those subsequent occasions as on the present one; the agents' *interpretation*, if you will, of their actions as being 'the same' on those occasions. Dramatising somewhat, we may express this by saying that the agents' interpretation generates this richer fact. A social fact does not acquire its richer content, however, in virtue of including introspectible goings-on in the agent's mind, as the phenomenologists would have it; Wittgensteinians such as Winch eschew any such notion. Rather, the action derives its richer meaning from reference to a more comprehensive social setting also generated by agent action.

It is important to appreciate the difference between the present use of Wittgenstein's rule-following considerations to make a constructivist point, and the more extreme ethnomethodological version which we examined in Chapter I. According to the latter, the community of language users as a whole defines some item in the world as (for example) 'a suicide' or 'a quasar' by reaching a consensus on its classification. This consensus is held to generate a fact on the basis of the reasoning I presented, and criticised, in Chapter I. By contrast, on the more modest argument examined here, a determinate meaning is conferred upon an action in virtue of the rule in conformity with which it is carried out. The rule adds something to the narrow and local description of the conduct, because a rule always extends beyond any finite segment of rule-conforming behaviour.

Note that this 'more' need not involve the agreement of the community, on the present modest interpretation. Hence this argument is not committed to the 'community' reading of Wittgenstein of which the ethnomethodological argument made so much play. This means that according to the present argument, a collective, social fact may be generated through a process that runs in the direction, individual-to-community: we ask each agent what he or she is doing, and the answer given, for instance 'performing a ritual burial', will be authoritative under normal circumstances. The extent of agreement between agents serves only to define the outer boundaries of the social fact, as it were; it shows who is participating in this particular social activity and who is not. On the ethnomethodological argument, on the other hand, the process of fact generation runs in the opposite direction, i.e. from community to individual: here we ask the community what it is up to, or, going further, we ask the community what NN is up to, for every member NN of the community. If the answers given are the same with respect to every member NN, those answers define what the community is up to, thereby establishing a social fact.

On the moderate argument, the individual agent does not have to consult the community to be apprised of the nature of his or her own action, as it were; the individual can speak with authority about this under normal circumstances. The hermeneutician may here cite Wittgenstein's view that it is a 'grammatical sentence', constitutive of the language game involving the notion of an intention, that agents know their own intentions (cf. *Philosophical Investigations*, section 247). Of course, this epistemic privilege is subject to the condition that the terms employed in the description are meaningful in the first place, and this calls for a minimal level of general conformity in their use. But such a requirement does not preclude our occasionally accepting the agent's avowal of intention, even when he speaks in contradiction of all of his fellows.

It is true, of course, that most social intercourse depends upon a certain mutuality of purposes and upon a minimal level of valid community member information about the aims of others. This is no metaphysical necessity, however, but a practical one. As a matter of fact, certain kinds of competitive social activities depend upon the interactants *not* having full and correct information about each other's intentions; such activities are the topic of game theory. Another kind of case is represented by the military commander who leads a squad on a top-secret mission, the true nature of which he has deliberately concealed from them to ensure that no breach of secrecy will occur.

Note, finally, that the fact-generating power vindicated by the moderate argument does not extend to the natural world at all: the community cannot turn lead into gold just by describing what they are doing in this way.

THE HERMENEUTIC ARGUMENT ACCORDING TO JÜRGEN HABERMAS

Considerable caution must be exercised when we talk about 'Habermas's version of the hermeneutic argument'. There are several lines of reasoning in Habermas, all intimately intertwined, which employ tenets from the hermeneutic tradition to establish a constructivist conclusion. We have touched upon the most radical of these arguments already in Part One. It employs what Habermas termed the *consensus theory* of truth, to the effect that truth, with respect to any particular issue, is the opinion that humankind would converge on were it to engage in an infinite and ideally refined investigation of that issue. Habermas gives this idea a Kantian twist by claiming that this hypothetical research process, like all human cognition, would be guided by *a priori* cognitive principles which impose certain necessary features on its object; unlike Kant, however, Habermas holds that there are a number of different sets of such principles, each inspired by a distinct 'knowledge guiding interest' and each aimed at a different domain of reality (Habermas 1972). One such interest is the 'practical' one which is at issue when the objects investigated are human actions. This knowledge guiding interest has mutual understanding and consensus among human beings as its *telos*, and this may be translated into *a priori* principles of understanding that are basically identical with those expounded in the hermeneutic tradition. Thus, the result of this marriage of Kantianism and hermeneutics is a radical constructivist position, maintaining that human cognition shapes reality, in particular with respect to those fundamental formal features that are imposed upon it by the knowledge guiding interest peculiar to each domain.

In Part One, I criticised one particular aspect of this grand speculative scheme, viz. Habermas's commitment to a consensus theory of truth, which carries the penalty of an infinite regress. Fortunately, there are other strands of reasoning in Habermas that are to a lesser degree laden with dubious metaphysics and *a priori* epistemology; I believe that they support a viable version of constructivism. The most attractive of these arguments draws upon findings in developmental and social psychology which form the basis of some simple philosophical reflections. Thus, of the two schools that have converged upon the hermeneutic position – the German school perpetuating the *Geisteswissenschaften* tradition and the Anglo-American one following in the footsteps of Wittgenstein – the former has in fact operated somewhat closer to empirical research, despite its traditional speculative leanings. Therefore, examples taken from this tradition more aptly demonstrate how the hermeneutic construal of the interplay between language and social fact can be used to support a moderate constructivist thesis.

The following quotes are taken from Habermas's treatise *On the Logic of the Social Sciences* (Habermas 1988):

> If action is linked with intentions in such a way that it can be derived from the propositions that bring these intentions to expression, then conversely the thesis is also true that a subject can carry out only those actions whose intentions he can in principle describe. The limits of action are determined by the range of possible descriptions. This in turn is established by the structures of language in which the self-understanding and worldview of a social group is articulated. Thus the boundaries of action are drawn by the boundaries of language.
>
> ...On the level of animal behavior...the moment of intentionality has not yet become detached from the modes of behavior and incorporated into symbolic contexts. Only the autonomy of intentional contents in language makes action possible. A more or less rigid system of instincts that defines meanings specific to a species from behind, so to speak, and attaches them to selected environmental conditions, is only freed from one-to-one correlations with the environment at the cultural level. Only then can the system of instincts be subjected in turn to new definitions, through a linguistic system with variable meanings. Whereas meanings that are signaled depend on need dispositions and merely indicate pre-selected objects of drives, symbolic meanings that have become autonomous in linguistic systems have acquired the power to interpret needs retroactively.
>
> (Ibid.: 71–3)

Habermas draws attention to a fundamental difference in the motivational constitution of animals and human beings. Animal behaviour is conditioned by purely physical parameters of the setting according to dynamic principles simple enough to be captured in a stimulus–response model. Human action, on the other hand, is determined by the world as interpreted through linguistic categories. In the process of psychological and motivational maturation, the instincts and drives with which the individual was born are overlaid with, and interpreted in terms of, linguistic typifications of the objects of desire. Human action comes to aim, not at something to which man is driven by instinct, but rather to that which linguistic typification sets before him as desirable.

As was mentioned above, Habermas adduces these considerations in support of a methodological recommendation for social science: approach human action through an interpretation of the linguistic categories in which the agents themselves describe it, and forgo any attempt at purely behaviourist analysis. But, as was the case with Peter Winch, Habermas's methodological stance rests upon an ontological thesis. That thesis is to the effect that social reality is thoroughly shot through with linguistic meaning; hence, to miss this meaning in the scientific study of social action would be to miss social reality altogether. Here, I want to draw out the implications of this ontological thesis for a constructivist position; these implications constitute what I call the *hermeneutic argument*.

To capture the phenomenon in its simplest and most perspicuous form, we may leave the realm of the ontogenesis of human motivation on which Habermas focuses and look instead at a simple, everyday case of an occurrent desire in an individual. Afterwards, we shall return to other, more socially significant cases.[10]

When you enter a restaurant, you will normally be in a fairly indeterminate state of hunger. You may vaguely feel in the mood for seafood; but in order to satisfy that vague desire, you must specify it and translate it into a determinate verbal form commensurate with the items on the menu. In the end, you must order something as specific, for example, as 'Lobster Thermidor'. Your desires concerning what you want to drink with the meal are likely to be forced into even greater specificity as you make a selection from the wine list.

One part of the process of rendering your desire determinate is construction, while another is causal determination and, hence, irrelevant to our current concerns. Let us get the latter out of the way before we proceed. By letting the pictures of the tempting dishes with their fascinating foreign names roll through your mind, savouring their taste in imagination, you may succeed in removing some of the indeterminacy of your culinary desires. This is a causal process in which you anticipatorily test your reactions to each of the options and compare their strength, with one dish finally emerging the winner. There is also another side to this determination, however, which is one of construction. In putting your culinary preferences into verbal form when placing your order, you registered a demand and made a commitment of a certain kind. You have entered into a short-term mutual understanding with the establishment: you agree to accept any dish satisfying a certain description and the establishment undertakes to provide it. If the dish is brought to you, cooked to your order in all particulars, you cannot (without overstepping your privileges as a patron) have the dish returned to the kitchen on the grounds that it did not give you the pleasure you anticipated. Your brute desire has been translated into a binding verbal request.

The little restaurant anecdote was chosen merely for clarity. A similar commitment is incurred every time we put our desires into words, not merely in the quasi-contractual situation of the restaurant patron. We incur the same kind of obligation to our interlocutors whenever we tell them what we want in the course of everyday conversation. Indeed, there is a related phenomenon involved in the one-person situation, although it will hardly do to call this a commitment towards oneself. In putting his desires into words, a person objectifies his desires, fixing them in a form in which he may afterwards consult them to monitor his progress in satisfying them. Before you leave to do your shopping, you may spend some time pondering what you want for dinner tonight, going through the same procedure as the restaurant guest above: letting the various foods sit on your tongue in imagined anticipation and selecting the ones you prefer. You may then write those items down on a shopping list. Once this list is made, it guides your purchasing transactions, in the very literal sense of being that which you consult on your way through the supermarket. It is the list that now determines what you 'want' in the only sense that matters socially, namely that of determining what your actions will be. As in the restaurant scenario, when you go home and cook the planned meal, you may find that it does not give you satisfaction. But this does not change the fact that the ingredients for this meal were really what you wanted, that is, demanded, when you did your shopping.

It becomes clear that the concept of a human desire is a hybrid between two ideas: the idea of that which a person actively tries to realise, or to get hold of, and of that which actually gives him gratification. The two are by no means identical, but either is an aspect of our concept of a desire; and that concept is only useful to the extent that the two aspects tend to accompany each other. The second element dominates in the case of biologically-founded desires, but loses importance as we move towards desires that have no obvious biological basis, but are cultural creations instead. A person's desire to realise some particular ideal of moral excellence may not give that person any satisfaction (or, at any rate, none remotely similar to the satisfaction of having a good meal). Still, that goal is the object of a desire on his part, in a suitably broad meaning of the word 'desire'. It is precisely at the interface between the biologically- and the culturally-determined aspects of desire that social construction creeps in. It does so via the process of translating mute biological desires into linguistically-typified demands. The linguistic typification of the desire will typically impose a degree of determinacy that was not present before, drawing a clear boundary where none existed previously. In putting our desires into words, we generate something that was not (necessarily) there before; in brief, we generate a new fact.

Note that the distinction drawn here is not the (Freudian) one between what a person *claims* he wants and what he *really* wants – that is, what his actions actually tend to bring about. The linguistically-constituted aspect of desiring is definitely real in the sense that it genuinely affects behaviour, by virtue of the agent consulting the description he has put upon his desires and letting his actions be governed by it. Of course, occasionally a person may deceive himself in the description by which he expresses his desires; his actions may belie his avowals, because certain subconscious tendencies get in the way of his conscious monitoring of his action, based upon the 'official' description of his desires. These aberrations from the norm are not our concern, however.

The little examples I have used so far to illustrate how desires are generated do not have very much to do with the construction of *social* fact, but rather belong within the sphere of individual psychology. However, we now may return to the context in which Habermas introduced considerations of the linguistic typification of desire. This was very much a social context; Habermas pointed out how, in the development of the individual's motivational structure during maturation, the descriptions from which he selects to formulate his desires are those that are available in his language. The categories that language provides are, in their turn, determined by general societal factors. Hence, the generation of desire has a genuinely social dimension, different societies making different things available to its members as possible objects of desire, via the language spoken in those societies.

EMPIRICAL WORK ILLUSTRATING THE HERMENEUTIC ARGUMENT

There is a sizeable body of empirical work in the social sciences that can be invoked to add empirical detail to Habermas's abstract reflections on the ontogenesis of human motivation. One line of research focuses upon the *emotions*.[11] Under the slogan that 'emotions are social constructions', social psychologists have pointed out that, contrary to the way we tend to conceive of them, emotions are not clearly identifiable phenomenal or somatic states. If we look for characteristic introspectible or bodily symptoms to constitute such emotions as love, anger, or jealousy, we draw a blank. For instance, it would be impossible to distinguish between jealousy or envy on the basis of phenomenal or somatic aspects. Still, to avow one rather than the other has significantly different implications. This is because avowing an emotion is to raise a certain claim within a social context of rights, liberties and obligations. For instance, to report that one is jealous of some person is to point to a right that one has in regard to something and to charge that this right has been violated by the person in question. Saying that one is angry with someone is to signal that one has a reason for having a negative attitude to that person and, hence, to justify, in a general way, whatever hostile action one will subsequently take. Strong emotions in particular are thought to justify certain actions, or at least to be an extenuating circumstance in the moral, and legal, assessment of those actions.

In most statements of 'the social construction of emotion', emphasis has not been on the aspect that renders it a constructivist position, in my terminology. Instead, attention is given to the *causal* aspect – that is, the way in which society inculcates in individuals a tendency to display particular emotions on appropriate occasions. The emotions are obligatory on those occasions; for instance, grief is prescribed on occasions when we bury loved ones; tender affections must be shown when mothers nurse their young; outbursts of patriotism are *de rigueur* when one's country is threatened. Here, I point to another aspect of the way that emotions are socially generated, namely, to *construction* in the technical sense. In all the cases mentioned, social construction works by the same linguistic mechanism that we investigated in the simple restaurant case above. Language puts at our disposal certain moulds into which we fill the raw material of our emotional life. Categorisation creates a social fact by bestowing upon the person's intentional state a determinacy that was not there before this self-typification. In putting his emotional state into a linguistic mould, a person commits himself to a certain pattern of conduct, at least parts and details of which were not subjectively given to him in anticipatory imagination, but are laid down by the very use of a linguistic label. A new fact is generated, since the person commits himself beyond any spontaneous inclination to act that existed prior to the commitment and *a fortiori* to any that are introspectively given to him. Here, we see the difference between the phenomenological and the hermeneutic approach vividly illustrated.

The thesis of the social construction of emotions should be understood to allow that the higher animals may harbour emotions. The behaviour of a dog or chimpanzee may be sufficiently similar to that of an angry person to warrant describing that state as an emotion, which we may call 'quasi-anger'. The qualification is due to the fact that, lacking a language, the animal is not capable of expressing its emotional state with such precision as to justify the tag 'anger'. In particular, it cannot express the idea that the object of anger has committed some transgression that must now be rectified. These normative ideas are beyond its intellectual repertory, since they require linguistic means for their expression. The doctrine of the social construction of emotions is the doctrine of the construction of emotions as finely-differentiated, finely-nuanced psychological states.

Another important domain in which social construction is at work, by virtue of the same linguistic mechanism, is that of sexuality and gender.[12] Gender identity is often depicted as a social category, or even a role: a predefined structure of rights, obligations and behaviours that the adolescent must adopt. This structure is embodied in certain salient linguistic tags that are socially sanctioned, such as 'a real man' or 'a true lady'. Gender identity is a construct in the precise sense that in accepting some particular, linguistically-typified role – say, that of a heterosexual male – the adolescent thereby creates the fact of being such a person: he takes upon himself the obligations inherent in this role, at the same time advancing certain claims concerning the way he wants to be treated by the rest of society. There will typically be some gap between what the young person spontaneously feels – his spontaneous reactions to concrete situations – and the reactions that are sanctioned by the governing sexual stereotype. The stereotype is an *ideal* which the youngster takes upon himself to live up to. Thus, the self-typification of a person as a male or a female is not a simple reflection in language of a pattern of reactions that existed prior to the typification. The gender label does not coincide with a sharply-defined reality existing beforehand, but imposes some determinacy where none existed before. By labelling himself a man, the person then and there commits himself to act in certain ways in future situations in which, without that labelling, he would have had no instinctive impulse to act in one way rather than another.[13] The gap between the (linguistically-typified) role and a person's spontaneous inclinations is clearly demonstrated by the occasional tension between them: a person may detect certain deviant tendencies in himself – shoe fetishism, or homosexuality – while at the same time playing the social role of a normal heterosexual male and, indeed, wanting to have the spontaneous reactions pertaining to this role.

The process of social construction is more visible in the case of sexual identity than in the case of the emotions, since social pressure is stronger in the former case. Emotions are often optional; a number of equally acceptable linguistic labels will be available to the agent. In many situations, the agent may decide if he will feel elated, homesick, or sentimental. In the case of sexual identity, on the other hand, there is one right and proper way, set against a spectrum of deviant ones of increasing depravity and social stigma. Thus, we have the phenomenon of construction via linguistic typification coinciding with, and being reinforced by, typification by social *role*. This important term of social psychology has already crept into the account given above and we must elaborate on it, if only to distinguish the issues it involves from the ones that occupy us here.

A *role* is a socially-prescribed pattern of conduct, to which specified kinds of individuals must conform in specified types of situations. The double qualification serves to distinguish roles from moral norms. While moral norms are not keyed to particular persons and particular situations, role specifications are addressed to people of a particular status: that of a public official, a suitor, a football coach, and so on. (No doubt this is a difference of degree, not of kind. A good case can be made that there are moral norms associated with certain statuses, such as being a parent.) Precisely in being thus defined in relation to social statuses that are themselves social creations, roles and the actions they generate might be thought to be excellent examples of social construction. However, this is not the case, given the definition of construction adopted here. Generation of fact through the specification of norms is a different thing from the construction of fact – in particular, construction by the Habermasian mechanism of linguistically-typified commitment. The two ideas are two-way independent (which is not to deny that they may both apply to the same case). First, there may be role-specific normative control of action without linguistic typification and, hence, without construction. An example is the way that the role of 'participant in a conversation' dictates the physical distance between the speakers. Empirical investigation has shown that there are strictly defined lower and upper bounds on the permissible distance separating parties to a conversation, transgressions of which create feelings of discomfort in the interlocutors. Moreover, these distances vary cross-culturally. This aspect of the role of 'participant in a conversation' is not linguistically constructed; the rule of proper distance in conversations is one of many social norms that function perfectly unconsciously. No ordinary social agent ever formulates it explicitly or obeys it deliberately. It manifests itself only in the discomfort felt in cases of transgression and in the adjustments that people subconsciously make to maintain proper distance. No linguistic codification is called for here, since the cognitive processes involved in obeying this norm are so simple that they can be carried out without the use of linguistic aids. It only takes a simple sensory and cognitive apparatus to ascertain whether the distance between two persons is above or below the permitted thresholds; a dumb animal could do it. (They do, as a matter of fact, as the remarkably equal spacing of a flock of swallows on a telephone wire demonstrates.)

Secondly, there may be generation of fact by linguistic self-typification, even in the absence of any normative prescription. This was illustrated in our initial example of the restaurant patron, who was under no normative obligation, role-related or otherwise, to choose one dish from the menu before any other. Still, his selection of one particular dish – his verbally formulated order – will generate a fact by construction, since it will impose a determinacy on his (momentary) preference structure that did not exist prior to the choice.

To the extent that the imposition of social roles generates social fact, it does so *causally*. In the process of socialisation, be it into society at large or into specialised social collectivities such as educational institutions, the workplace, or the street-corner gang, the community causally forces the individual's conduct into a particular approved shape. It does so by means of the familiar instruments of reward and punishment. This is a causal process, not a process of (linguistically-based) construction, although very often the two will go hand in hand. It contrasts with the specific way of generating social fact that we are trying to analyse here.

FURTHER FUNCTIONS OF LANGUAGE IN SOCIAL CONSTRUCTION

It is time to add a further twist to the hermeneutic argument. In the examples examined above, social fact was seen to be generated when human agents interpreted 'raw' desires in terms of linguistic labels that transcend their behavioural or introspective backing. It was supposed that the agents grasped the meaning of the terms used and, hence, understood precisely the extent of the commitment incurred by using them. There are, however, even more radical cases of linguistic generation of social fact, in which a person commits himself by using a term he does not fully understand.

For the necessary background to understand what goes on in such cases, we must briefly look at some recent developments within the philosophy of language. Philosophy of language has recently taken a social turn; it has repudiated its formerly held dogma of seeing linguistic meaning as essentially and inherently an individual phenomenon, located in the speaker's mind, and has come to appreciate that the subject of linguistic meaning is, rather, the linguistic community as a whole.

To cite a slogan coined by one of the instigators of this recent development, Hilary Putnam, 'meanings ain't in the head'; rather, they are distributed across the linguistic community in virtue of what Putnam aptly calls the 'division of linguistic labour' (Putnam 1975). Not every language user contributes equally to the social institution of language; like most other institutions, this one has its specialists and experts as well as its lay members. The experts know the precise meaning of certain terms used by the entire linguistic community, the meaning of which, however, is not known to the average member of the community.

As is the case with any kind of division of labour, the division of linguistic labour raises to new levels the generative powers of the single individual in a given activity. The division of manual labour means an increase in the number of pins that a worker may put out at the production line; the division of linguistic labour augments the effects a person may bring about by the use of language. I may inform somebody that the fore gaff-topsail needs to be trimmed for scudding. These words may have no meaning to me – I act solely as a go-between, having been told by the captain to take this message to a member of the crew. To him, the message is replete with meaning and practical import; he hastens to make the adjustment. For my statement to have that meaning, it is important that my interlocutor understands that I am using that word as the captain uses it – if not, the message is of no use to him. In other words, it must be understood that I use the words 'fore gaff-topsail' and 'scudding' according to what Simon Blackburn has called a 'deferential convention' (Blackburn 1984, ch. 4.6). I use it to mean what somebody with special expertise on sailing vessels uses it to mean. Perhaps the only content I associate with the word 'fore gaff-top sail' is 'a sail located near the top of the mast'. There are likely to be several items answering to this description on a big sailing-boat; as for the term 'scudding', I may associate no particular meaning with it whatsoever. Hence, it is vital that the crew presuppose that I use these words deferentially.

To see how these insights support a constructivist position, we may again look initially at a simplified example and then, afterwards, turn to full-scale instances with genuine social significance. Here is an example adduced by Tyler Burge in a recent debate between individualists and holists within the philosophy of psychology (Burge 1979). Suppose Smith is suffering from arthritis of the wrist and of the fingers. Later, he develops a painful disease of the thigh. Now Smith is a layman with only a very incomplete knowledge about the nature of arthritis. In particular, he is ignorant of the fact that arthritis afflicts only the joints. So Smith forms the belief that the arthritis has spread to his thigh as well.

Next, consider another situation largely identical to the one just described, but involving another individual, Jones. Jones's state of health is supposed to be exactly the same as Smith's in the situation described above. He has the same ailments, including the painful condition of the thigh. Like Smith, Jones refers to this ailment as 'arthritis'. Here, however, we introduce the difference: we suppose that the medical profession in this alternative scenario uses the word 'arthritis' to designate not just inflammations of the joints, but also various rheumatoid ailments of the limbs, including the condition falsely called 'arthritis' by Smith in the first scenario. (Let us call this condition 'tharthritis' for ease of reference.)

The point is that we could not correctly attribute to Jones the belief that he has contracted *arthritis* of the thigh. Instead, we must attribute to him the belief that he suffers from *tharthritis*. We were only justified in attributing the former belief to Smith because he was the speaker of a language in which the word 'arthritis' means arthritis. This condition no longer holds in the Jones story; here, 'arthritis' means *tharthritis*. We have to modify our belief ascription accordingly.

The difference between Smith's and Jones's beliefs is due solely to the language of which they avail themselves. Viewed in isolation, Smith and Jones may be supposed to be perfectly similar; we may even stipulate that they are in exactly the same physiological condition. Still the mental states involved are different: Smith believes himself to be suffering from *arthritis* of the thigh, whereas Jones has no such belief; instead he believes himself to suffer from *tharthritis*. The two individuals differ in being members of different linguistic communities, which give different semantic value to the terms that they use to express their beliefs and, hence, different interpretations of these beliefs.

To link up this case with those previously discussed, we may add the further element to our story that Smith not only harbours beliefs about his arthritis; he also has various desires pertaining to it, prominently the desire that it go away. These desires, too, may only be attributed to Smith courtesy of the linguistic community of which he is a member. His desires are social creations, in a double sense. Not only will the linguistic articulation of the desires (turning them into 'demands') go beyond anything for which there was a spontaneous behavioural impulse prior to the articulation. It will even go beyond anything of which the agent has any proper understanding.

Thus, language and the division of linguistic labour add an extra dimension to the way that people's thoughts fix the content of their (social) actions and, hence, the way in which those thoughts generate social facts. In this manner, we move beyond the crude picture of social reality as being made up locally and piecemeal, that is, out of the behaviour of the inhabitants of each narrow tract of the social world plus the mental concomitants of that behaviour. Instead, we get a much more holistic picture; the nature of any local region of the social world will be co-determined by what goes on in and between people who are not inhabitants of that region at all, and may be far removed from it. Moreover, it is not only determined by facts directly involving human beings, but also by the contents of books and computer files.

The clearest examples of this kind of construction will be cases where the linguistic authority coincides with an ordinary societal authority. Take the Catholic Church and its dogmas as an example. The average Catholic is called upon to accept certain articles of faith, the precise content of which he cannot be assumed to understand fully; he does so on the strength of the authority of the Church. This authority extends beyond pronouncing upon the truth value of such tenets. The Church lays down even the meaning of the terms that occur in those tenets – and not just what the words mean in the books, as it were, but even as spoken by the lay members of the Church. The Church bestows upon these words a meaning that goes beyond anything that occurs in the lay speakers' heads. The situation is the same here as in the case of the arthritis patient in Burge's example above, with the medical doctors replaced by the catholic clergy.

The concept of 'transubstantiation' is an illustrative case. This is the idea that the bread and wine offered during the Eucharist are really the flesh and blood of Christ. They are so, not in their immediately perceptible qualities, but in their underlying substance. Underneath the perceptible attributes of bread and wine, the underlying substance has now turned into that of Christ's bodily parts. This doctrine makes use of a sophisticated philosophical vocabulary, namely, the Aristotelian system of substances, essences, and attributes. It is not to be assumed that the average Catholic layman has a full grasp of these concepts, if any at all. Still, when the Catholic layman declares his faith in transubstantiation, the phenomenon thereby credited is the one the Church defines in Aristotelian terms. The word, 'transubstantiation', as spoken by the Catholic layman, signifies the specialised Aristotelian notion. It does so because the lay Catholic uses the term according to a deferential convention, in such a way that the term means, as spoken by him, what it is taken to mean by the authorities on Catholic dogma.

We have seen examples of the way language extends the scope for generation of social facts by, as it were, giving every individual vicarious powers of thought, borrowed from other parts of the community. But language also enhances the constructive powers of social agents in ways that do not depend upon such loans. In language, concepts lead their own lives, at least partly liberated from that connection with non-linguistic human action through which concepts get their meanings in the final analysis. Certain concepts are attributed to an individual in virtue of his ability to use correctly certain linguistic terms; they could not be attributed to a creature that lacked linguistic means for their expression. Evidently, such concepts will tend to be highly abstract. Still, the issues they serve to formulate may have the capacity for tangible social consequences.

Mathematics is a case in point. Within the community of mathematicians, we find concepts creating social reality, in the sense that conceptual structures and connections generate social relationships in the groups investigating those structures. Normally, those social relations will be professional, abstract and highly specialised, for instance, like the relationship between two teams of mathematicians competing to be the first to produce a proof of a particular theorem. Sometimes, however, those relationships may attain a broader social significance. The point is well illustrated by the notion of *incommensurability* in classic Greek mathematics. The Pythagoreans sanctified numbers and formed a religious society dedicated to their study; this society even gained a certain political influence. The Pythagoreans held that all things were made up of mathematical 'units', the number of units being characteristic of each type of thing and thereby expressing its essence. Hence, it was a great shock to them to discover that the world cannot be construed as a determinate structure of such units. This was the discovery that the diagonal of a square is not commensurate with the sides: if the side is given a precise numerical value, it can be proved that it is impossible to give the diagonal a precise numerical value, expressible as a finite fraction. The upshot is that the world is not mathematically expressible and, hence, not rational. The Pythagoreans declared this scandalous result a secret, not to be divulged to the masses. (Legend has it that the first members of the society who broke this ban suffered the wrath of the gods; their ship sank and they perished.)

What we have here is a social fact being constituted by the logic of the concept of number. In particular, the crisis of the Pythagorean society upon the discovery of irrational numbers (as they came later to be called) and the decision to keep the discovery a secret are contingent upon the concept of such numbers. So far, this is a trivial observation – in principle, no different from the observation that fist fights between soccer fans over the eminence of their respective clubs are not possible without the concept of soccer. The distinctiveness of the mathematical example, however, lies in the independent life that mathematical concepts lead, which is owed to their essential linguistic embodiment. A person could probably possess and manifest the concept of soccer without being able to express it verbally in soccer-related discourse; all it takes is the ability to play the game, including a willingness to abide by its rules. The rules of the game can be followed by a person who does not know how to put them into words. For the higher reaches of mathematics, however, the situation is different. It makes dubious sense to attribute a grasp of the incommensurability of irrational and rational numbers to a person who has only behavioural, non-linguistic ways of manifesting that understanding. To understand these concepts, a person needs the command of a specialised mathematical language in which the relevant result can be proved; presumably, this even has to be a written language. A good mathematical formalism increases the power of thinking by providing a concrete, tangible model of abstract logical processes. Relationships between (written) symbols offer a sensory simulacrum of abstract relationships between concepts; manipulations of symbols stand in for abstract transformations of thought objects. The formalism offers a handle for thought, which would otherwise lose its grip on these abstract conceptual connections.

Another, less esoteric, example is science. In the development of science, abstract theoretical speculation is as important as the gathering of experimental data. The most abstract scientific conceptions can only be entertained if an appropriate language is available. Remember the way that certain important scientific breakthroughs came about through reflection upon the meaning of words. Thus, Einstein's special theory of relativity grew out of an analysis of the concept in classic physics of 'simultaneity' and the way it is established. The conduct of science would clearly not be possible without the existence of abstract conceptual structures, embodied in linguistic form.

Thus, it is the existence of a language in which the requisite background assumptions can be expressed that makes one all-encompassing social fact out of the disparate activities of those thousands of people engaged in large-scale scientific projects, such as the testing of the Grand Unified Theory of matter at CERN. Take away the public language in which those background theories are expressed and that overall social phenomenon dissolves into a confusion of discrete local acts without meaning: people hurrying to and fro, pushing buttons and looking at dials, scrutinising computer printouts, and so on. The whole thing will have no more meaning than the scurrying about of ants on an anthill. We may appropriately call this the Babel effect. Yet, what we consider here is something more drastic than the divine intervention that deconstructed social fact at Babel. There, a public language was still in existence, but it was not a universally shared one. Here, we consider the even more dramatic result of a sudden collective aphasia, as it were, erasing all abstract notions in the language.

The CERN example illustrates a point distinguishing the phenomenological and hermeneutic variants of the argument from 'meaning'. Whereas the former presupposes that all meanings are located in one or another human consciousness, this is not so for the hermeneutic argument. We may correctly attribute to such large-scale institutions as CERN certain aims that are not realised in any human consciousness. They may, for instance, be written into the charter of the institution. No one taking part in day-to-day activities at the institution need know them; we may hypothesise a situation in which the officials who formulated those documents are long dead. Still, to the extent that such documents exist, and that recourse will be had to them in certain situations (such as political struggles over the future direction of the centre's activities), it will be natural to say that they still determine the centre's purposes.

We may mention one more way that language helps generate social fact. Certain socially salient issues are linguistically conditioned, not just because they could not be conceived without language – as was the case with mathematics and science above – but also because (unlike mathematics and science) these issues may be suspected of having no content apart from language. They are, as it were, empty linguistic forms that are held by the participants to express genuine issues. A case in point might be the Catholic doctrine of transubstantiation, discussed previously, which is the attempt to interpret the dogma of the real presence of Christ's flesh and blood in the Eucharist by means of ontological categories derived from Aristotle. We may suspect that there is no content to the claim that some items possess all the properties definitive of bread or wine, yet are different substances (namely, flesh and blood). The doctrine of transubstantiation is made possible by a (philosophical) misunderstanding of a certain feature of our language – to wit, its subject–predicate structure, which apparently sets the 'thing' or substance over against (even the total sum of) its properties. Still, this issue, for all its abstractness, was socially potent: it gave rise to factions within the Catholic Church that were demarcated solely by their stand on this issue. On a larger scale, the issue was among those that divided the Catholic and Protestant wings of Christendom. There is no need to belabour the importance of that rift in European history. (Evidently, the disagreement over transubstantiation was not the most important issue dividing Protestants and Catholics, nor should the Reformation be seen solely as a spiritual struggle; more tangible political and social concerns were at work as well. On the other hand, there is no doubt that the doctrinal issues served to give a particular shape to the competition between these societal forces, thereby generating social facts.)

CHAPTER VII

The Argument from the Symbolic Nature of Social Facts

Social science frequently claims that social phenomena are essentially *symbolic*. The social world is a symbolic order, created by human beings in and through their symbolic dealings with one another; even the physical setting in which these dealings take place and the objects and tools that are used as their props are deeply imbued with symbolic meaning. This observation provides material for another argument in favour of the construction thesis.

The most important source of the symbolist interpretation of social reality is Durkheim's *The Elementary Forms of the Religious Life* (1915). Here, Durkheim declared that 'social life, in all its aspects and in every period of its history, is made possible only by a vast symbolism' (p. 231). The primary focus of Durkheim's work was on the status of religious belief and ritual. Durkheim's view of religion as essentially symbolic was intended to reconciliate two *prima facie* opposed attitudes. The first is that (primitive) religious beliefs are false (and most of them glaringly so); they seem, in Durkheim's words, to be nothing but a 'fabric of errors'. The other was the conviction that a mode of thought that has dominated human thinking and informed human action for millennia cannot be altogether illusive; it must contain an element of validity. Durkheim's solution to this dilemma was to declare that religion does indeed contain truth, but a truth that is missed if we interpret religious doctrines in a literal way. Instead, this truth is apparent once we see religion as a symbol of an entirely different domain, namely the social realm. Religious beliefs are really about society and religious rituals are in fact communions with, and celebrations of, that higher being: society.

In *The Elementary Forms of the Religious Life*, Durkheim moved in the border area between sociology of religion and social anthropology, since his main concern was with primitive religion.

The focal object of investigation was totemism, which Durkheim considered to be the most primitive stage of religion and which he examined by means of ethnographic material collected among Australian tribes. As a matter of fact, in recent times, Durkheim's influence has been stronger among social anthropologists than among sociologists and psychologists concerned with religion. For reasons to which I shall return, symbolist interpretation has been less popular in the study of religion and primarily has been advanced in connection with the interpretation of magic.

The symbolist interpretation of magic in social anthropology was meant to controvert a previous orthodoxy concerning the nature of magic, represented by such pioneer social anthropologists as Frazer and Tylor. The problem of specifying the distinctive features of magic, as a form of thought characteristic of preliterate societies and in contrast to the mode of thinking prevalent in modern industrialised societies, was a chief concern of these early British ethnographers. They construed magic simply as misguided scientific theorising and magical action and ritual as primitive technology. (We examined this tendency in Part One under a slightly different heading, as that of the rationality of native thinking.) Like technology, magical action was held to be *instrumental*; that is, it is designed to bring about a change in the world, distinguishable from the very performance of the action and remaining after the action has been accomplished.

According to the alternative, symbolist interpretation, on the other hand, represented recently in its pure form by social anthropologist Edmund Leach (Leach 1976), Frazer and Tylor committed a crude ethnocentric mistake in assimilating magic to certain practices dominant in our culture. Magical action is symbolic-expressive; it is not designed to bring about a change in the world, but is consummated in its very performance. In carrying out a magical action, an act of symbolisation has been achieved and the agent has manifested a certain attitude to the thing symbolised; but nothing remains after the action has been performed. According to this conception, native magical action is primarily designed to communicate with the universe, not to manipulate or change it. The natives express their deference to spirits or deities, but do not try to impose their plans and schemes on the world by manipulating these beings.

The symbolic interpretation of religious and magical practices would seem to offer a very direct avenue to a social constructivist position. Symbols, including symbolic actions, we may agree, are constructed by the thoughts people have about them, in the same sense of 'construction' that we dealt with in the preceding chapters: namely, construction by composition. Certain thoughts and intentions in the people involved in symbolic practices form a *part* or *aspect* of the phenomenon of symbolism. Hence, the present argument is closely related to the phenomenological argument in particular, but has distinctive features that warrant separate treatment.

The argument from symbolism may be considered as a particularly pointed version of the phenomenological argument. This is so because symbolic action is especially relevant to a constructivist interpretation, more so than the broader class of actions to which the phenomenological and hermeneutic arguments apply (and which comprises symbolic action as a sub-class). This is precisely because purely symbolic action is exhausted by its very performance. Once a person has bestowed symbolic meaning upon an action, no result or further cooperation on the part of the physical universe is required to make the action succeed. Symbolic actions are prime instances of constructed reality.

Let us consider a thumbnail version of the argument that facts involving symbolism are social constructions (a preliminary formulation to which we will return later). For some item (including an action) to be a symbol is simply for that item to *stand for* the thing symbolised. The notion of 'standing for' we next construe as the circumstance of one item directing thought towards another item. Given these assumptions, a symbolic relation is certainly generated by the belief that that relation exists. In believing that some item S stands for some other, specified item O, a person has *eo ipso* been made to think of O. In recognising something as a symbol for another thing, a person is reminded of that thing and thereby has actualised the symbolising relationship. (It may be argued that the collective beliefs of a multitude of persons are required to make something into a symbol, properly speaking; but this condition is easily satisfied, since the beliefs we are dealing with here are typically socially shared ones.)

A fuller account of symbolism and symbolist interpretation as a constructivist thesis will follow, but let us first briefly examine the ways that religious and magic practices have been thought to involve symbolism. The correct scientific interpretation of the empirical facts is still a matter of some controversy in this area, and we must take a stand: we must decide upon a plausible construal of the claim that magic practices are symbolic, if only for the purpose of the subsequent argument.

THE SYMBOLIST INTERPRETATION OF RELIGION AND MAGIC

Durkheim's theory of religion, the ancestor of symbolist interpretations of magic in social anthropology, holds that human beings are under a systematic illusion with respect to the nature of their religious beliefs and practices. Whereas believers are convinced that they are in communion with a suprasensible and supranatural being, the real object of worship is human society, transformed in such a way that its true identity is disguised. When participating in religious practices, the worshippers feel the supraindividual power of society guiding and controlling them, which induces increased powers in themselves. These powers they project on to a super-sensible realm, failing to see that such powers actually spring from the collectivity of which they themselves are a part. They are the victims of an illusion.

Still, Durkheim does not conclude that religion is wholly an illusion. As we saw, he wants to rescue religion from such a charge; the saving manoeuvre is symbolic reinterpretation. In religious ritual, a god as object of worship is somehow the symbol of society; by worshipping the symbol, the votaries worship what the symbol stands for, that is, society.

Durkheim's theory of religion faces a serious problem, however, which is that the votaries are not aware of the deity as a symbol of society. While Durkheim at times may profess that the true object of religious worship actually is dimly grasped by the faithful, his construal clearly does not coincide with the everyday interpretation of religious belief, whether it be the lay believer's understanding or the official doctrine expounded by institutionalised religious authorities. Most votaries would insist that they seek communion with a transcendent being and would resent the suggestion that society as such is the true object of their zeal. Official church doctrine also maintains that religious beliefs and activities are directed towards a suprasensible, transcendent reality, not to objects of this world. Indeed, in the standard view, the worship of society would be condemned as idolatrous. Hence, Durkheim has to introduce the idea of unconscious symbolism, declaring that society is the unconscious object of worship. This is, however, a highly dubious doctrine. Freud may have shown that the general idea of unconscious symbolism cannot be dismissed out of hand; but then the Freudian interpretation is backed up by evidence in the form of behaviour and dream material in which the symbol stands for the object symbolised. There is no similar detailed evidence to back up Durkheim's claim.

Durkheim's construal of religious activity actually would seem to reflect a conflation of causal and intentional accounts of the phenomenon. Let us grant that, when participating in religious ritual, man believes himself to be somehow *en rapport* with a source of power that he terms 'God'. Let us also, for the sake of argument, grant Durkheim that the actual source of power involved is society, although the worshipper does not realise this. But these premises do not allow us to infer that the object – that is, the intentional object – of religious belief is really society. In sentences expressing beliefs (and other 'propositional attitudes'), we cannot replace a term referring to an object with a non-synonymous term referring to the same object and still expect the sentence to retain its truth value; this is the so-called intensionality of propositional attitudes. For example: if a religious devotee wants to worship the bones in the shrine in front of him, believing them to be the relics of a holy man, but these objects happen, alas! to be the bones of a pig, we cannot infer that the devotee wants to worship the bones of a pig.

Thus Durkheim's theory of religion is undermined by a fundamental fallacy, and his followers within social anthropology have generally adopted a more moderate line. In the first place, they typically focus on action and symbolism of a more local nature, this being a result of the shift of attention from religion to magic. Having abandoned the global claim that religion symbolises society, anthropologists now deal in a piecemeal fashion with particular religious and magical rituals involving correspondingly local and limited objects of symbolisation. The symbolic nature of the practices in question are normally fully understood by the practitioners; hence the anthropologist can largely avoid invocation of 'unconscious symbolisation', a conceptual oddity at best. Second, with the exception of a few hardliners such as Edmund Leach, anthropologists no longer claim that religious and, in particular, magical rituals are *purely* symbolic. These rituals are rather held to be symbolic-cum-practical; that is, the symbolic element is combined with, and auxiliary to, a practical purpose (cf. Beattie 1970).

In adopting this interpretation, the symbolists steer towards a compromise with the 'intellectualist' position of Frazer and Tylor. According to the compromise position (which comes in many different versions), the essence of magic lies precisely in the combination – we might even say conflation – of an instrumentalist and a symbolist point of view. The natives symbolise certain objects, events, or states of affairs and believe that, by manipulating them, they gain some kind of causal control over the things symbolised. Another, related conflation lies in the natives' belief that they can bring about changes in nature by the same means that suffice to bring about new facts in society, that is by performative speech acts such as commands or appeals. Again, it is a case of misunderstanding the power of symbols – this time the power of language.

A lucid and carefully worked-out version of the compromise interpretation of magic is found in John Skorupski's *Symbol and Theory* (Skorupski 1976). In the following, I shall borrow extensively from Skorupski's exposition, which I consider the best philosophical account in the field. Skorupski does not present us with only one interpretation of magic, but offers a number of plausible proposals, all sharing the implication that magic is expressive-cum-instrumental. These accounts should not be seen as rivals, but rather as complementary: different analyses will fit different kinds of magic. Moreover, a magical practice will often be seen to have features corresponding to several accounts. Here, I shall only examine the two main interpretations offered by Skorupski.

The interpretations in question can trace their ancestry back to James Frazer's analyses in *The Golden Bough* (Frazer 1911). The first one is especially germane to magical acts of the type that Frazer termed *sympathetic magic*. In such acts, the sorcerer (or other practitioner of magic) creates an object that is thought to have some special affinity with the target of the magic and then performs an operation upon this object, the result of which is expected subsequently to transfer to the target through some sort of causal link. For instance, the sorcerer fashions a wax effigy of his enemy and proceeds to pierce its chest with pins. This treatment is presumed to afflict the enemy with a corresponding wound that kills him.

According to Frazer, it is the natural, non-anthropomorphic relation of *similarity* between the effigy and the target that is held (by the sorcerer) to channel the causal power. Skorupski, aligning himself with such later anthropologists as John Beattie, puts a symbolic reinterpretation on this kind of magic. The symbolic aspect lies in the status of the effigy as *standing for* the target, a relationship that serves to focus the effect upon the latter. The causal effect rides on the back of an essentially man-made relation of symbolisation or representation. Thus, the magical actions falling under this heading are symbolic-cum-instrumental. They aim at achieving practical effects, such as the death of an enemy. Clearly, there is no opposition between the symbolic nature of the action and its practical goal: the action is expected to achieve its goal *by virtue of* its symbolic power. On the other hand, it is doubtful if the action can be called expressive, at least if this implies that the action releases some real emotion on the part of the practitioner. Often, magic is performed by 'professional' sorcerers, who exhibit a detached and businesslike attitude to the spells they cast.

Another symbolic interpretation of magic developed by Skorupski focuses upon spells and incantations and the role played in these by a symbolic system, namely *language*. In magical rituals, the sorcerer addresses the magical potions and directs them to perform certain tasks. Here, magic is a speech act – the commanding of personalised forces or spirits to do certain things. The sorcerer, for instance, will address the ulcers that afflict his client's legs, telling the sores to leave the client and go searching for another victim. He will address the seeds that he puts into the ground and impel them to turn into a bountiful crop, and will tell the poisonous substance used in a bird oracle to take or spare the chicken's life in such a way that its survival or death will provide a positive or negative answer to certain questions posed as part of the ritual. All these actions are symbolic in their attempt to bring about an effect by means of a symbolic medium; namely, language.

Such actions may all naturally be described as *expressive*. The sorcerer expresses or displays his wishes and intentions to the supernatural agencies, thereby hoping to persuade them to intercede on his behalf. This aspect becomes more prominent the more the activities gravitate towards what we would call (primitive) *religion*. Here, the sorcerer's attitude towards the agencies addressed is not commanding, but pleading or entreating. The magic is only thought to work if the sorcerer displays the proper deferential attitude to the deities, who demand that the client pay homage to them before they will heed his pleas. This ceremony is part of an overall conception of the world, in which men, spirits and deities are each assigned their own proper place; these relative positions are expressed and affirmed through the ceremony. This expressive character does not preclude that such actions have a practical side, however. The magician expresses his deference to the deities so that they will reward their loyal devotee with a successful hunt or a plentiful harvest.

The above examples are merely illustrative and cannot show that all kinds of magic possess the instrumental-cum-symbolic duality; as a matter of fact, Skorupski takes pains to indicate that his various construals of magic may not attain full coverage of what is customarily so labelled. It is safe to say, however, that Skorupski presents a very persuasive case that his categories of symbolic action encompass a wide range of magical practices as reported in the ethnographic literature, and that their subsumption under these categories reveal that these magical actions are not purely symbolic, but symbolic-cum-instrumental.

The ironic fact is that purely symbolic-expressive action is not the hallmark of native communities, but precisely of modern, industrialised society. In modern societies, we have come to realise the impotence of symbolic-cum-instrumental actions and have replaced them with purely instrumental interventions. We no longer cast spells on our fields to make the crops grow, but spray them with fertiliser; we treat our sick with medicines rather than put them through the ordeals of exorcistic ritual. However, this shift has left a residual class of actions in which the expressive component is very strong. This group of actions has been pushed to the opposite end of the conceptual spectrum and is now viewed as *purely* symbolic. Examples are the ceremonies performed by royalty, clergy, or prominent citizenry on national holidays, such as flying the flag, standing at attention while the national anthem is being played, placing a ribbon on the tomb of the unknown soldier, and so on. At least some of these actions were once considered to have instrumental efficacy; the actions of kings or of heads of the religious hierarchy were somehow thought to have beneficial effects for the people. There was a time when kings were judged by the plenitude of the harvests that they brought their subjects, but today we no longer blame royalty for the exigencies of the climate.

SYMBOLIC ACTION IN MODERN SOCIETY

The category of symbolic action has much wider application, however, even in our modern, rationalised society, than the rather trite examples mentioned above. The same stereotype that represents native action as purely symbolic, rather than symbolic-cum-instrumental, misconstrues large segments of the conduct found in modern industrial societies in seeing it as purely instrumental. A closer look will reveal a further aspect: concomitant with the instrumental part of human social action, there is often a symbolic side in which certain other facets of social existence achieve expression.

Facts in this range make up the field of *semiology*. Semiologists heed de Saussure's call for a general science of signs and their life within society. Some segments of social reality that have been subjected to semiological analysis are clothes, food and kinship systems. No doubt, the richest field for semiological analysis is clothing. Clothes have a utilitarian function in protecting the human body from the exigencies of the climate. But their design is only loosely constrained by their intended function; when that function has been fulfilled, there is immense scope for variation. This variability has long been an arena for social symbolisation. Clothing makes a commentary upon the ongoing social spectacle, typically by *enhancing* or *amplifying* the distinctive traits of the social happening in question. We use certain kinds of sombre clothes to emphasise the solemnity of a burial; we use light materials and bright colours to underline leisurely, free-time sports activities.

Beyond providing amplifying commentary upon ongoing social activity, dress symbolism also keeps us mindful of, and thereby affirms, certain socially salient categories and distinctions among people. This is a topic of symbolism not bound to particular occasions; it cuts across local and temporal symbolisation. A crucial topic of symbolism is the distinction between male and female. This is not only marked by the familiar opposition between trousers and skirts, or buttoning on the right versus the left side, but also in terms of such more subtle differences as quality of fabric (which tends to be coarse and heavy for men, soft and delicate for women) and in the colours (which are typically bright for women, more subdued for men). Another socially-salient distinction, marked in clothing, is that between young and old. There are also the endlessly ramified and eloquent ways to express the distinction between upper-class and lower-class status, between wealthy and poor, between those in power and those without it, and in general between the 'haves' and the 'have-nots' in any walk of life. Here, the opposition is largely built around the contrast between expensive and inexpensive items, but also between items that are derived from work clothes versus clothes that are conspicuously unsuitable for work.

The most sustained effort in the genre of semiological analysis remains Roland Barthes's essay, *The Fashion System* (Barthes 1990). Barthes describes clothing as a veritable 'vestimentary language', a symbolic code with clearly-defined syntactic structure and great semantic richness. According to Barthes, clothes make statements about the settings in which they are used and about their wearers. He adds a particular twist to the general approach in that he does not focus upon the stable connections between certain kinds of clothes and their symbolic reference (such as those mentioned in the previous section), but instead on the symbolic meaning of shifting fashions that operate in the slack left by these symbolic constraints. Barthes shows how, according to the changing dictates of fashion, particular combinations of clothes are required for certain specified settings and situations and, hence, symbolise both those settings and certain characteristics of those wearing the clothes.[14]

Another aspect of social life that has been subjected to semiological analysis is food (cf. Claude Lévi-Strauss 1970; Marshall Sahlins 1976). Like clothing, food has a basically utilitarian function. But food, like clothing, has a richness of variation that goes far beyond purely alimentary needs. This redundant area is invaded by social significance and turned into a field of symbolism. As in the case of clothes, the meaning of food symbolism may be local and context-bound, or it may be more general. It is local when symbolising the nature of some current activity, as an abundance of fine foods signals a festival, or, the opposite, frugal foods marking a religious fast. Signification is more general when it points to permanent features of the people involved, such as differences in wealth or education. Such class distinctions are subtly reflected at the alimentary level in the contrasts between wine drinkers and beer drinkers, between beef eaters and pork eaters, between people who like to sample foreign foods versus those who stick to 'home cooking', and so on. In this way, the biological function of eating is made the vehicle for subtle social messages.

Clearly, many other features of social life possess the duality of a utilitarian basis plus a morphological richness that invites symbolic use. Barthes himself mentions furniture, housing, and cars as examples; one could add leisurely activities such as sports, vacations, and many others. However, I shall forgo any detailed treatment of these. They have never, to my knowledge, been subjected to serious scientific study, but receive more anecdotal treatment; for example, they are a favourite topic of journalists writing about changing trends in 'lifestyle'. There is no doubt, however, that there are symbolic functions here, too. One need only look at American cars, especially from the 1950s, to recognise the tell-tale exaggeration of such features as tail fins and grilles that have no practical function. Again, a utilitarian object has become weighted with symbolic meaning.

Indeed, exaggeration is the essence of the kind of symbolism that is parasitic upon a utilitarian function; I shall refer to it as *concomitant symbolism* in the following. I believe that we can have a better understanding of this kind of symbolism, including its characteristic exaggeration, as we explain the role of such symbolism in modern society. We may distinguish between two sub-types, mentioned above, one symbolising occurrent, local features of ongoing social happenings, the other symbolising more permanent and global social concerns, not specifically related to a current social encounter. Let us dub them *occasional* and *non-occasional* symbolism, for short.

INTERACTION RITUALS

If social interaction is to proceed smoothly, people must be able to establish quickly what kind of social scene is being enacted at any given time. The nature of a social encounter is often not directly correlated with obvious external signs, however, but rather with what goes on in people's minds; this was the point on which the argument from subjective meaning was based. Hence, in order to clarify a social encounter, the participants' thoughts must be externalised. A simple and systematic way of doing this is by exaggerating certain – natural or conventional, but in any case non-symbolic – manifestations of those inner states (Skorupski 1976, ch. 6).

The so-called interaction ritual is a simple illustrative case. When people meet, it is important for them to define their social roles and synchronise their practical plans without unnecessary waste of time. Hence, a general code has developed governing the processes of people initiating, maintaining, and finally terminating, face-to-face encounters. This code is largely expressive and symbolic; the interactants indicate to each other their willingness to engage in interaction and to work towards some joint outcome by certain tacit signals. These are typically exaggerated versions of natural signs of goodwill: a wide smile and a cheerful tone of voice. It is fully appreciated on all sides that these indications of friendliness, although derived from natural reactions, need not correspond to any genuine and spontaneous feeling in order to fulfil their social function. They only need to be a reliable predictor of the nature of the responses, whether spontaneous or not, that will be forthcoming from the interactants.

The point of such trivial examples carries over to more specialised and complex social encounters. Recall again that it is what goes on in the minds of the participants that determines whether a social occasion counts as a religious service, the swearing-in of a foreign ambassador, or something completely different. This mental activity is not immediately observable. Hence, there must be some symbolic way of making it known – for example, the deference shown towards the deity, or the respectful attitude towards the ambassador as the representative of a country. Once such symbolic means of expression are instituted, they take over the role of the mental states they symbolise. Such mental states need not be really present as long as their symbolic representations are displayed and as long as the interactants behave in a way consistent with the presence of such states.

This account of occasional symbolism allows us to give a more precise analysis of the representational mechanism of concomitant symbolism. The symbols, or symbolic aspects of actions, 'stand for' social activities by *emphasising* or *enhancing* them, stressing the features by which they contrast with other social activities. Certain features of the natural expressions of the relevant mental states are reproduced in a form exaggerated beyond any functional rationality and thus point, as it were, towards the specific character of the social event in question.[15] Notice the difference between concomitant symbolism and the kind of symbolism, mentioned earlier, in which the object of symbolisation is represented by some proxy: an unknown soldier is an anonymous proxy for those killed in a war, the flag is a tangible stand-in for the homeland, and bread and wine represent the body and blood of Jesus Christ (according to a Protestant interpretation). In concomitant symbolism, on the other hand, a thing will typically symbolise *itself*, through the mechanism of exaggeration. (Of course, these are 'ideal types' only. The two modes of symbolism will often be mixed in a number of ways.)

Non-occasional symbolisation can be given a similar functional explanation, although some theoreticians might prefer an alternative account. The functionalist explanation insists that smooth and successful interaction between people requires that the interactants possess certain crucial items of information about each other with respect to age, gender, class background, education, and general level of knowledge, as well as more specific items of information. Most of this information lies hidden from immediate view; hence, it must be externalised – this service is rendered by non-occasional symbolism. Cynics would object that many of the features that are most eloquently symbolised in social life are not very material for the practical purposes of interaction, for example, the class differences between the interactants, or their income levels. Instead, they would point to a general human desire to derive affirmation of self-identity through social encounters. The symbols serve to present a social identity, a persona, to which the other interactants must then pay tribute. There is no reason for us to try to adjudicate between these two theories here – in fact, the truth may well be found in some combination of them. In either theory, the business of symbolism is to make available salient information about social events and their protagonists.

We see that the mechanism of non-occasional symbolism is once again exaggeration: if a social class is defined by the wealth of its members, the members will demonstrate and exaggerate this feature in their clothing and general deportment. They will eat lavish meals and drive ostentatious cars; in brief, they will engage in what Thorstein Veblen called 'conspicuous consumption'.

THE DRAMATURGICAL INTERPRETATION OF SOCIAL ACTION

The account just given has themes familiar from the so-called *dramaturgical* view of social action, introduced by Erving Goffman and his collaborators (Goffman 1959). The idea, briefly put, is to see social interaction as a matter of the carefully-conducted presentation of the interactants and their roles in the encounter. Goffman develops a rich vocabulary to describe this representational function, using the theatre as a guiding metaphor. He describes how people performing a representation of self often construct a setting, or stage, on which to perform. This stage may be the impeccably clean living room in which the housewife entertains guests, or the stylish locales in which patrons are served in a restaurant. These contrast with the 'back stage', to which the audience is not admitted: the bedroom in which the housewife keeps the mess cleaned out of the living room, or the kitchen area in which the waiters and other staff behave with less grace than in front of the patrons.

Goffman at times writes as if self-presentation were the ultimate purpose of all social interaction, rather than just an aspect of it; as if the only reason why we deal with other people is to foist upon them a certain definition of ourselves and our station in society – both typically somewhat inflated. Social interaction, in this picture, has a goal purely intrinsic to it; any extrinsic, practical ends drop out of sight. However, this impression is due to rhetorical exaggeration on Goffman's part: he often enough shows an awareness that the symbolic side of social interaction is parasitic upon a non-symbolic basis, typically comprising actions directed towards practical ends. Moreover, Goffman shows clear awareness that the function of such symbolism is to provide clarifying information not otherwise available about social activities. It does not detract from this insight that Goffman is fascinated by, and untiringly documents, the way this information is often used for misrepresentation and manipulation.

This is a suitable place to sound a note of caution about the concept of symbolisation. In the writings of certain social scientists, this concept tends to swallow up everything not (purely) instrumental. The resulting dichotomisation of social action seems simply false (if the terms are taken in their normal sense) or unhelpful (if construed as an implicit proposal for redefinition of the term 'symbol'). Many actions are non-instrumental without being symbolic. We may here mention Weber's famous distinction between instrumental and 'value-rational' action, where the latter kind is non-instrumental but typically not symbolic (Weber 1947); perhaps we should add traditional behaviour as a further example of non-instrumental, non-symbolic action. An example of value-rational action might be the keeping of a promise to a friend even after his death, in a situation in which no negative consequences would follow for anyone from non-fulfilment of the promise. Such action has no instrumental purpose. The social significance of this kind of action becomes evident once we remind ourselves that action in obedience to moral principles without any utilitarian purpose constitutes a large element of the religious life in a community. This is an important part of the culture, but should not by that token be called symbolic. Not all religious life is symbolic worshipping of the deity, but may consist of observing divine prescriptions. This is not to deny, of course, that many actions in adherence to prescriptive rules are symbolic. Such actions are distinguished precisely by their exaggeration: the abstention from certain kinds of food in certain periods (fasting) may be said to be largely symbolic, since it seems excessive in its pointlessness (in contrast to an action such as not harming one's neighbours). It is a symbol of one's obedience to the divine commands and, hence, is expressive.

Another example: Marshall Sahlins (1976, ch. 4) makes much of the fact that there are certain restrictions on permissible foods in modern American (and European) culture that are not 'instrumental' – in other words, do not serve any obvious nutritional end. For instance, eating dogs or cats is not allowed, whereas consumption of pigs and cows is permitted; horses occupy an intermediate position. Sahlins seems to consider these rules part of a dietary symbolic code, created so that the difference between foods highlights differences in the consumers' social standing: the well-to-do eat beef, the less well-off eat pork, and so on. However, it would seem that the taboo on eating horses is just a (non-instrumental) norm imposed upon people's eating habits; it is not in itself expressive. Similarly, much action that semiologists would see as purely expressive is not solely so. For instance, the quiet and muted action required at funerals in Western societies is not solely meant to express the fact that this is a funeral, nor yet to express respect towards the deceased or his beloved ones. It is simply thought to be the appropriate thing to do, since noisy and boisterous activities would disturb and grieve the mourners. This point is not contradicted by the observation that, in other societies, noisy grief and loud mourning are regarded as being appropriate on such occasions.

SYMBOLISM AND CONSTRUCTION

So much for the role of symbolism in social life and for its standing as a theoretical concept in social science. We must now return to our real concern, which is with the issue of social constructivism. Is symbolic action a social construction, generated by the way human beings think about it? To answer that question correctly will require some caution.

Let us for the moment return to the quick argument offered at the beginning of this chapter, which seemed to point towards a positive answer to our question. A symbol, we agreed, is a thing (or action, process, or whatever) standing for another thing – that is, directing thought towards that thing. Hence, in thinking that some item S is a symbol of the object O, our thought is directed towards O, since O is part of the content of this thought. Ergo, S is indeed a symbol of O.

There is an obvious objection to this line: it will give the concept of a symbol an overly-wide extension. Any thing that is in any way related to another thing, and so able to be taken as an indicator of that thing, will be a sign of the latter. Thus, dark clouds will be a symbol of rain (and rain of dark clouds); red spots will be a symbol of measles (and vice versa). To avoid this consequence, we might try to add that the symbol must be man-made. But even this restriction is not enough, since it will make, say, motorways symbols of human existence, and this is not intuitively the case. Surprisingly, many anthropologists happily endorse such broad notions of symbol, or related ideas like 'expression'. An example is Edmund Leach, who states that even the act of breathing is 'expressive' – it 'says' that the breathing person is still alive (Leach 1976: 9). One may doubt the fruitfulness of inflating the term so radically that it applies to absolutely everything that is related to something else – that is, to anything at all. Hence, the term does not mark a contrast and is, for that reason, without meaning, precisely according to the logic of those structuralists and semiologists who sometimes promote it. This ought to give them pause. Intuitively, what is wrong with the broad notion of symbolhood is that is overlooks the necessity of a communicative intent in the concept of a symbol. For a thing to be properly called a symbol, it must not only call up another thing, but must be *meant* to call up that thing.

To develop an analysis of symbolism in terms of human intentions, we may seek assistance in the writings of Paul Grice. Grice has never offered an analysis of symbols, but rather of linguistic meaning – in particular, sentence meaning (Grice 1957, 1969). The salient point of that analysis may be transferred to the case of symbolism, however. Here is first a thumbnail sketch of Grice's theory of (sentence) meaning, which I shall afterwards transform into a theory of symbolism.

Grice first demarcates the intended sense of 'meaning' from such occurrences of the term as, for instance, in the sentences 'Dark clouds mean rain', 'Money does not mean anything to me', and so on. He refers to these kinds of meaning as *natural*, since they may pertain to natural objects such as clouds. The intended analysandum, 'non-natural meaning', on the other hand, is a kind of meaning that calls for the mediation of a human being (or another conscious creature). It is the meaning that accrues to something when someone means something by it; and this, according to Grice, happens when someone uses it to generate some effect – understanding or a behavioural response – in an audience. Let us focus on the situation where the meaning is that of a declarative sentence (an assertion). In this case, the effect engendered is that of belief, according to Grice. Grice proposes, first, that for some item to mean that p (in the 'non-natural' sense) is for some person to use that item to generate in his audience the belief that p. We immediately realise that we have to refine this. If I arrange that the detective finds McX's handkerchief on the murder scene, thereby inducing in him the belief that McX is the murderer, we should not say that (my placing) the handkerchief *means that* McX is the murderer. What is wanting, according to Grice, is that the detective understands that the handkerchief is not, as it were, 'natural' evidence, but is placed there by me with the intent that he form a certain belief. Moreover, it is required that he form this belief at least in part because he grasps this intention of mine. In other words, for (my placing of) the handkerchief to mean that McX is the murderer, I must intend the detective to form the appropriate belief and to form it because he understands that this is what I intend him to do.

In more general terms, for an utterance X to mean that p, as addressed by a person U to an audience A, what is required, according to the Gricean analysis, is that:

(i) U utters X intending A to form the belief that p.
(ii) U intends that A should recognise this intention in U.
(iii) U intends that the effect mentioned in (i) be achieved because of this recognition.

The Gricean model can be modified in various ways with respect to the effect to be engendered in A, thereby making it cover such non-assertive speech acts as orders, questions or requests. We need not go further into this, however, but instead turn to consider what a Gricean analysis of symbolhood might look like, constructed according to the same principles. Here is a suggestion: for a thing (or state, process or action) S to be a symbol of another thing O, as used by a person U, is for U to want S to call up the thing – not by some natural likeness between the two, but because the recipient of the symbol realises that this is what U wants to happen. Putting it in the above format, we may say that S is a symbol of another thing O, as used by a person U, *vis-a-vis* some audience A if and only if :

(i) U confronts A with S, intending S to call up O in A.
(ii) U intends that A should recognise this intention in U.
(iii) U intends that the effect mentioned in (i) be achieved because of this recognition.

The second and third clauses in the definition are meant to cater to the fact that we will not, intuitively, call something a symbol even though it is consciously designed by someone to call up the idea of something else in the audience, if the latter is not intended to recognise this. For instance, if the sight of a carnation makes Smith think of his wedding day, this does not make the flower a symbol of his wedding day, even if Mrs Smith shrewdly exploits this connection to make her husband remember their anniversary. For this, it takes an understanding between the Smiths, such that the cause of Mr Smith's thinking of the anniversary will be his recognition that this is what Mrs Smith wanted him to think of when she placed a carnation in his lunch box.

Notice that this rather complicated definition of symbolhood safeguards the connection between being thought to be a symbol and actually being one. Symbolhood is achieved whenever the 'sender' of a symbol thinks of it as a symbol – that is, intends it to evoke the thought of the thing symbolised in some audience, by means of recognition of the intention. It is not required that the intention be actually fulfilled, that is, that somebody actually grasps the meaning of the symbol. However, it is a significant fact about symbols that this result is very easily and directly achieved, too. By the very fact of A's (the audience's) thinking that U (the 'sender'), in using the symbol, meant A to think of the thing O by means of A's recognition of this intention in U, U's intention will be achieved – for in thus thinking, A will indeed have thought of O and will have done so as a result of, or indeed even as a part of, his recognition of U's intention in using the symbol.

We might if we like expand the analysis of 'symbol' in such a manner that, for something to count as a symbol, it is not only required that it be accompanied by certain intentions on the part of the 'sender' but that these be recognised (regularly or normally) by the intended audience. Here, I have chosen to stick to the simple definition, to keep in as close conformity with Grice's definition as possible. I believe that this issue is largely a terminological one. There is, moreover, no need to pursue it in the present context since, given the stated purpose of our investigation, we are in any case restricted to dealing with communal processes of social construction. The use of symbols falls within the purview of our project only to the extent that such use forms a social practice which will no doubt, in any actual case, involve a multitude of both senders and receivers of symbolic messages. Hence we may sidestep the issue whether a private or idiosyncratically employed symbol deserves to be called a 'symbol' at all.

A further objection may be made to the above analysis, similar to one sometimes directed against Grice's analysis of linguistic meaning (see, for instance, Schiffer 1972). It is simply not the case, it is pointed out, that the average user of a symbol has such a complicated thought in mind as the one indicated here. After all, it took several centuries of philosophical reflection to produce the analysis of linguistic meaning upon which it is modelled. Symbol users think of symbols simply as things that *stand for* other things; they do so due to human intervention, not because of natural properties.

To handle this objection, we may invoke the results concerning the division of linguistic labour introduced in Chapter VI. A thing can be made a symbol if its user subsumes it under a term that means *symbol*, even if he is not capable of giving any precise semantic analysis of this term. The link between this description and the notion of symbolism is then supplied through the division of linguistic labour in a way analogous to the arthritis case on p. 156. The lay speaker uses the term 'symbol' according to a deferential convention, to the effect that it means the same as spoken by him as when spoken by experts concerning symbolism. Hence a person may believe that something is a symbol, thereby contributing to making it one, without really knowing what this idea means, so long as there are others in the community who have a better grasp of it – not necessarily the kind of conception that would receive the admiration of a semiologist, but at least a substantial idea.

We have offered an analysis of the notion of a symbol, an analysis that supports the intuition that symbolic facts are generated by human thoughts about it. In other words, it supports a constructivist position with respect to social symbols and symbolic acts. The irony is, however, that this analysis of symbolism does not support the constructivist thesis with respect to the kind of conduct for which is was traditionally proposed, namely for magical action of the kind investigated by anthropologists. As the above analysis showed, typical magical action is not purely symbolic, but symbolic-cum-instrumental, and the element of instrumental effectiveness is certainly not brought into existence just by the native belief that magic works. No amount of native conviction will make it true that the ritual dance really makes the rain return, or that the spell makes a woman fertile. Hence, native beliefs about magic are not made true by those very beliefs. (In the terminology of Chapter V, those beliefs possess 'external implications'.)

Constructivism comes into its own, however, when we turn to the kind of purely symbolic activities found in modern industrial society. Here, all the essential features of the ritual action are guaranteed to exist by the very beliefs of the participants that those elements are present. This is due, of course, to the fact that such action is *purely* symbolic-expressive and, hence, is not held by the participants to have any implications beyond itself (external implications). The participants' shared belief that the flag being hoisted symbolises their country *does*, indeed, make that flag symbolise the country. Their joint belief that, by hoisting that flag and singing the national anthem, they honour their country, ensures that this is really what they do. Today, we no longer believe that such ceremonies really bring about the well-being of a country, but adopt a purely symbolic outlook.

There is a final twist to this development: occasionally, such purely symbolic-expressive actions have been made symbolic-cum-practical once again. Sociologists and anthropologists have long taught us that such ceremonies often have latent functions, such as strengthening the society's morale and enhancing social cohesion; as a matter of fact, this was an important element of Durkheim's theory of religion. With the dissemination of this knowledge, latent functions sometimes turn into explicit goals: ceremonies are deliberately used by political parties, institutions and organisations to generate attitudes of community and loyalty in their members.

Presumably, most of the symbolic action going on in modern societies in the category of 'symbolisation by proxy' as described above will count as *conventional*. In the next chapter, we shall see that the phenomenon of convention by itself provides an avenue to a constructivist position. What has been demonstrated in the present chapter is that the symbolic status of a given social phenomenon involves a distinctive process of social construction, regardless of whether the symbol in question is conventional or not. Symbolisation is a sufficient condition for social construction to occur.

While the inference from a symbolic status to a constructivist conclusion is fairly obvious with respect to (pure) cases of 'symbolism by proxy', there may be some hesitation to accept the same conclusion when we turn to the kind of actions that I termed 'concomitant symbols', investigated by Goffman and co-workers. The crux of the matter is the propriety of holding that these actions are rendered symbolic by human thought. We saw that the *modus operandi* of such symbolism is the exaggeration of natural features of the action in question. The symbolising relation is somehow naturally related to that which it symbolises, namely the exaggerated action, and might thus be held not to be generated by thought. This reluctance would nevertheless reflect a confusion involving our present notion of 'generation by human thought' and certain related notions sometimes referred to by the same words. One such is 'convention'. But 'constituted by human thought' does not mean 'conventional'; conventionality is a narrower, more specialised concept: a subcategory of the class of facts generated by thought. The observation that the basis of concomitant symbolism is somehow 'natural' would count against it being conventional in either the classic or in David Lewis's interpretation, which we shall examine below; the same observation would not, however, count against its being generated by human thought.

Consider a parallel: human beings have a tendency to interpret an extended arm as an indication of an object at the end of the arm; this is no doubt a natural, biologically-determined trait and, hence, not a convention. Yet, the gesture of pointing is still a matter of the thoughts accompanying the outward behaviour. In a world in which human beings did not ever construe the person extending his arm as having certain intentions in so doing, it would make no sense to describe this manoeuvre as an act of *pointing*. Similarly, human beings probably have a natural propensity to regard exaggeration of a certain activity as a referral to that activity, thus rendering the symbolising relation non-conventional. That relation, however, is still grounded in the thoughts of the people involved. Thus actions manifesting concomitant symbolism count as socially constructed, too.

We may conclude that the argument from the symbolic nature of (some) social phenomena does indeed establish a constructivist thesis with respect to these phenomena. Symbolic actions invite a constructivist interpretation, because the conditions for their successful performance are much less demanding than acts with an instrumental, practical aspect. We also make the somewhat surprising discovery that the argument from symbolism gets much more purchase when applied to modern societies, where acts of pure symbolism are frequent, than when applied to those tribal societies that originally inspired the symbolic interpretation of social facts.

CHAPTER VIII

The Argument from Convention

With respect to many phenomena in the social world, anything short of a constructivist account would seem clearly out of place. Moving through society, we encounter people making promises to each other, individuals with licences to carry firearms, people with academic degrees, Bank Holidays, tradesmen paying for goods with paper money, constitutional monarchies, Courts of Appeal, acts of the European Union, and so on. Is it not blatantly obvious that these things are social constructions? After all, none of them are natural items or conditions. Being a monarch is not a natural physiological state, something that could be detected by a biopsy done on the regent. (We do not believe any more that royalty are distinguished by their blue blood.) The value of money is not a mysterious power that resides in the physical coins or paper slips and is somehow depleted when inflation sets in; a driving licence or a licence to carry a gun do not give the licensee increased opportunities of action due to features of the actual plastic card or the photograph upon it; a promise does not bind the promisor by virtue of certain acoustic properties of the spoken vow. These are all clearly social constructions. The mechanism of construction is *convention* – the agreement between the members of a community that such-and-such is to be the case.

In the following pages, I shall examine social construction by convention. Two issues will be in focus, beyond the critical examination of the very claim that convention is a case of social construction. First, what is the nature of convention? Second, is social construction by convention, if we accept it, just an example of 'construction by composition', that is, the way in which a set of external, observable events and items – human behaviour and artefacts – are transformed into social happenings by the meanings with which the agents accompany them? I shall argue that, although we may view the argument from convention as a special case of the familiar argument from the meaningfulness of action, it possesses such distinctive properties that we are well-advised to study it under a separate heading. The argument from convention adds an extra level of construction to that which follows from the arguments from meaningfulness.

HISTORICAL ROOTS: THE SOCIAL CONTRACT DOCTRINE

If we look for the historical ancestry of the argument from convention, our investigation will take us within the disciplinary boundaries of political philosophy. In this discipline, a strong tradition traces the foundations of the state and other social institutions back to human agreements; this is the study of liberal democracy and its roots. The concern of political philosophy with the way social institutions are based upon the consent of the governed can be traced back to the early political theoreticians of the Renaissance and the doctrine of 'natural rights' possessed by every human being. Among these is the right of self-determination, safeguarding the autonomy of every individual; the problem for political philosophy is how to explain how this self-determination may exist alongside the state and its *de facto* and *de jure* authority over the individual.

These issues were addressed by Thomas Hobbes, John Locke and other proponents of the Social Contract doctrine. The Social Contract theorists were primarily concerned to show that the state and its powers do not spring from sources independent of and above those ruled; in particular, these powers have not been bestowed by God directly upon an autocratic ruler. Instead, the powers of government derive from the *consent* of the subjects, who thereby empower the state to enforce (some of) their natural rights. Or, as we might prefer to put it, the fact that some society has a particular structure of legitimate political institutions is solely constituted by the fact that the members of that society agree to the installation and perpetuation of that structure.

Thus, the classic conception of society as conventional (consent-based) is to a large extent shaped by the historical circumstances of its emergence in the seventeenth century. As the classic conception has it, convention is the explicit agreement about some issue or decision, among a group of persons affected by that decision. The fathers of the political revolutions in the seventeenth and eighteenth centuries wanted to secure a political system in which the populace was consulted in all important political matters and in which institutions existed through which the public could impose its will upon the ruler. On a more general level, the practical–political concerns motivating the idea of society as consent-based means that this entire conception is not purely theoretical; it is as much normative political philosophy as an account of the political life actually encountered. This normative-cum-descriptive duality will pose a problem when we move on to assess whether convention suffices to generate social fact, as we want to use the term 'fact' in such a way as to exclude the normative. We shall have to eliminate the normative side of the consent theory of society when we get to this point.

To the political theorists of the seventeenth century, the model of agreement, or convention, was the *contract*. A contract is a device whereby individuals explicitly design and freely take upon themselves certain obligations, in return for obtaining commensurate rights. The contract became the focal notion of the liberal conception of society, expressing a new political ideal and, indeed, a new metaphysical conception of humankind. Human beings came to be seen as free, autonomous individuals, responsible for their own lives and at liberty to engage in their own individual 'pursuit of happiness'. The idea of equality comes with these ideas, since all partake equally of the fundamental freedom. The liberal conception was developed in step with crucial social and economical changes in Europe, its emergence marking the end of a society in which relations between human beings were rigidly determined by their membership of estates, guilds, and crafts. Instead arose a class of free economical entrepreneurs – and, as its reflection, the abstract idea of a political subject, the *citizen* (even though mainly as an ideal rather than a political reality).

Locke used the model of a contract to elucidate two points about the nature of civil authority (Locke 1970). First, there is the Social Contract proper, the agreement between free individuals in the state of nature to form a body politic, the better to protect their lives and property, as they have a right to do under natural law. Second, this body enters into a contract (or, rather, a trusteeship) with a limited group of individuals to serve as the executive branch; this arrangement is called *government*. Hence, all the powers of government derive from the consent of the subjects. If government exercises power in tyrannical ways, or otherwise acts against the will of the subjects, the population has the right to rebel against that government. The conduct of government will then be in breach of the contract by which it was installed, rendering that contract null and void.

The classic Social Contract doctrine was a contribution to a political struggle, a plea for the political rights of a new propertied class. Indeed, *Two Treatises of Civil Government* was a political pamphlet, intended to justify the Glorious Revolution of 1688. Locke advances, *inter alia*, the claim that political obligation is created when, but only when, individuals agree to entrust a political authority with the enforcement of their natural rights. Thus, this part of Locke's doctrine essentially belongs within a normative discourse: it is a claim about the conditions under which societal obligations and constraints may legitimately be imposed upon a population of autonomous individuals. The investigation we are currently conducting, on the other hand, belongs within the philosophy of social science and deals with the conditions under which social facts are generated. Without delving into the difference between facts and norms, or between description and prescription, we may safely assert that our present undertaking is different from Locke's examination of the prerequisites of political obligation.

Locke's political philosophy, however, comprises an implicit contribution to the social construction issue that concerns us here. To identify this contribution, we may recast the chief tenet of Locke's political philosophy into the following principle: a political system only exists rightfully if it is installed through a process involving the consent of the governed. This may be reformulated thus: the fundamental facts concerning the political system of a society obtain by right only provided they were instituted through a process involving the consent of the governed. We now realise that this formulation implies that social facts can come to obtain, and that their maintenance can be assured, through the agreement among the subjects, that is, they can obtain through a process of social construction. This is the implication of Locke's theory that interests us here.

This inference from Locke's theory presupposes that the normative and descriptive features of his theory can be split neatly apart. It is indeed natural to assume that, within any normative claim made within the framework of Locke's political philosophy, to the effect that a given political system prevails by right, there resides a purely descriptive statement to the effect that that system exists in the first place. I believe that this assumption can be upheld. We should not be deterred by the observation that this existence claim is very vague, which means, *inter alia*, that concrete judgements of existence are particularly susceptible to normative influence. For instance, the criteria determining when a government could be said to be established within a given territory require (*inter alia*) that the putative government exercises a certain minimal level of control over the population of that territory; but there may be endless disagreement over what constitutes a sufficient level of control. Answers to this question might be expected to vary with people's ideological predilections; a person favouring dramatic social change might be tempted to describe a revolutionary movement struggling to consolidate power as a government, although it had not yet established ascendancy over the old rulers. The reason for viewing this problem as one of vagueness only (apart from its political overtones) is that it is always possible to obtain definite answers by resorting to a more detailed level of description. A concrete investigation of the level of control secured by a would-be government in every local area would establish the extent of its rule with any desired precision. The issue of whether or not a government should then be said to exist at all is thereafter a matter of semantics.

Assuming that such questions of vagueness can be resolved, we may conclude that the 'argument from convention' succeeds in establishing a constructivist conclusion for certain social facts. The argument from convention is simply the observation that, when stripped of its normative aspect in the way demonstrated, the Social Contract doctrine makes an implicit contribution to the social construction issue. The Social Contract doctrine demonstrates, *inter alia*, how people generate social facts through mutual agreement – in brief, how civil society is a social construction.

The transposition of Locke's ideas from the context of political philosophy to social science was actually undertaken already by Herbert Spencer, who used this conceptual framework to describe society as it could be observed in his day (Spencer 1893). According to Spencer's social evolutionism, the highest stage of social life is represented by what he called 'industrial society', which is the stage approximated by certain countries in western Europe (in particular, England). Industrial society is characterised by a particular mode of social organisation constituted by contractual relationships. Not only is the sphere of production based upon private contracts between entrepreneurs, so are the other dominant social relationships; this is even the case for the military services, which men join voluntarily and on contractually specified terms. (To Spencer, the ancestor of the industrial society was the 'militant' form where, conversely, all social relations, even within the sphere of production, were modelled upon the military system of command.) Thus, where Locke focused on the fundamental constitutional contract between the citizens and the governing body, Spencer was more interested in the network of civil contracts between citizens that grows out into the space created and protected by government.

Two circumstances made possible the shift from a normative to a descriptive context: first, the idea of purely descriptive social theorising, neutral with regard to the concerns that express themselves in political philosophy, had now acquired a firm foothold. Comte was the first to formulate this project clearly and had coined the term 'sociologie' to cover it; Spencer introduced this term into the English language. Second, the conception of a social contract was a contested political idea when Locke composed the *Two Treatises of Civil Government* in the wake of the Glorious Revolution; the social order established by the installation of King William still enjoyed only a precarious existence. By the time Spencer wrote his *Principles of Sociology*, the political struggle had been long won. He could use the same framework of concepts to describe a social order that was firmly entrenched.

The argument from convention makes a very persuasive case for the construction thesis by virtue of the transparency of the model upon which it is built; the private contract is as compelling a paradigm of society-construction for us today as it was for Locke three hundred years ago and for Spencer in the past century. But although the argument thus generates a very strong presumption that *some* social facts are constructed by convention – for, after all, it seems indisputable that contracts create facts – familiar problems exist in extending the contractual model to other social phenomena that we would intuitively call conventional, but which are not created by contract or other explicit agreement. We must look into those problems in order to get a better estimate of the scope of the argument from convention. Eventually, those problems will force us to adopt another model of convention than the contract. Before we go on to examine those problems, however, we shall look a bit further into the different forms of fact-generation by convention.

We do so in the expectation that our difficulties with the analysis of conventional facts can afterwards be resolved.

ELEMENTS OF CONVENTION

To say that convention is a matter of agreement among people is not yet to say that every instance of conventional conduct, and reality-generation by convention, requires the collaboration of all the parties to the convention. Conventions typically comprise the (conventional) election of small groups or individuals empowered to carry out conventional acts on behalf of all. In this way, the power of generating social fact by convention trickles down from the highest level of political authority, embodied in the populace as a whole, to the lowest and most concrete levels of social function. As a matter of fact, most of the parties to the convention are barred, individually and collectively, from performing concrete official functions and thereby from creating the corresponding facts. For instance, the populace as a whole cannot hand down judicial sentences; only its especially-appointed officials, known as judges, can do that. Above, we saw this phenomenon of power delegation illustrated by the second element in the Lockean model of political society – namely, the forming of a government to serve as the executive arm of the body politic.

Moreover, in any society, there will be agencies that can generate social fact by convention, but do not possess this power by delegation from the central political authority and, ultimately, from the population as a whole. There will be associations and societies such as trade unions, political parties, or private clubs, each with a domain of authority and the power to make decisions and thus generate social fact. In such social groups, too, the ultimate subject of authority is the totality of the members or participants. But everyday decisions are made by proxy by especially-certified officials and, by the same token, so are social facts.

Just as not all conventions are enacted by the population as a whole, not all conventional acts are expressed by means of some linguistic device like, 'We hereby agree that . . . ' or, 'We hereby agree to . . .'. Once the overall conventional framework is in place, conventional acts are carried out by means of linguistic tools that do not recapitulate the original acts of agreement. Acts of convention may be carried out, by the appointed agencies, by such expressions as, 'I hereby name you the *Arctic Explorer*', 'I hereby declare you man and wife', 'The court sentences you to twenty years of hard labour', and so on. The umpire may simply yell, 'Out!' or just wave a hand to call a ball out in a tennis game.

Analytical philosophy of language has coined a special term for the linguistic devices through which conventions are enacted: 'performatives'. The point of this label, introduced by J. L. Austin (1962a), was precisely to stress that, in uttering an expression of this type, the speaker is doing something, rather than (merely) saying something. He is *naming* the boat the *Arctic Explorer*, instead of just *describing* himself as naming it; he is *wedding* the couple, rather than *describing* himself as doing so, and so on.

In performing these acts, the speaker generates social facts that linger on after the action has passed; it is henceforth a fact that the boat's name is the *Arctic Explorer* and that the man and woman are husband and wife. Performatives are the instruments *par excellence* of social construction, tools for generating social facts by the simple device of declaring them to be the case. Of course, the use of performative expressions is effective in generating fact only if a broad, social background is presupposed. The words, 'I hereby declare you man and wife' will not produce a married couple if spoken on stage, as a joke, or otherwise by a person who is not suitably authorised to institute wedlock. In the final analysis, authorisation derives from an agreement between all the members of the community to delegate powers to a given individual. Thus, much of the concrete and local construction of social fact by convention is based upon, and is somehow a concrete articulation of, the fundamental construction of a community out of a multitude of individual agents. This unity is formed through a convention by which each individual agrees to delegate some of his decision-making powers to the community. It is, in other words, formed by a 'social contract'.

PROBLEMS WITH FACT-BY-CONVENTION

Above, I sketched an argument in favour of social constructivism, based upon the traditional concept of convention or agreement that comes down to us from seventeenth-century political philosophy. There are difficulties, however, in the view that human beings create fact by convention. We must now look into these difficulties, as they will give us a better understanding of convention and will eventually lead to a conception of convention that is superior to the classic one, allowing us to save the constructivist position (although in a somewhat restricted form).

Some might be reluctant to accept that there is room for philosophical doubt here, or, indeed, for philosophical assessment at all. They might object that the view that social reality is (in part) generated through convention is commonplace, a plain empirical fact that philosophical analysis could not possibly discredit. This, however, is an illusion; we need only remember how the theory of convention and consent, in the hands of Locke and others, was very much a *philosophical interpretation* of contemporary political events. That interpretation involved elements of a rather dubious empirical standing; after all, there never was an occasion on which people in the state of nature convened to form a civil society. Nor do people who join a society by birth ever contract with the rest of society to become a member. So, notoriously, Locke had to invent the notion of a *tacit consent*, supposedly given by those who decide to live in a society and enjoy its benefits. Now it is quite clear that we are dealing with a philosophical construal, not with plain empirical fact.

Of the facts that are generated by convention, some belong to a *kind*, other instances of which could exist even without convention. Some of them seem at first to be natural facts, but natural facts somehow embedded in a social context. The worlds of sports and of law are replete with examples. This raises with especial clarity the problem of understanding how agreement creates fact. For instance, when a group of officials declare that the horse Mayflower was the first to cross the finish line, they are apparently commenting upon a purely natural fact: the muzzle of a certain animal was the first to touch a certain imaginary geometrical line. On the other hand, this fact has a strong component of convention to it, within the setting of the race. If all the officials are agreed that Mayflower did indeed cross the line first, and if this verdict is confirmed by photos, Mayflower is declared the winner, in an unassailable manner. Even though later evidence might throw doubt on this verdict, it is allowed to stand – at least, unless there is evidence of fraud.

There seems to be something magical here. How can agreement between people interfere with reality in this way? Admittedly, what the officials are after is not the ultimate scientific truth about the matter; they only want to establish which horse was first across the finish line *for the purposes of the race*, as we might put it. This observation really creates more problems than it solves, however, for what does it mean for some (natural) fact *to be so-and-so for the purposes of a certain institution*? That notion is hardly self-explanatory.

If we have a closer look, we see that what convention dictates is not really the fact – not even one relative to the institution of the race – that Mayflower was the first horse to cross the line. What is established is rather the fact that Mayflower is the *winner* – that is, is to be awarded the prize and be allowed to go on to further races. Thus, what is agreed on by convention (on a concrete occasion) is that certain *actions* are to be performed by certain appointed persons, as a consequence of certain conditions being satisfied. Similarly, when a general convention is instituted, what comes into existence is a general linkage between certain conditions and certain actions; we might say that the convention consists in a commitment to carry out certain actions (or to abstain from certain actions) under certain circumstances. For instance, the convention states that a horse satisfying such-and-such conditions is to be awarded the prize and is to be allowed to participate in further races.

On this point, I find myself in agreement with an analysis of conventional facts that has recently been proposed by John Searle (Searle 1995). A caveat should be entered before I proceed to give a brief sketch of Searle's account. Searle does not present his analysis as pertaining to *conventional* facts under this very label, but rather to *institutional* facts, and at one point he even contrasts conventions with rules, where the latter seem to be the component that specifically defines institutional facts. (ibid.: 28). The formula whereby institutional facts are created, according to Searle, is obviously very close to that (traditional) definition of convention I have adopted above, however, since Searle's formula calls for agreement between social agents. Searle does indeed go on to describe institutional facts as conventional. He also proposes that the particular power of institutional facts be referred to as 'conventional', to distinguish it from physical power. Thus, I believe that the difference between Searle's account and the one I have presented above is chiefly terminological; at any rate, it is obvious that what Searle refers to as institutional fact overlaps to a large extent what I have referred to here as conventional facts. We may safely assume that his analysis of the former carries over to the latter. But it must be kept in mind that when I talk about conventional facts below, the term used by Searle is *institutional* facts.

Searle's avenue into the issue of social construction is rather different from the one I have followed here. My concern is to examine how an acceptable construal can be put upon the intuitive idea that social facts are somehow dependent upon the way human beings think about them, a construal that does not lead to general idealism and, hence, paradox. Searle, on the other hand, starts out with the question of how social facts can exist at all in a world which, under its most fundamental description, is comprised of nothing but physical particles moving around in fields of force. Searle's answer is, very briefly, that the material universe possesses further higher-level properties that ride on the back of the physical ones – and social properties constitute the highest level of this hierarchy. A crucial stage on the way from the purely physical level to the social is constituted by mental states. In the evolutionary process, creatures are generated that are endowed with brains of a highly complex neural composition; these are seats of consciousness. Some of these conscious states possess intentionality and are thus to be described as propositional attitudes (cf. the discussion on pp. 118–19).

Social reality is generated when human beings (and other animals) develop what Searle terms *collective intentionality*, which is intentionality expressed by humans in sentences whose subject is 'we', as in, 'We are going to build a house this summer'. Next comes what Searle terms institutional facts, which roughly coincide with what I have here called conventional facts. These arise when human beings agree to bestow a particular status and an attendant function upon some object or person. The logical form of conventional facts is captured in the formula, 'X counts as Y in C', where Y refers to a function, X is some item to which this function is attributed, and C is the social setting within which this attribution is valid. A particular filling-out of the formula might be, 'This slip of paper with the characteristic engravings (X) counts as a means of commercial exchange and a repository of purchasing power (Y) within the jurisdiction of the Bank of England (C)'. This formula expresses a convention whereby money is created.

Searle goes on further to analyse the formula defining conventional (institutional) facts. This analysis brings to light that the real subject of a conventional fact is always a person, although it may ostensibly be a thing (such as a paper slip that conventionally counts as a five-pound note). What we attribute to this person is always a power to do something, or the obligation to do something (or abstain from doing something). Thus, the general formula of a conventional fact is 'We accept (S is enabled (S does A))', or, 'We accept (S is required (S does A))'. If we translate our above example involving money into this format, we get this: 'We accept (S, the bearer of X, is enabled (S buys with X a quantity of goods up to a given fixed value indicated on X))'. Thus, on Searle's analysis, as on the one I have proposed above, conventions are essentially agreements among people to do something – *inter alia* agreements to empower some third person to do something, or to require that person to do (or abstain from doing) something.

Searle's analysis is more specific than the one I have proposed, as Searle asserts that what a person is empowered to do is always to perform some *function*. Searle declines to give a precise definition of a function in terms of necessary and sufficient conditions, but he seems to have the standard philosophical sense in mind; among his examples are screwdrivers, hearts, money, and others. I fail to see, however, that there is any substantial sense of 'function' in which all conventions can plausibly be said to assign a function to something. Take the above example from the world of horse-racing. In what sense can it be said that Y refers to a function in the formula, 'The first horse to cross the line (X) counts as the winner (Y) in the game of horse-racing (C)'? The same goes for many of the other conventions that define events in the world of sports; take, for instance, Searle's favourite example, which is the rule that defines a touchdown in football. I believe that the weaker formula I proposed above is the strongest that can be sustained; this formula characterises convention as the agreement to carry out certain actions (or to abstain from certain actions) under certain circumstances. This is not to deny, of course, that the stronger formula, involving the notion of a function, applies to many cases, and arguably the most interesting ones, from a sociological point of view. But it is not of universal application. (On page 65 of his book, Searle seems to make the formula true by definition, in the face of a convincing counterexample. One may doubt if such a ruling on the term 'institutional fact' is a fruitful one.)

The observation that conventional facts are a matter of agreement among people to *do* something might assuage some of our scruples about generation of fact by convention. It is less worrying to accept the idea of such generation once we realise that what is generated is not solid natural fact, but precisely something involving action, over which man is, of course, the master. We might say that convention has been shown to be an agreement *to* rather than an agreement *that*; it is an agreement to do something, rather than an agreement that something is the case. This feature is quite plain in the classic concept of convention in political philosophy. When Locke talks about the Social Contract, he clearly means an agreement to do something – for instance, to empower a central agency to undertake certain kinds of preventive and punitive actions – rather than an agreement that something is the case.

A RESIDUAL DIFFICULTY

Unfortunately, even the idea of 'agreement-to-do' is open to a classic objection that philosophers since Hume have levelled against the Social Contract doctrine (cf. *A Treatise of Human Nature*, Book III, part II). This objection is that, rather than being explanatory of the fact of social order, the idea of forming a society by agreement already presupposes some kind of social order. This is so, whether we construe the 'social contract' as a historical reality, or merely as a fiction useful for laying down the features of a just society. At least, it presupposes the existence of a language and an institution of giving and honouring promises. But, how could such instruments be available without a modicum of social order already being in existence? Both language and the making of promises are social institutions; they could not be present prior to, and be instruments of, the formation of civil society.

The problem is not resolved in Searle's analysis of conventions (i.e. institutional facts), as presented above. Searle emphasises that language is constitutive of institutional reality and himself points to the quandary in which this seems to put us. Since language is itself an institutional (that is, conventional) fact, the language dependency view seems to lead us into circularity or an infinite regress. Searle resolves this difficulty, to his own satisfaction, by simply declaring that 'language doesn't require language because it already is language' (1995: 72): that is, the condition that conventions always presuppose the existence of a language is *trivially* satisfied when the convention in question is language itself. (It appears that in Searle's analysis the temporal priority of language *vis-à-vis* any conventional order, which worried the early critics of Locke, has been replaced by a logical one.) What this comes down to is that language does not need a further conventional device to mark it as conventional, because language is self-identifying as a convention. We are brought up in a culture where we learn to treat the sounds that come out of people's mouths as having representational power, that is, as standing for something or other; we do not need an additional symbol system to signalise that language is language.

But this shows that Searle's account of convention, while avoiding regress or circularity, suffers from a lacuna, since it points outside of language to an element that Searle so far has not specified. We need an account of what it means (tacitly) to *treat* something as (conventionally) standing for something or other, a notion that does not in its turn reduce to the idea of declaring this thing to stand for another thing.

We are at an impasse; it seems indisputable that conventional facts are ubiquitous in social life and, indeed, make up the basic fabric of society. Unfortunately, the traditional philosophical interpretation of such facts, which supports a constructivist interpretation of convention, seems defective on closer scrutiny, and, therefore, we must go looking for a better one. We have a special ambition: we hope to find a mode of construction that goes beyond the one already established in the argument from the meaningfulness of action. There is no doubt that conduct in compliance with an explicit agreement may be subsumed under the argument from meaning and thus be shown to involve a social construction of fact. A social fact is created whenever a pattern of outward behaviour – which might in itself just be habitual, or accidental – is traced back to an inner 'meaning' (belief) to the effect that this pattern of action was agreed on in a community-wide decision and should be adhered to. Out of these elements arises a fact of the form, 'It is a convention in this community that ...'. Even apart from the problem that not all conventional conduct can be viewed as springing from such explicit agreement, however, we are looking for a specific mode of 'construction by convention', a mode that will not collapse into the 'construction by composition' previously examined.

AN ALTERNATIVE CONCEPT OF CONVENTION: DAVID HUME

The alternative conception of a convention that we shall examine can be found in embryonic form already in Hume, where it is propounded as a solution to the puzzles that face a Lockean notion of convention. Hume's alternative is found in two versions, of which one represents a rather modest deviation from the doctrine of convention by explicit agreement, the other a far more radical departure.

According to the modest version, verbal declarations retain an indispensable role in the formation of conventions. Conventions arise in situations where a plurality of agents each stand to gain if a certain regularity in their conduct is instituted, or perpetuated. More precisely, each of the agents stands to gain by following a certain principle of conduct with respect to the rest, provided that the latter adopt the same policy with respect to him. Each agent is required to express his insight into this mutual interdependence of interests, and each is supposed to be aware that the others have expressed themselves in a similar manner. In this situation, a convention will form, since the circumstance of mutually inter-locked interests and the expression of insight into this circumstance will give everyone a reason to act in accordance with the same principle. But no promise will have been made nor any obligation explicitly accepted; Hume's analysis is precisely meant to show how the institution of promising can be assumed to have arisen and thus cannot avail itself of that instrument. Hume puts it like this:

> This convention is not of the nature of a *promise*: for even promises themselves, as we shall see afterwards, arise from human conventions. It is only a general sense of common interest; which sense all the members of the society express to one another, and which induces them to regulate their conduct by certain rules.
>
> (Hume 1888: 490)

Hume goes on to illustrate this with an example:

> I observe, that it will be for my interest to leave another in the possession of his goods, *provided* he will act in the same manner with regard to me. He is sensible of a like interest in the regulation of his conduct. When this common sense of interest is mutually express'd, and is known to both, it produces a suitable resolution and behaviour. And this may properly enough be call'd a convention or agreement betwixt us.
>
> (Ibid.: 490)

This version only partially solves the problems involved in Locke's conception; notably, it fails to give a coherent account of the emergence of linguistic conventions, since language still seems to be required for conventions to arise. And language, as Hume of course will agree, is itself conventional. ('In like manner are languages gradually establish'd by human conventions without any promise' (ibid.: 490).)

Thus our attention is shifted towards the more radical account of convention, which, however, is not textually marked off from the first one in Hume's presentation. This version is identical with the less radical one, except for the clause about the declarations of mutual interests. In the second version, what is involved in convention is just a regularity in conduct among a plurality of agents, in which everybody is supposed to have an interest in the perpetuation of the regularity, and so a willingness to perpetuate it, on condition that everybody else does the same thing.

In the course of discussing justice as a conventional virtue, Hume expresses the matter like this,

> And thus justice establishes itself by a kind of convention or agreement; that is, by a sense of interest, supposed to be common to all, and where every single act is performed in expectation that others are to perform the like.
>
> (Ibid.: 498)

A few pages earlier, in fact, Hume presents a simple example of convention that illustrates the point. This is the famous case of the two rowers, who will hardly fail to find a common cadence to their rowing, even though they have not explicitly agreed on any particular rate of strokes and even though neither one sets the cadence by explicitly calling out orders. The rowers agree on a suitable rhythm, but without a word necessarily being uttered.

DAVID LEWIS'S ANALYSIS OF CONVENTION

In recent years, an analysis that is essentially a refinement of the Humean account has been proposed by David Lewis (Lewis 1969). Lewis's analysis shows in detail how the idea contained *in nuce* in Hume's more radical proposal will allow us to sidestep the objection directed at the historical concept. However, it will not assist us in showing that conventional facts are *sui generis*; rather the opposite, since Lewis's account is reductionist and shows conventions to be built up out of such facts that were already dealt with in the phenomenological argument. Fortunately, we shall be able to supplement Lewis's story with additional considerations that demonstrate a *sui generis* status for certain conventional facts.

Lewis's point of departure is the idea of a *coordination problem*. Human beings often find themselves in situations where success in reaching their goals depends upon their correctly predicting the actions of other people and shaping their own conduct accordingly. Some of these interactions are what game theorists call *games of pure conflict*, in which the agents have opposing interests and try to predict each other's actions with an eye to tripping each other up. Others are *games of pure coordination*, in which the interactants have coinciding interests. They have the same ranking of the various possible outcomes on their preference scales, and can thus join forces in realising them. What Lewis refers to as coordination problems are close to the latter type of collective choice. They are specifically distinguished by having solutions that Lewis terms *coordination equilibria*, which are favoured outcomes in the sense that none of the interactants would have been better off if any single one of them had acted differently. They are outcomes in which no one would have wanted, retrospectively, to have acted otherwise (or would have wanted any single *other* interactant to have acted otherwise). Coordination is rendered non-trivial by the fact that several coordination equilibria are available; hence, the task facing the agents is to pick the *same* one. Moreover, it is assumed that the agents cannot simply achieve coordination by the expedient of communicating with each other and agreeing upon a solution. If this complex predicament holds generally in a group of persons, those persons are said to have a *coordination problem*, in the technical sense, in relation to each other.

Lewis's concept of a coordination problem may appear rather *recherché*, but is seen to point to a very familiar phenomenon when we look at concrete examples. It applies, for example, to the situation of a group of persons who all want to meet and who do not care where they meet (among a number of possible alternatives), as long as they all show up at the same spot. Unfortunately, they cannot get in touch with each other beforehand to arrange a meeting place. It also describes the situation of a group of strong conformists who are invited to the same party and who all want to dress identically, do not care which way – casual or formal – as long as it is the same for all, but again have no opportunity to negotiate a solution. Or, think of the situation of automobile owners who do not care which side of the road they drive on – the left or the right – as long as all drive on the same side.

If they happen to find a solution to their puzzle, none of the participants in these situations would want to act differently, as long as the others acted as they did. Nor would they want any of the others to act differently. We would all hate to find ourselves driving down the right-hand lane on British roads; we would be almost as disturbed to witness somebody else being in the same predicament. However, if everyone else switched to driving on the right-hand side of the road, any individual motorist would want to do it, too. The actual pattern of conduct – driving on the left – is the solution to a coordination problem that has another, equally good, solution. Moreover, any coordinated action pattern is better that any non-coordinated one (for instance, people driving on either side they choose). Hence, this is genuinely a coordination problem, in Lewis's sense.

Lewis suggests how coordination might be secured in such situations, on a basis other than that of explicit agreement. Suppose two people are cut off in the middle of a telephone conversation. Both want to resume the conversation; to achieve this, they have to coordinate their actions. If each calls the other back simultaneously, the line will be busy; if neither makes the return call, nothing will happen. The connection can be re-established in two ways: either the original caller calls back while the other waits, or the other way around. Of these two ways, the first one might be favoured by the speakers, on the grounds that the original caller may be expected to have the telephone number readily available. Now suppose that, some time later, the same two persons are once again interrupted in the middle of a telephone talk. Again, the caller re-establishes the conversation while the other waits. This time they act with more confidence, since each now has better grounds for believing that the other will act in a complementary way. Added to the grounds they had originally, there will now be, for each of them, ego's knowledge that alter remembers that they previously managed to establish the connection according to this formula and that this might give alter an increased tendency to act in the same way again. If we assume that the two individuals go on to share a long history of interrupted phone calls over the years, each rectified by the original caller on the background of the suggested reasoning and with steadily increasing confidence based upon previous experience, we may expect that they eventually come to re-establish interrupted talks according to the above formula as a matter of course. Whatever the original deliberation was behind the caller calling back and the other person waiting, that deliberation will now have receded into the background. The chief motivation will now be the rich precedent of this strategy. Each caller remembers countless previous occasions on which the original caller re-established the connection and knows that his interlocutor does so too; this gives either a reason for following the same policy. The two individuals have now established an understanding – that is, a *convention* – to the effect that, if they are cut off while talking on the phone, the original caller calls back. A symptom of this might be that, if the original caller failed, for no particular reason, to re-establish contact after an interruption, the other might feel deceived – *as if* an explicit agreement had been broken. Still, no explicit agreement was ever made.

This simple two-person example shares many features with familiar, large-scale social conventions, such as that of accepting certain tokens, in themselves almost entirely without value, in exchange for goods and services. This is the convention of using *money* as a means of exchange. Here, we have coordination of action among individuals who have no previous knowledge of each other. Nor is the coordination based upon specific knowledge of particular precedent – cases where this, that, or the other named person accepted coins or bank notes for goods. Instead, a buyer or seller has a knowledge of *general* precedent, knowing that traders in general have accepted money as legal tender and expecting the next one encountered to do the same. He expects this, since he knows that other traders have had similar experiences in the past; he expects them to draw similar conclusions from their observations. So he himself acts in the same way.

Lewis sums up his reflections upon these and similar examples in the following definition of convention:

> A regularity R in the behavior of members of a population P
> when they are agents in a recurrent situation S is a convention
> if and only if, in any instance of S among members of P,
>
> (1) everyone conforms to R;
> (2) everyone expects everyone else to conform to R;
> (3) everyone prefers to conform to R on condition that the others
>   do, since S is a coordination problem and uniform conformity
>   to R is a proper coordination equilibrium in S.
>
> (Lewis 1969: 42)

Lewis proceeds to add certain complications, into which we need not go, to this definition. Instead, let us stay with the simple idea and see if we can solve our original problems about convention and its reality-generating powers within the framework of these ideas.

Before we do so, however, we may mention that Lewis's and similar analyses of convention based upon game theory have not gone unnoticed by social scientists. It is significant that political science has not adopted these tools, as one might have expected, given the history of this conception. The reason would seem to be that contemporary political scientists are more concerned with the antagonistic aspects of the political process than with the consensual ones – that is, the agreed framework within which political rivalry takes place. It is the struggle between different segments and classes in society, and the competition between political parties to secure the vote, that interests them.

Instead, it is economists who have adopted similar analyses; this, of course, is a natural extension of their occupation with those game-theory models of action that inspired Lewis's analysis of convention in the first place. A fine example is Robert Sugden's *The Economics of Rights, Cooperation and Welfare* (1986). In this book, Sugden shows how such social conventions as the traffic code and those pertaining to money can be analysed with the aid of game-theory conceptions that are very close to Lewis's; in particular, such analyses enable us to explain the genesis of those conventions. Sugden's definition of convention is not exactly the same as Lewis's, but stays safely within the bounds of the intuitive sense of the term. Basically, Sugden dispenses with the final clause of Lewis's definition, which specifies that uniform adherence to some pattern of action R is a coordination equilibrium in the community. This implies, as we saw, that no one would be better off had any one of the participants acted otherwise. This relaxation allows Sugden to extend the basic analysis to cases of conventional action that are not fully cooperative, but show some element of competition. An example is action performed within the institution of *property*, where individuals are indeed rivals and where persons in a disadvantageous position would often be better off if property owners did not stick rigidly to the conventions of possession; most notably, if owners occasionally deviated from the central principle that a person retains possession of whatever was in his possession in the past, redistributing their goods according to (for example) principles of need. Yet, a convention remains in force that individuals already in possession of goods are entitled to retain their ownership.

Sugden's explanatory ambitions are correspondingly wider than Lewis's; he wants to explain the emergence not only of social patterns of conduct that are standardly recognised as conventions, but also the emergence of social phenomena that are not considered to be conventions. In Sugden's opinion, these can be seen as derivatives from, or descendants of, original conventions. To this class belong the moral norms that are held to pertain to the institution of property. Such norms are not held to be conventions, but rather to express some deeper normative truths; occasionally, they are even elevated to the status of 'human rights'. Sugden tries to exhibit the mechanisms that will, in time, gradually bestow the appearance of autonomous norms upon certain conventions.

THE PROBLEMS CONCERNING CONVENTIONAL FACTS ADDRESSED

If we now return to our original problem about convention and its fact-generating powers, we will recall that the problem was that political society cannot be built upon convention, since convention, in the classic analysis, requires the prior existence of social institutions, such as language and the commitment to honouring contracts and promises. There is no doubt that the Lewisian analysis takes care of this problem (which, indeed, it was expressly designed to do). Lewis shows how conventions (at least some of them) grow out of simple situations of coordination of human action. At no stage in the emergence of those conventions need explicit promising, or a setting up of contracts or agreements, occur. The idea of a social convention is built of simpler conceptual materials.[16] Notice also how, in construing convention as the solution to a coordination problem, Lewis embraces the idea that convention is a question of agreeing *to* rather than agreeing *that* (of course, with the proviso that agreement in a literal sense does not occur). Thus, Lewis's analysis is impervious to the problems raised by the apparent conventional creation of such facts as, for instance, that a particular horse is the first to cross the goal line in a race.

Another issue touched on earlier did not pertain to the notion of convention as such, but to our use of it to support a distinctive version of constructivism; we hoped to find a specific mode in which social fact is created through the mechanism of convention.

Lewis's analysis is less helpful here; indeed, the very point of that analysis is to show how the concept of convention is built up out of such familiar elements as human intentions and desires – although highly complex specimens – and certain regularities in human behaviour springing from them. These are precisely the elements out of which social reality is constructed by what I termed 'construction by composition', as demonstrated by the phenomenological argument in particular. As a matter of fact, Lewis's analysis of convention is a fine illustration of what the phenomenological argument is all about, since it shows how the social essence of a certain observable phenomenon – a certain behavioural regularity – is determined by the 'inside' of intentions and beliefs with which social agents accompany those external events. Conjoined with certain other intentions, the very same behaviour might have constituted purely habitual action or perhaps action considered morally incumbent upon the agents and, hence, non-conventional. Moreover, the analysis satisfies the non-triviality constraint that we imposed upon constructivist proposals, since Lewis's analysis is anything but trivial. Still, in the investigation we are currently undertaking, we are not satisfied by merely finding further examples of construction by composition, however fine the specimen, but are looking for a new mode of construction.

To get ahead with this undertaking, we must first become aware of a lacuna in Lewis's analysis of convention. That analysis does not explicitly provide for the distinction between a *correct* and an *incorrect* way to proceed within a convention, which creeps into all human conventions once they move beyond the most rudimentary stage (nor, on the other hand, does the analysis exclude the distinction). What is true or correct within a convention cannot in most cases be identified straight away with what people happen to do or think within it. Mistakes may be made in applying the rules; for instance, the people elected to carry out some official function may not have the proper credentials.

The point is most readily discernible in complicated and intellectually demanding conventions. The prime examples of such conventions are found in *institutions*. Institutions are defined in terms of another and cruder sort of independence: they are systems of conventions that are independent of the particular identities of their subjects at any given time. Institutions have a certain permanence; in a hundred years we shall all be dead, but most of our major current institutions will probably still persist. This permanence is not merely a question of physical hardware lingering on, but is rather a question of the continuity of certain operations and functions and the continued validity of the charter given to the original institutions.

The independence we are about to examine, however, is a different, rather more subtle one. It resides in the distinction between what is true or correct according to the rules of an institution and the actual decisions made by its members. The point is neatly illustrated by the institution of *law* and the debate among legal theorists concerning under which circumstances we should say that such-and-such is *the law*. The issue here is precisely to determine what is necessary for a particular social fact, within the sphere of law, to have been constituted. In this debate, a radical brand of constructivists, the so-called *legal realists*, urge that the law is simply that which the courts would actually decide in concrete cases. Or more precisely: the law is what Supreme Court judges would actually decide. Here, we have an analysis of institutional facts (facts concerning the institution of law) leading to facts about a certain human practice and, eventually, to facts about the behaviour of certain designated persons and the motives and deliberations from which their behaviour springs.

This extreme form of legal constructivism creates insoluble problems, however, precisely because it denies the full normative force of legal rules in the process of deciding what is legally valid. (We are not talking here about the normativity of the rules in guiding the conduct of the ordinary legal subject, but in guiding the judges in passing sentences.) In declaring that decisions of Supreme Court judges determine what the law is, legal realists overlook the fact that judges, including those of the Supreme Court, try to *conform* to the law and to *discover* what the rules actually dictate. The judges treat the rules as norms to be adhered to and do not consider themselves at liberty to *create* law in passing sentence (cf. Hart 1960, ch. 7). Indeed, the realist construal renders it impossible to make sense of what Supreme Court judges are doing when they enter into subtle arguments to decide a complicated case. Their deliberations are clearly not attempts to *predict* what they will themselves decide in the case in question, or else judges would be chasing their own coat tails forever.

A proper understanding of the judicial process must allow for a distinction between what the judges happen to decide and the true content of the law. This involves recognising that courts may reach a wrong verdict. Although it is true that the verdict of the Supreme Court settles matters, as far as purely practical consequences are concerned – people going to jail, or reparations being made – the verdict does not settle the theoretical issue of what the law really and truly is. There is room for legal scholars to dispute the correctness even of Supreme Court verdicts; such dissension cannot be dismissed on the grounds that the Supreme Court *defines* what is right. This is as much as to say that what is really and truly the law is not identical with the actual judicial decisions (although the two will, of course, typically coincide).

Thus we see that in societal institutions, especially in institutions with codified rules, the simple distinction between a right and a wrong way to proceed with respect to a social convention is deepened and extrapolated into a distinction between how subjects, even the totality of subjects, *actually* proceed, and how they ideally *should* proceed. The right way is no longer defined by what people will eventually agree on or by what some authoritative individual will decide, but is idealised and projected beyond the horizon of actual social practice. An idealised conception of 'correctness' has been instituted and, with it, a class of facts that reflect the ideally correct way to proceed in conformity with institutional rules.

There is another, less dramatic, way in which the content of a convention (an institution) may fail to coincide with a human practice: the convention may determine facts that human practice has so far not made operative (and perhaps never will). The law provides answers to certain legal issues that have never been raised and will, perhaps, forever lie dormant. Here, we are not dealing with a discrepancy between actual application of the conventional rules and their true content, but with rules extending further than human practice has ever gone and will ever go.

The distinction between what is the true content of a convention and what it is thought to be is particularly clear in the legal case, but has a broader field of application. In most conventions, a distinction exists between the ideal content of the convention and people's actual decisions and consequent action. There is no hope for a general analysis of convention-based social fact that will simply identify it with a certain pattern of human actions and the structure of intentions from which they spring. Conventions, especially the kind we call institutions, typically represent an idealisation of human thinking and an extrapolation of social practice; hence, they forever transcend the concrete thought and action upon which they are based. On the other hand, the independence is limited; no conventional fact would exist if there were no actual social practice to sustain it. Thus, the independence does not threaten the status of conventional facts as social constructions.

We have located a version of social constructivism that goes beyond what was previously presented in the argument from the meaningfulness of action and its corresponding mode of construction, *construction by composition*. The idea of convention is the key to a realm of social facts that are not reducible to facts about human practice – that is, to the unity of behaviour, intentions, beliefs, and desires. Conventions, in particular of the form we call institutions, allow a distinction between what is valid and what is actually done. The autonomy of conventional facts rests precisely in the gap between the two. Certain complicated clusters of social facts, themselves emerging through compositive construction, come along with a 'halo' of further facts around them, which are the idealised counterparts of the former facts. We may appropriately call this new mode of social construction *construction by idealisation*.

The observation that institutional facts outstrip their base in human action and thought has so impressed certain philosophers that they have held these facts to be occupants of a special ontological realm. Thus, Karl Popper places such facts in what he calls the Third World, which is, among other things, the realm of mathematical objects, scientific theories, and the senses of linguistic terms (Popper 1972). It stands in contrast to the First World, which is the world of physical objects, events, and processes, and the Second World, which is the realm comprised of individual mental experiences (or, as we might say, the world of psychological facts).

Popper's terminology may be useful in dramatising the autonomy of certain classes of facts that I have emphasised above; but his way of putting the point may pose dangers. In the first place, talking about 'worlds' invites reification and may mislead us into spurious speculations about how these worlds are interrelated, *inter alia* in their causal aspects; in fact, Popper seems actually to have fallen into this trap. Second, and more pertinent to our current concerns, Popper's doctrine of the Third World seems to lump together things, or facts, that are better kept distinct. The Third World comprises both facts that are social constructions (in virtue of *construction by idealisation*) and facts that are not constructed, but instead reflect eternal verities; with the latter we may count the truths of logic and mathematics. According to Popper, however, *all* occupants of the Third World are actually social constructions or, as he prefers to put it, 'man-made', even the truths of logic and mathematics. But there is a clear intuitive difference between the body of facts that make up, say, the British penal code, and the truths of elementary number theory. Any fact in the former category may be said to have been made true at a certain date, typically the date a certain law was passed in Parliament; this is so even though legal facts transcend the concrete basis of their legal validity, such as documents enacted by Parliament. No such time dependence holds for the truths of number theory.

This distinction can be upheld even if, like certain intuitionist mathematicians, one holds that truth in mathematics is dependent upon the availability of proof: a mathematical sentence is only determinately true once a proof of that sentence has been devised. On the most plausible construal of this position, proof in mathematics is 'retroactive': once the sentence has been proved, the proof counts as demonstrating that the sentence was already true before the proof was available; it is indeed an eternal truth. This is not so in the world of legal facts. When a legal ordinance is passed making smoking illegal in public places, this can hardly be construed as proof that lighting up was always illegal in such areas.

LANGUAGE-BASED CONVENTIONS

Lewis's analysis of convention is inimical to the claim that language is essential to convention; this is an important element in his attempt to dispose of the traditional conception of convention as explicit agreement. Lewis has shown that convention is basically a matter of people *acting* in accordance with certain mutual expectations, but grants no essential role to language.

Lewis's theory does not preclude, however, that certain especially complicated conventions (in particular, the kind we call *institutions*) are contingent upon a command of language among the parties to those conventions. We have just seen, in the preceding section, that complicated conventions involve difficult decisions of correctness. Such decisions can hardly be made without explicit discussion in a verbal medium. Consider the reasoning involved in trying to reach a correct judicial decision. This involves subtle deliberations concerning the similarities of precedents and the proper reading of legal statutes. Such issues necessarily involve discursive reasoning that must be conducted in language (even apart from the fact that, in the latter case, the *objects* of reasoning are themselves verbal formulations).

Moreover, many conventional phenomena by nature could not exist without language, even when we disregard the use of language in discussing the formal correctness of conventional enactments. Parliamentary democracy is an example. Without language, raising political issues and determining what stance a majority of people adopt towards them would be impossible. Terms must exist that roughly mean 'topic for a vote', 'majority', 'minority', or 'vote of no confidence', and so on; these terms must be applied in systematic ways during the proceedings. If not, we do not have a parliamentary democracy.

Thus, we may resolve that a certain range of societal phenomena could not exist without the availability of an appropriate language. However, we must grant Lewis that this is not, strictly speaking, due to the fact that they are *conventions*. Rather, it springs from the complexity and sophistication of the social practices that sustain those conventions, making them contingent on the existence of a language with which to give them some sort of concrete manifestation. This is a phenomenon that we examined before under the heading of the hermeneutic position, at which point we dealt with social phenomena that are linguistically conditioned, but not (necessarily) conventional.

We saw above that, in *The Construction of Social Reality*, Searle takes the stronger position that conventions ('institutions', in his terminology) *eo ipso* presuppose a language. It turns out, however, that the issue that occupies Searle is slightly different from the one discussed here, since our concern is with the relationship between convention and natural languages such as English and French, whereas Searle examines if conventions require any kind of symbol system, not restricted to natural languages. Searle eventually answers 'yes' to this question. The argument is that conventions involve the attribution to a thing of some function that it cannot perform by virtue of its mere physical properties; money, for instance, does not serve as an instrument of economic transactions by virtue of its purely physical features. Hence, some kind of marking of the object is necessary to indicate that it is invested with powers over and above its purely causal efficacy; and this marking is symbolic. In the face of a number of counterexamples where natural items are invested with conventional powers without being especially marked, Searle seems to fall back on the position that

211

any kind of object conventionally invested with some power is *thereby a symbol of that power* and thus a part of 'language'. I fail to see that this move is compelling, unless it is turned into a definition of 'symbol'. Take the convention (which we might well call an 'institution') discussed by Lewis that it is incumbent upon the original caller to re-establish the connection when a telephone conversation is accidentally interrupted. This does not seem to impose a symbolic status upon anybody or anything; it would be highly artificial to say that the original caller *symbolises* the function of conversation re-establishment, or indeed symbolises anything. Or, for example, take the convention of driving on the left side of the road in England; it would be curious to describe this practice as a symbol of anything – even of safe driving!

This is an appropriate place to make a brief comment upon the relationship between the argument from symbolism and the argument from convention, once again with a view to safeguarding the distinctiveness of the latter. My reflections above show that these two arguments, far from being identical, do not even have coextensive ranges of application: actions exist that are conventional, but not symbolic. Nor, conversely, is all symbol use conventional, by Lewis's criterion. We realise this if we compare Lewis's theory of convention with the analysis of symbolism presented in the previous chapter. Symbolic action may be *ad hoc*, since an individual action may possess the intentional structure indicated on p. 180 without being embedded in the elaborate practice and network of reflexive interpersonal intentions that make up conventions, according to Lewis. Towards the end of the previous chapter, we hypothesised that the kind of symbolism using exaggeration is its instrument of symbolisation is biologically based and, hence, not conventional.

LANGUAGE AS A CONVENTION

The relationship between language and convention may also be explored in a direction opposite to that of the previous section. We may investigate in what sense, and to what extent, language itself is conventional. That language *is* conventional is a truism that needs no support, but yet has proved remarkably resistant to explication. In the case of language, the inadequacy of the traditional conception of convention is blatant. Language could not emerge out of explicit agreement between human beings to use specified spoken sounds or written marks to refer to specified things, since a language would already be needed to formulate the agreement. We saw above that the problem is not adequately resolved in Searle's 'neo-classical' theory of convention. For although Searle is not saddled with an infinite regress of languages, whether synchronically or diachronically, his analysis at some stage invokes the idea of a *use* of language that is not further explained within his system.

As it happens, David Lewis's efforts to develop an alternative theory of convention are ultimately motivated by the desire to explicate the conventionality of language without invoking explicit agreements, and we may once again borrow from his analysis. Conventions, for Lewis, are regularities in behaviour. The regularity that is relevant for defining the concept of a language (and related concepts, such as meaning or reference) consists of speakers' never or rarely uttering false sentences; at least speakers try to avoid such sentences, although they will, of course, sometimes fail to do so. In other words, the convention underlying the use of language, and the convention that defines meaning, is the convention of *truthfulness*: the convention of avoiding sentences that are false according to the semantic rules of their particular language.

Like other conventions, linguistic conventions are solutions to a coordination problem. This time, however, the problem is not narrowly defined, but is perfectly general. At every turn of everyday social life, agents will have desires concerning what their fellow human beings should do. Language is a general-purpose tool for solving such coordination problems. By using language, we can impart information to others that is likely to change their conduct; we may warn them of dangers and alert them to useful opportunities for action. Such use of language is in the indicative mood. But language also offers other, special tools for the direction of behaviour. There are such non-indicative moods as imperatives, interrogatives, permissives and commissives (these are the terms used by Lewis). We may *order* people to do things (the imperative mood), or get them to give us information by *asking* them (the interrogative mood). We may also influence their conduct by making rewards contingent upon performance of desired actions – for example, we may *promise* them those rewards (using the commissive mood).

Successful use of language is a coordination equilibrium in the sense defined by Lewis. When a regularity in language use is established, everybody prefers uniform adherence to this regularity to occasional deviance. People who sometimes lie are a threat to the overall usefulness of speech. If lying were to become widespread, the usefulness of language would vanish and the convention would dissolve; nobody would be willing to act upon the assumption that someone else's utterances had any special link with the facts (that is, were *true*). Moreover, language use also satisfies the condition of a possible alternative: the linguistic regularity actually adhered to in a population is only one among an indefinite number of other, equally good solutions. Speakers of English realise that they could accomplish their purposes equally well by speaking a different tongue, such as French.

Being thus conventional, language is a social construction. Things do not have names, or the predicates that apply to them, as an inherent property, but receive them only as part of a social practice. The whole domain of language and meaning is a social construction. To put it another way, the whole semantic realm is a construction that exists only because human beings, collectively, use certain complex sounds and inscriptions with certain specific and complex intentions. Language is a particularly significant social construction, since linguistic facts are instrumental in generating other social facts, as we have seen. By virtue of the existence of a language, other social entities (in themselves non-linguistic) are created. Perhaps, however, it is better to say that we are dealing with a mutual dependence here: the use of language makes possible intricate social practices (such as science, mathematics, or metaphysical and religious speculation), which in themselves make possible sophisticated uses of language unthinkable apart from those practices. Social practice and language use are indissolubly fused in what Wittgenstein termed 'language games'.

LANGUAGE AS AN INSTITUTION

In the preceding section's, we saw that many conventions, especially those termed 'institutions', enjoy a certain independence of the concrete social processes that sustain them. Conventional (institutional) facts are somehow idealisations or extrapolations of those social facts and, hence, transcend them. They cannot be reduced to those social facts. This leads naturally to the question if facts about language enjoy a similar status. May facts about language and meaning outstrip our explicit grasp of them? Or are the meanings of linguistic expressions essentially and necessarily only what we, as users of language, take them to be? Was Humpty Dumpty right in insisting that words mean what we make them mean (with the important correction, however, that linguistic meaning is not determined by the beliefs of individuals, but only of the entire community)?

I believe that the answer is, once again, that a convention may transcend the explicit understanding of the individuals who take part in it. The key factor is that most words are learned ostensively, and that linguistic knowledge is tacit knowledge, manifested in the *use* of terms and not in the verbal explication of their meaning. An infant learns most terms in language through being presented with paradigmatic specimens and being told that this is a 'tree', a 'car', or a 'chair'. Only later comes an ability to explicate the general characteristics that constitute the defining features of treehood, carhood, or chairhood. Such explications are the products of analysis, the correctness of which one may genuinely doubt, even where simple everyday terms are concerned. There is a famous altercation in philosophy over the meaning of the term 'solid', which we all learned by being made to notice the difference between such things as rocks and table tops, on the one hand, and sponges, loaves of white bread and soap bubbles, on the other. But, is resistance to penetration or compression enough to make a thing 'solid', or is it also a part of the term's meaning that a solid thing is homogeneously composed of matter and has no cavities? In the latter case, rocks and table tops are not solid after all, since they contain mostly empty space and a little mass that is located mainly in the nuclei of their atoms; indeed, no observable things are solid. The philosopher Susan Stebbing leaned towards the former opinion, the philosopher-physicist Eddington towards the latter, and they once had a famous quarrel about it; what interests us here is not who was right, but rather the very fact that sophisticated and fluent speakers of English could differ irreconcilably over the issue. At least one of them must have been wrong, a testimony to the possibility of such error (Eddington 1928; Stebbing 1944).

The example above concerned one of the simplest terms of everyday language. The point is much more compelling when we turn to more complex terms. A notorious example is mentalistic idiom, the vocabulary by which we describe our mental life. These are terms that we use every day with perfect assuredness and precision; we rarely feel hesitation or doubt when we say things like, 'I have a slight toothache', 'I am thinking about the next election', or 'I fear what will happen after the match'. Still, after 2,500 years of pondering, there is radical division among philosophers over the semantics of such terms. Only one claim commands general assent: it is that most philosophical theories on this issue have been woefully wrong, and that speakers of ordinary language tend to replicate the philosophical errors as soon as they start to speculate about their own linguistic practice. The common man is especially berated for giving credence to something called the myth of the 'Ghost in the Machine', the conception that the human body is inhabited by an elusive and mysterious entity – a mind or soul, which directs the body; this myth is claimed to have its roots in the teachings of René Descartes. There is, however, no agreement about what to substitute for this illusion. Gilbert Ryle, who coined the pejorative phrase about the 'ghost' (Ryle 1949: 17), claimed that statements about mental items are really about dispositions to perform certain actions, but this answer has few friends today. Some claim that mental terms refer to brain states; others insist that mental states can be reduced neither to action nor to physiological states, which sounds reassuring until it is added that mental states are really fictions, generated by certain modes of speaking that are pragmatically useful, but do not have any genuinely reportive function.

There is no reason to dive further into the deep waters of the philosophy of mind; the above suffices, I believe, to illustrate the point that linguistic expressions may defeat our best efforts to explain their meaning and that any given consensus concerning their meaning, even one shared by the entire community, may be wide of the mark. Language is genuinely an *institution*, something that may transcend the explicit understanding of the human beings who operate within it at any given time. Still, it is a social construction, since it has no being apart from a social practice that sustains it.

Summary of Part Two

We now have examined constructivist positions based upon the distinctive features of social facts. These arguments proved more successful than the more general arguments examined in the previous part.

Social facts rest upon a stratum of facts about individual human actions. Such actions possess a dual nature, comprising behaviour plus something else that bestows meaning upon the behaviour, thereby turning it into action. This dual nature makes room for a new type of argument in favour of constructivism, supporting a version that I called 'construction by composition'. The 'meaning' side of action combines with the purely behavioural side to form a new unity: action. By thus generating human action, meanings generate social facts, too, to the extent that the latter are composed, *inter alia*, of human actions.

We looked at several versions of the argument from meaningfulness. The *phenomenological argument* adopts a narrowly psychologistic construal of the 'meaning' of action, conceiving it as a concrete item in the agent's consciousness that is re-experienced by a person who understands the action. Against this, I recommended recasting meanings as propositional attitudes, a format of description in which the purely cognitive content in mental states is extracted and expressed in propositional form. Understanding action means grasping this content. Such a reconstrual moves us close to another, more sophisticated version of the argument from meaningfulness, which assimilates the meaning of action with the meaning of linguistic items; this I called the *hermeneutic argument*. We examined several examples of the way in which the meaningfulness of language adds to the meaningfulness of action, concluding that the hermeneutic argument suffices to establish the reality of construction by composition.

217

Next, we examined the *argument from the symbolic nature* of social facts, which we may consider either a version of the argument from meaningfulness or an independent line of reasoning. The argument is that, by virtue of the unique logic of the notion of a symbol, a symbol is created by the very thought that something is a symbol. The thought that S is a symbol of O directs attention towards O, which, in conjunction with certain further conditions, suffices to render S a symbol of O; hence, a constructivist position ensues. We accepted this argument, but pointed out that the scope for such generation is narrower than is often thought, since purely symbolic action is rarer than certain social anthropologists would have us believe.

Finally, the *argument from convention* is a distant relative of the argument from meaningfulness, but possesses special features that call for separate treatment. The argument directs attention to the way in which social reality is generated as the result of human agreement. We rehearsed the traditional objection that 'agreement' cannot be taken in a literal sense here, as this would lead to paradoxes. Instead, the argument from convention should be recast in terms of an alternative reading of convention, proposed by David Lewis. According to Lewis, conventional conduct reflects certain mutual and interlocking expectations, among the members of a group of interactants, about how the other members will behave. Given Lewis's analysis of convention, we may, indeed, accept that conventions are social constructions. However, so far, this amounts to a special case of the argument from meaningfulness: the particular meanings with which people accompany their behaviour – in this case, hierarchies of intricately interrelated expectations and intentions – transform behaviour into social action and, hence, social fact. Still, the phenomenon of convention has an aspect permitting us to go beyond the argument from meaningfulness and construction by composition. I called this *construction by idealisation*. Once a conventional human practice is established, it generates a reflection of itself (as it were) in the realm of abstract ideas. This is the idea of ideally correct conduct according to a convention, purified of the errors and imperfections with which the actual practice will inevitably be afflicted (or, as we might also put it, the notion of convention as an idealised norm of conduct). Idealised convention exists only as an extrapolation from actual conventional practice and, thus, is a social construction to the extent that the practice is one.

Summary

The social constructivism vindicated on the basis of the Narrow Arguments is metaphysically moderate. It eschews the unsound principle at the core of all the Broad Arguments, a principle that brought about their downfall: that human thought may generate reality as its *object*. Instead, the moderate constructivism that emerges reflects the insight that social facts essentially involve human thought (or 'meaning') as a *component* or an *aspect*, which implies that human thought generates social fact by being a part of it.

Part Three

Methodological Implications of Constructivism

In conclusion, I shall briefly sketch some methodological implications of the moderate constructivist position presented in Part Two. As an instructive contrast, I shall first point out the methodological impasse that would result if any of the Broad Arguments were accepted; this should further strengthen resistance to those arguments.

According to the Broad Arguments, social facts are generated as the *objects* of the social members' cognitive efforts. This doctrine has an obvious methodological corollary: in order to get at the social facts, we must first get at the agents' thoughts and from these move on to the facts. Here, trouble strikes. It is impossible to get access to the thoughts if we take the Broad Arguments at face value. The Broad Arguments share, by definition, a general premise that collective thought generates its object. This premise is not limited *per se* to social fact; this restriction in the present book simply reflected our current narrower interests. Hence, if the Broad Arguments are adopted, we must accept that physical reality, too, is a social construction; this is an implication that many proponents of constructivism have been happy to endorse.

With this result in mind, let us now examine how a social scientist must proceed in identifying agents' thoughts. The only way for the researcher to learn what social agents think and what they mean by what they say is to observe the agents and record their comments. The researcher will then attribute such thoughts as seem suitable to account for the observed behaviour, and will identify the meanings of native utterances by establishing correlations between the agents' verbal output and items in the setting.

Unfortunately, if the Broad Arguments are taken as read, this way of getting access to the agents' thought and language is blocked when those agents have a largely different culture, a situation that will often occur, for instance, in social anthropology. Since the natives do not share the anthropologist's culture, they live in a differently constructed world – indeed, not only a different social world, but even a different physical world. Hence, the anthropologist cannot identify the thoughts that will explain their behaviour with respect to the observed setting, nor decipher their language by recording how they apply sentences and terms to their surroundings, as the researcher does not share the same setting. Thus, one society can be hermetically closed to a social scientist belonging to another.

As a matter of fact, the situation is even worse under the terms of the Broad Arguments. Societies also become hermetically closed to the infants born into them. In principle, infants learn language in the same way an anthropologist tries to break a native code. It is a question of aligning speakers' utterances with aspects of the occurrent scene. However, an infant does not yet live in the same world that his parents and other speakers inhabit; an infant must be presumed to be pre-social (unless we adopt the utterly implausible theory that children are somehow primed, at birth, for the specific culture into which they are about to be born). Hence, an infant cannot undertake a pairing between utterances and features of the setting, since he is not acquainted with the setting (and, by the way, not with the utterances either, as these are part of a more inclusive setting). Hence, how children ever learn their native language becomes incomprehensible. I consider this one more fatal flaw in the Broad Arguments.

This point is useful to show how the Broad Arguments differ from the Narrow Arguments, to which we now turn. The two types of argument have the same methodological implications at the initial stage. The Narrow Arguments, too, imply that social science must capture the agents' subjective point of view, on pain of failing to come to grips with social reality. The Narrow Arguments do not drag us into the ontological collapse to which the Broad Arguments inexorably lead, however, nor do they render social reality impenetrable to inquiry. They are far more conservative from the ontological point of view. There were two principles of fact-making in the Narrow Arguments, namely 'construction by composition' (in the arguments from the meaningfulness of action, including the argument from symbolism) and 'construction by idealisation' (in the argument from convention). Both are distinct from the 'construction by objectification' involved in the Broad Arguments. According to 'construction by composition', social reality is generated by the conjunction of two elements: human behaviour, described in purely behavioural terms, and certain 'meanings' accompanying that behaviour. (To the former should be added the physical 'hardware' of society, such as houses, roads, bridges, books, newspapers or coins.) According to the arguments from the meaningfulness of action, the items of the former kind are not themselves generated by construction, but enjoy an independent existence; they are only turned into social items once a 'meaning' is bestowed upon them, however. This 'meaning' defines their (social) nature. Hence, behaviour is available for the inspection of an anthropologist, offering a wedge by which to enter the meaningful 'inside' of a culture. 'Construction by idealisation' occurs when general canons of logic and rationality are applied to a given human practice, drawing implications from the practice that may go beyond anything of which the agents themselves are explicitly aware. Only the idealised extrapolation of the concrete practice is generated in this way, while the practice itself has a more elementary mode of existence and is cognitively accessible to an outsider. (The practice, too, will be a construction, namely, by composition out of a purely behavioural part and a meaningful mental component, but we have just seen that this does not hinder an anthropologist's interpretive efforts.)

Hence, we avoid the impasse. For either kind of construction, a stratum of unconstructed facts exists, which the scientist can use in his effort to get at the constructing processes and, through them, at the constructed facts. We can penetrate to the 'meaning' behind social agents' outward behaviour by carefully observing that behaviour (in particular, details of how it is conditioned by the surroundings). Once the 'meanings' are fixed, so are the social facts they define. Similarly, we reach the idealised facts generated by the agents' concrete conventional practices by observing those practices and determining the rules governing them. General canons of logic and rationality then are invoked to project those rules beyond the limitations and imperfections of their actual application. The version of constructivism that follows from the Narrow Arguments makes generated social reality essentially accessible.

The question of whether or not the agents' own meanings should be adopted, or even recognised, in social science has generated much debate. (Recall that some of the constructivist arguments we have examined in this essay were derived from work that was originally addressed to this issue; this goes for the contributions from Alfred Schutz and Peter Winch.) The Narrow Arguments support a positive answer to this question by a very simple consideration. They point out that agents' conception of social reality is *a part* of that very reality; hence, a failure to capture that conception in a social scientific description would be a failure to capture a part – we might add, a crucial part – of the object under study. The agents' meanings structure social reality as a whole by supplying the identity conditions for social events, states and processes. The presence of a certain 'meaning' (belief or intention) turns a certain bodily movement into the social act of signing a contract, or casting a vote, and turns a piece of paper into a means of economic exchange. In brief, 'meanings' transform colourless movements and lifeless physical objects into human reality. Hence, social science should encompass the agents' own understanding of their actions, at least as a point of departure.

Still, opponents of an agent-oriented methodology might not be persuaded by this argument. Two names are bound to come up when discussion turns to the status of the agents' own descriptions in social science: Émile Durkheim and Vilfredo Pareto. These two founding fathers of sociology were concerned to show that social agents' own explanations of the meanings of their actions are often shallow, if not downright mistaken, and should hence be superseded in the scientific account of a society. Pareto pointed out how the very same social practice may exist in neighbouring societies, but with entirely different respective native rationales. This creates a suspicion that the native explanations are spurious and that the real ones should be sought elsewhere. Pareto introduced the concept of *derivation* for such rationalisations of conduct. Durkheim declared that our common-sense ideas, including our ideas about society, are 'like a veil drawn between the thing and ourselves', concealing rather than constituting social reality (Durkheim 1938: 15). In an important passage from *On the Elementary Forms of the Religious Life* (Durkheim 1915: 417–18), he compares everyday social terms with such terms as 'heat' and other secondary qualities that have been made redundant in modern physical science, suggesting that the everyday action explanations are equally outmoded.

This comparison challenges a subjectivist approach to social science and the constructivist argument in its favour. It reminds us that the mere existence of an aspect of reality is not enough to secure it a place in scientific theory. Heat, colour and taste undoubtedly exist as phenomenological qualities; still, modern physics has no room for them in its ontology. This is because they have no *explanatory* import; all explanation of natural fact may be achieved using such terms as mass, acceleration and force. The secondary qualities are superfluous from this point of view.

I believe that the constructivist argument in favour of adopting the subjective view is not undercut by this reasoning, however. The commitment to the agents' point of view that follows from the Narrow Arguments is neither unconditional nor naive. In Chapter V, we distinguished between the agents' verbal rendition of their meanings and the true meanings; the two need not coincide. We also insisted that social science seek the true meanings. Now, the true meanings are precisely those that we must postulate to explain the observed actions; hence, no wedge can be driven in between the agents' meanings and the true motivating forces behind their actions, rendering the former irrelevant for explanatory purposes. What we call 'agents' meanings' are already defined as items that have explanatory import (or rather, 'agents' meanings' *include* such explanatory meanings, but are not exhausted by them). Even agents' misconstruals of their own behaviour will be of interest to science as a part of social reality and in so far as they explain certain surface features of social action, namely the features by which agents hide from themselves the true nature of their actions. These could be called 'secondary elaborations' upon social action.

In the article 'Psychosis or Social Sanction' (Kroeber 1940), the American anthropologist A. L. Kroeber tells a fascinating story about a social phenomenon that might prompt a social scientist to go beyond natives' own descriptions. Among American Indians, shamanistic powers are thought to manifest themselves through seizures or trances, during which gods or spirits communicate with the shaman. As Kroeber notes, these hallucinatory conditions are very similar to what we in our civilisation would classify as acute states of psychosis. As in such cases, we would often in anthropology feel justified in questioning the agents' self-descriptions – even with respect to what I previously termed the *internal implications* of these descriptions. (Obviously, we want to dispute the *external* ones, if we do not believe that spirits exist and may communicate with people.) We would often dispute even the declaration that the person *believes himself* to be under the guidance of spirits, at least as a full and exhaustive account of the event. Such a straightforward description fails to do justice to the deviousness of the psychological state involved, as revealed in the characteristic purposiveness of the messages received by the shaman. Often these messages serve obvious self-interests on the part of the receiver, or contain wise counsel on the part of the tribe. It is tempting to conclude that we are being confronted with a short-term personality split, in which one (suppressed) part addresses the conscious part, speaking as the advocate of suppressed individual desires or of communal interests that cannot otherwise get a hearing. Does this not parallel cases of neurotic individuals in our own culture, who do things characterised by an obvious goal-directedness that they themselves refuse to recognise, but that can plausibly be construed as the manifestation of suppressed desires? In both cases, we must reject the agents' own self-interpretation as the full story and insist that they are *doing* something of which they are not aware: they are trying to further their own interests in ways that would not be socially permissible if not apparently sanctioned by the spirits, or are giving counsel that would never receive a hearing if not backed up by supernatural authority.

Of course, the researcher may have occasion to question self-interpretations in our own culture, too. If Jarvie is right in his analysis of the phenomenon of class (see pp. 131–3), people who perpetuate a class practice do so in bad faith; they claim to base their recognition of somebody as belonging to a certain class – in particular, their own – on certain objective distinctions. The truth is that, at least on certain occasions, they will accept someone who fails to satisfy those criteria as a member of their class, even someone whose failure is so blatant that ignorance of it is not possible. In other words, the members of the higher, coveted classes conceal from themselves the fact that their social prominence and their mutual recognition is not based upon objective merit, but, to some extent, upon arbitrary consensus. Class practices fulfil the social function of distributing goods and privileges among the members of society, typically in invidious ways. Hence, the belief in classes is *ideological* – and while subjects of ideological beliefs are not necessarily in bad faith, in the original Marxist conception, a good case could be made that things are different with the concept of social class in its normative and discriminative use, since this concept has been the target of endless denouement. Nobody today can be totally ignorant of the attempts to debunk it. A social researcher might plausibly consider as being in bad faith the self-interpretation of a person today who took class distinctions at face value.

Does not the introduction of explanatory concepts of the

researcher's own device secretly subvert the entire rationale of the agent-oriented approach? After all, we get the researcher's concepts rather than the agents' own. Someone who worries about this overlooks the fact that these concepts are subject to strict constraints, designed to guarantee that the resulting action interpretation is the agent's own, even if only subconsciously. Only concepts whose attribution is warranted by the agent's conduct are allowed. Moreover, the social scientist does not have a free hand to devise explanatory concepts and explanatory hypotheses, but is constrained by strict hermeneutic principles that secure the authenticity of the interpretation.

Reflection on the two examples above reveals that the loyalty to the agents' point of view following from the constructivist argument is not a highly-confining methodological principle. The commitment is only to the agents' own interpretation as the *starting* point for social research, not as the inevitable end point of the efforts. Once a body of social facts defined in terms of the agents' own interpretation has been established, those facts may be accounted for in terms of explanatory devices that far transcend the agents' own horizon and conceptual resources. The explanation might invoke the substructure–superstructure duality of Marxism, or might be of functionalist form. For instance, there is room for a functionalist interpretation of shamanistic trances: presenting radically novel ideas as counsel provided by benign spirits is the only legitimate way to get them accepted in societies in which tradition is the source of all authority. There are fascinating reports in the literature about how American Indian tribes have been brought close to extinction by the rigidity of their traditional mores in the face of changing external conditions and how only timely advice from the 'spirits', imparted to a shaman during a trance, made possible a radical social transformation that saved them. It is very tempting to see the shamanistic trance as a socially-induced and socially-endorsed mechanism for introducing novel ideas, and for advancing controversial individual claims, in a traditional, rigidly-controlled community.

There is another reason why the methodology that follows from the constructivist argument does not dictate the indiscriminate recording of individual agents' subjective interpretations. In contrast to a naive social phenomenology, the methodology suggested here does not accord every agent the same weight in defining the nature of a social situation and does not view the meaning of a social encounter as defined by the 'lowest common denominator' of the subjective meanings of everyone involved (that is, those elements of meaning shared by all involved). The present methodology recognises the phenomenon of *social authority*, not only determining what the agent must do in a given social situation, but also defining what that situation *is* in the first place.

We illustrated this phenomenon with the example of the Crusades (see p. 138). The lay participants in the Crusades will have had scant knowledge of the theological disputes that (at least in part) led to these campaigns, or of the ultimate objectives. Still, it is true to describe the laymen as *participants in the Crusades*, in a full sense, because they had (as it were) delegated responsibility for defining the events to the agencies organising those campaigns. The same holds true for such everyday events as church services, formal dances, club meetings, and so on. The average participants in such events may not have sufficient knowledge of the proceedings to tell precisely what is going on at any moment; if one could look into their minds, one would not be able to guess what was happening, socially. Lay agents qualify as participants only by deferring to the authorities' definition of the current social situation – the 'authorities' here simply being the group organising the events.

This observation, I believe, should make the subjectivist position somewhat more palatable to its critics. It accommodates the realisation that, for the nature of most social encounters, what goes on in the mind of the common participant is largely immaterial. The events are defined by the way certain select people in positions of authority conceive them, not by what goes on in every individual mind, or even in the majority of minds. Hence, it remains legitimate to refer to large-scale social events by such names as 'the Crusades', or 'the French Revolution', without implying that every participant realised the full ramifications of those events. By the same token, it is also methodologically legitimate for social science to investigate these events without looking into every individual participant's conception of the course of events.

CONSTRUCTIVISM AND THE INDIVIDUALISM/ HOLISM ISSUE

The claim that social facts are determined by what agents think suggests that social facts can be analysed and explained by reference to individual human actions, thoughts, and intentions. In other words, it points in the direction of an *individualist* approach to social research. The arguments from meaningfulness would seem to dictate that social science proceeds by investigating the mental contents of individual agents – in the sophisticated and selective way indicated above – building up a picture of social reality on this basis. We should determine whether further examination of the argument will bear out this first impression.

First, we may note that this result is sufficiently sturdy to survive an obvious countervailing consideration. On closer examination of the hermeneutic argument and the argument from symbolic meaning, agents' intentions appear to be largely determined by the representational powers of language. The average social agent is only in a position to have thoughts and intentions about such things as arthritis, transubstantiation, or irrational numbers, by virtue of being a speaker of a public language in which these items are singled out for reference. The same thing is true of symbolism. We argued that if social agents think of something as a symbol, this is sufficient to make it one; however, most agents are not capable of giving any very precise account of the content of this thought. They can only be said to have the thought that something is a symbol by virtue of being speakers of a common language in which a term with the meaning of 'symbol' is used. Thus, it might seem that the support for individualism from the idea of the meaningfulness of action was only apparent, as we have to invoke certain holistic entities – namely, language and linguistic meaning – in order to describe what goes on in the minds of individual agents.

Closer analysis, however, shows that the individualist picture is not threatened after all; we can break down the macroscopic, holistic units that figure in this picture of construction, providing a more fine-grained account in its stead. The coarse-grained picture showed an abstract, general entity, language, determining individual human intentions. If we analyse this abstract entity, however, facts about individual intentions and beliefs come to light, although these are other intentions and other beliefs than those that are shaped by language. Beliefs that determine the meaning of language are socially distributed in characteristic ways; linguistic meaning is fixed by the experts in the field to which the terms in question belong. Thus, what emerges to replace the holistic picture is one in which a particular set of facts about individuals (concerning the beliefs and intentions of the experts and authorities in a given field and the meanings they give to certain linguistic terms) determines another set of individual facts (namely, the linguistic meanings of the same terms as used by lay people).

So far, we have found much in social constructivism to please a methodological individualist and nothing to offend him. Are we entitled to conclude that our results provide a vindication of methodological individualism, in the form of reductionism? I shall argue that the answer is no. Our analyses in Part Two actually identified an element of social ontology resistant to individualist reduction. This obstacle to reductionism is posed by *conventional facts*. Conventional facts, especially the ones involved in *institutions*, go beyond anything that is given in the practice that sustains them. Before I can demonstrate this in detail, however, I must make clear the sense in which I shall be using the term 'individualism' and its opposite, 'holism', since these terms have been used to cover a multitude of different, often rather vaguely defined, positions.

Holism is the position that explanation of social facts, including facts about the interaction of individuals, cannot be achieved without reference to items at the social level (groups, states, classes, and so on) and their properties. Statements about such social items cannot, in their turn, be analysed into statements about individuals and their actions. *Individualism*, as I use the term here, is a type of reductionism, claiming that statements about social reality can be analysed as statements about individual human actions and be explained in terms of laws referring only to individual action in simpler contexts. It reflects the intuition that society is, after all, nothing more than human individuals and their actions. Let us look more closely at reduction to see how this pre-theoretical intuition can be given a more precise sense.

The reduction of one theory to another is a familiar thing in science and is normally considered a crowning achievement. It is of two kinds: the *reduction of concepts* and the *reduction of laws*. The two are not completely independent. Within the reduction of concepts, we may again distinguish between two kinds, translational and material. *Translational* reduction of concepts is achieved through the demonstration that certain terms of the reduced theory, in this case social terms, have the same meaning as some (cluster of) terms from the reducing theory (in this case, terms referring to individuals and their actions); hence, they can be translated without loss of meaning into the latter. Reduction is effected when the original terms are replaced by their translations.

An example from social science is the replacement of the term 'average birth rate in population S' with its individualistic translation, say, 'the number of births in S per annum, divided by the number of individuals in S, and multiplied by 1,000'. (This formula, which defines the so-called 'crude birth rate', is clearly trivial and merely serves an illustrative purpose. I shall argue below that non-trivial definitions are hard to find. Note that the argument against individualism provided below, based upon the notion of institutional facts, does not extend to the definition of average birth rate, since this term is not an institutional one.)

Material reduction of concepts, on the other hand, consists of replacing one term with another that is found by experience to stand for the same thing, although the two terms do not have the same meaning. A celebrated example from natural science is the identification of the concept of heat (of a gas) with the mean kinetic energy of the molecules of that gas; another, more familiar, one is the identification of water with a compound consisting of two hydrogen atoms and one oxygen atom. These were empirical discoveries, not the result of semantic analysis; one could never have established that water is H_2O just by pondering the meaning of the term 'water'. The reducing and reduced terms are connected by so-called *bridge laws*, which state that the substance or phenomenon referred to by one term is identical to the one referred to by another; thus, in the present case, 'water = H_2O'.

Let us now turn to the reduction of laws. The reduction of a law A to another law (or group of laws) B, is achieved by deducing A from B (in conjunction with further premises). The classic example in science is the way in which Galileo's law, which specifies the rate of acceleration of an unsupported object near the earth's surface, could be deduced from Newton's laws (in conjunction with premises specifying certain relevant features of the earth, such as its mass). This shows that Galileo's law can be regarded as a special case of Newton's laws (at least as an approximation). Another classic example is the derivation of Boyle–Charles' law (which states that the product of the volume and pressure of a gas is constant at a given temperature) from the laws of statistical mechanics proposed by Boltzmann.

Note that translational reduction of concepts is independent of the reduction of laws, whereas there is a close link between the material reduction of concepts and the reduction of laws. For instance, even if we grant that a triad is translationally reducible to the notion of a group of three persons, and this again to 'a set of three persons who have a high level of mutual interaction, and who stand in status and role relationships to one another',[1] it is not a foregone conclusion that the laws describing processes in a triad can be derived from the laws governing the conduct of people in a simpler social situation – that is, the dyad. As a matter of fact, this is clearly not the case: the social processes within triads are characterised, among other things, by the formation of shifting *coalitions* between two members against the third. This feature of triads is not inferrable from the principles describing the processes in dyads, where coalition formation is (of course) impossible.

In contrast, the material reduction of concepts is closely tied to the reduction of laws. What justifies us in replacing some concept, say, 'heat' or 'water', with other concepts, is the fact that we can *identify* the prior concept with the new one. The warrant for this identification consists in the existence of laws, featuring the new concept, that explain the facts that were explained by means of the prior concept, and that also explain the (approximate) validity of the laws using the prior concept. For instance, our warrant for identifying heat with mean kinetic energy of gas molecules is the fact that the laws formulated by means of this concept permit us to explain heat phenomena, and do so by showing that the laws that we previously established in this area (for example, the Boyle–Charles law) can be seen as crude approximations to the superior laws using the new notion. Thus, the material reduction of the concept of heat to that of mean kinetic energy is contingent upon the reducibility of laws about heat to laws about mean kinetic energy.

With our terminology fixed, we may now examine how our analysis in Part Two, though it follows a familiar individualist path for a while, eventually delivers an argument against this position. The best way to proceed is to trace out the individualist line of thought and see precisely where it breaks down. Let us do so by looking at an individualist–reductionist position proposed by Hugh Mellor on the basis of considerations very similar to those sketched above (Mellor 1982).

Mellor uses Maurice Mandelbaum's well-known example of a bank clerk to illustrate the reducibility of social properties (Mandelbaum 1955). Mellor argues that what makes a person a bank clerk is precisely the psychological fact that he himself, his colleagues and his customers believe him to be a bank clerk and act accordingly. Hence, we can analyse the fact of somebody's being a bank clerk into those belief states and the actions they generate and can explain all facts concerning bank clerks by explaining those beliefs and actions.

There is a standard objection to this position, raised by Mandelbaum in the article cited and addressed by Mellor: the actions of an individual or a plurality of individuals only count as acts of the social entity of which they are members if the setting is right. Only the actions the clerk performs *ex officio*, in his capacity as a bank clerk, count as the bank's acts. The same actions performed outside of the proper setting – say, by the bank clerk during a party – would not count as an act of the bank. This forces us to introduce the general notion of a social *function*, or *role*, to distinguish those individual actions that count as acts of a social unit from those that do not. This means, however, that we cannot define social acts in terms of individual actions, for the ideas of a function or a role are themselves social ideas, which means that their inclusion in the definitions would defeat the purpose of individualist reduction.

Mellor's rejoinder is, in effect, that the social setting that surrounds any particular human social action can itself be reduced to psychological (and physical) facts, too. However, a closer look shows that this is not so. I would argue that, to the extent that the setting involves *institutional* facts – which are indeed ubiquitous in social life – no such reduction is possible. Our examination of institutional facts showed that the type of construction operative here is more complex than those described in the phenomenological argument and the hermeneutic argument. In simplistic terms, those arguments showed that certain social facts consist of behaviour and the subjective 'meanings' with which the agents accompany them. But, as we saw, institutional facts are different, in that the idea of correctness of standards and norms enters as a further aspect blocking reduction to individual action (according to the following formula: social action = individual behaviour + individual 'meanings'). We saw this clearly illustrated in the case of legally valid acts. It was tempting to define such acts simply as those in accordance with the verdict upon which a specific group of social agents (namely, Supreme Court judges) would eventually agree. This will not work, however: judges reach their verdicts on the basis of reflections upon independent standards of correctness. Hence, legal validity cannot be defined as that upon which judges eventually settle. The argument transfers to the case of Mandelbaum's bank clerk. The circumstance of everyone believing that a person is a bank clerk does not make the person in question a bank clerk. That belief must be weighed against certain institutional standards of correctness – for example, the correctness of an appointment procedure. This evaluation may show that the belief is simply in error – perhaps the person whom everyone believes to be a bank clerk was never formally hired.

However, we must not move too fast here. The above argument only shows that we cannot *define* institutional action in terms of individual actions alone. However, this does not rule out a *material* reduction of institutional action to individual action, working by means of bridge laws linking clusters of individual action to institutional actions, much the same way that bridge laws link processes of molecule swarms to processes of heat transmission. (As a matter of fact, this is the kind of reduction Mellor envisions; see Mellor 1982: 51–2.)

The rejoinder to this suggestion is that much of the force of the criticism remains even when we consider other sorts of reduction than the translational kind. Let us try to examine what would be required for there to be material bridge laws between institutional facts and clusters of individual facts – that is, laws constructed on the model of 'water = H_2O'. We saw that the distinctive traits of institutional facts reside in their implicit reference to certain standards of correct procedure. Institutional actions emerge from individual actions when the latter have been performed according to relevant operative norms. To put it even more succinctly, institutional action equals individual action plus a warrant that the latter is in accordance with applicable norms. This means that bridge laws connecting the individualist and the social (institutional) levels would prevail if it were possible to specify, in individualist terms, those intellectual procedures through which such warrant is established. The question is this: can we provide specifications of the intellectual procedures carried out by individual human beings engaged in the interpretation of social norms, such that, when these procedures are adhered to, they guarantee the truth of the conclusions that they produce and, hence, the institutional validity of those actions? And could we, conversely, for any such truth, define a cognitive procedure that would be guaranteed to arrive at that truth as its conclusion?

When the issue is reformulated in this way, it is clear that the answer must be no. It is the second condition in particular that creates trouble, since it presupposes a strictly algorithmic theory of truth: it presupposes that, for any question within the area at issue, there exist cognitive procedures guaranteed to lead to a true answer to that question. It is known today that such algorithmisation of knowledge is not generally possible. We cannot formalise, once and for all, the kinds of arguments and inferences we will find valid. This has been shown to be the case in the field for which the belief in such algorithms would otherwise seem most plausible, namely, mathematics, in the epoch-making work of Kurt Gödel and Alan Turing. Gödel's and Turing's work shows that, in any formal deductive system of more than minimal content, there will always be truths that are inaccessible through the proof procedures specified for that system. Intuitively, this negative conclusion holds true even more strongly for such less strictly defined areas of discourse as law, or mores.

I have argued the untenability of individualist reductionism, as defined above. Clearly, other variants of individualism exist, and have not been affected. For instance, our deliberations do not show the impossibility of a non-reductive kind of individualism that does not aspire to build counterparts to holistic, societal concepts out of non-holistic elements, but simply tries to *explain* social facts in terms that are not themselves social. The non-holistic elements would be, on the one hand, purely individual terms and, on the other, the ideas of *truth* and *validity* – that is, the validity of certain inference rules and certain standards of rationality that supply the correctness involved in institutional facts. An analogy with a completely different realm will illustrate the difference between the suggested individualist approach and the one we criticised above. We cannot translate such terms as 'distributor', 'sparking plug', or 'camshaft' into purely physical terms, for these are *functional* terms, characterising an automotive part in terms of the job that it performs. For instance, a distributor is any component of a combustion engine that transmits electricity to the sparking plugs in such a temporal pattern that combustion occurs in proper sequence. There are endless devices, some mechanical, some electronic, that can perform this task; thus, no finite characterisation of such devices can be given in purely physical terms. This will not lead us to conclude, however, that distributors (or sparking plugs, or camshafts) are somehow partly non-physical and, as a result, transcend physical explanation. We firmly believe that any process involving distributors will be explainable in physical terms. The point is merely that this explanation will not invoke laws in which such terms as 'distributor' occur. The explanation will bypass such terms altogether and go straight to a detailed physical description of the distributor, subsuming it under the laws of physics.

There is another way to express this conclusion: as individualist reductionism and holism do not exhaust the spectrum of possible views, our elimination of the former has not left the latter alone on the field. We must remember that holism is defined as the position that explanation of social facts, including facts concerning the interaction of individuals, essentially requires reference to (non-reducible) social collectivities and social properties. My result above concerning individualist reductionism did not show the need to use holist terms in the explanation of social facts, but rather the falsity of reductionist individualism (which is not tantamount to holism, since there are other options). As a matter of fact, our analysis suggested such an alternative view – namely, that institutional facts refer to individual thoughts, intentions, and actions *to the extent that* they satisfy certain requirements of validity and correct procedure. This is not tantamount to a reduction of institutional facts, since correctness cannot be reduced to adherence to a limited, pre-specified number of cognitive standards; the idea of correctness, or truth, is essentially open-ended. Nor, on the other hand, are correctness or truth essentially holistic notions. Hence, my dismissal of reductive individualism does not oblige me to accept a view of society as a mysterious entity, over and above human individuals and their actions.

Notes

INTRODUCTION

1 As previously mentioned, the notion of construction is often taken to apply to social reality only, whereas the world of natural facts is thought to have an independent status as somehow more autonomous, more objective, than the world of social fact. But notice, to further adumbrate the difference between these ideas, that the notion of reification does not engage with any such distinction. To the extent that the notion of 'reification' is used to mark that which is man-made (and hence changeable by man) as opposed to what resists such influence, this cuts across the distinction between human fact and natural fact. Some natural facts may allow easy transformation, should people decide on it, and may often owe their perpetuation to the interests of certain parties involved. It is a *fact* that certain regions of the earth are arid and do not allow any kind of cultivation; this condition nevertheless might be said not to possess genuine reality (in the privileged sense), as it could be rectified by a minor effort by man, such as digging water canals for irrigation. Often there are obvious economical and political explanations for the inaction. Similarly, it is a *fact* that large tracts of the earth are today covered with rain forest, but this fact, we know only too well, is very fragile and very much in the hands of man. It is protected by certain segments of society, but is under attack from opposed interests that may well prevail in the end. In brief, to talk in this sense about what is real and what is merely a reification is to distinguish facts that man can change, and perhaps would change if he was not overly influenced by certain partisan interests, from facts that man is powerless to do anything about. This distinction and the theoretical concerns it serves are different from the ones motivating this study.

2 Important texts expounding the science constructivist position are: Collins (1992), Knorr-Cetina (1981) and Latour and Woolgar (1979). As a reading of these works will demonstrate, the science constructivists are a motley company, representing highly divergent approaches to social science which cut across their shared commitment to constructivism.

237

PART ONE THE BROAD ARGUMENTS

1   It is only on the basis of the constructivist premise that ethnomethodology is genuinely distinguishable from close relatives, such as symbolic interactionism. Symbolic interactionists, too, stress the creative, non-predetermined character of social action. But symbolic interactionists stop at the first premise; indeed, they normally go no further than the first level of that premise, i.e. that the dictates of normative social rules and codes are not determinate before they are fixed in the group. They do not normally share the ethnomethodologists suspicion of the semantic determinacy of descriptive terms. The differences between the two schools clearly emerge from the debate between Norman Denzin, Don H. Zimmerman and D. Lawrence Wieder (cf. Denzin 1971; Zimmerman and Wieder 1971b).

2   See also Harold Garfinkel and Harvey Sacks (1970: 348), M. Pollner (1987: xiii); Alan Bloom (1971: *passim*). Harold Garfinkel, in kindly commenting upon the present chapter, stressed that the quasi-Wittgensteinian argument that I sketch out is not the one intended in his writings; the precise nature of the difference, however, was not made entirely clear. I remain convinced that the argument outlined in the text is the most plausible argument, based upon Wittgensteinian ideas, that may be advanced in support of a constructivist position.

  It should be noted that after having marshalled many of the same premises as are found in ethnomethodological writings on rule-following and having reached some of the same results on the way, Wittgenstein settles for a different final conclusion concerning the reality of rules. As for the idealist position, it is repudiated elsewhere in the Wittgensteinian corpus.

3   The regress argument to be presented in what follows has been raised against constructivist positions before. For an elegant and compact statement, see Martin Hollis (1982); a rather more cumbrous version is found in Collin (1985: 161–6); the latter was arrived at independently. The fountainhead of all these arguments, however, is Frege's famous suggestion that all attempts at defining truth in substantive terms will lead to a regress (cf. Frege 1967).

4   See also Horton (1970). Horton has since modified his position somewhat (Horton 1982), introducing complications to which I cannot do justice in this brief exposition. The basic point remains the same, however.

5   A good place for the interested reader to pursue these issues is in Putnam (1983).

6   For an excellent critical discussion of the science constructivists and the 'new wave' in the sociology of science, see Brown (1989).

7   See for instance the exchange between Steven Yearley, Harry Collins, Bruno Latour, Michel Callon and Steve Woolgar in Pickering (1992).

8   The best-known contribution is Davidson's 'On the Very Idea of a Conceptual Scheme' (Davidson 1974). Other important contributions are Putnam (1978) and Newton-Smith (1981). For a criticism of some of the arguments of these works, see Feyerabend (1987, ch. 10).

9   Nor is it troubled by the circumstance that, in virtue of the same principle of construction, this availability must itself be linguistically expressible in order to succeed, since this condition is easily satisfied: it takes only a minimal linguistic vocabulary to express the fact that a certain term P exists in a language and is used to describe the world. This observation takes care not only of the availability of P, but also of the terms used to assert that very availability; indeed, it takes care of the whole infinite series of descriptions, each of which refers to some linguistic terms at the level below it and is itself referred to by some description above it. All these descriptions make use of the same finite linguistic vocabulary. A simple phonetic alphabet would do, or, even better, an exact scientific vocabulary of phonetic transcription. Hence, if there is a regress here, it is a benign one.

PART TWO   THE NARROW ARGUMENTS

1   Dilthey (1907–10)
2   I am aware, of course, that Schutz, like Husserl, would see the phenomenological enterprise as precisely an antidote to psychologism. According to Schutz, what is recorded in phenomenological analysis is not incidental mental items that happen to occupy the mental scene, but structures essential to the phenomenon under investigation; hence, phenomenological analysis is not psychological description but the intuiting of essences. I believe, however, that this is a distinction without a difference and would agree with the charge that phenomenology falls prey to psychologism – at least in the broad sense of the attempt to throw light on philosophical issues through the analysis of introspective data.
3   It is true, of course, that awareness of one's bodily movements and some reflective awareness of one's thoughts and intentions are normally present. This is not always the case, however, which testifies that it is not a conceptual necessity. Patients who have suffered a stroke occasionally lose their kinaesthetic sense, with the result that they cannot tell, without looking, what bodily movements they have performed. We may imagine that on occasion such patients succeed in performing certain actions, while being ignorant that they have done so. As far as meanings are concerned, it is a well-known fact that people may occasionally be ignorant of this crucial component of their actions: Freud taught us that agents are on occasion ignorant of their real motives.
4   This description may strike the reader as psychologically invalid. When we monitor our conduct, we do not conceive of that conduct as pure motion that is only turned into action by that very concomitant consciousness; we think about it as already *action*. I may grant this point without abandoning the general structure of the argument. In a more careful description, what is turned into an action of a particular kind – for instance, the action of fetching a bottle from the top shelf – is always another action, but an action of a simpler sort, which is

instrumental in reaching the goal of the action under its more comprehensive description. In the case in question, it might be the action of stepping up on a ladder. This answer, in its turn, is saved from a regress of still simpler actions by the fact that one soon comes to what philosophers have termed *basic acts* – acts that are not performed by doing some simpler act, but are simply *performed*. Stretching out the arm might be such an act. It is no argument against the existence of such acts that we normally do not think of our action in these terms. The point is, we can get down to basic acts analytically.

5   The account dates back to Aristotle, but has been reintroduced in recent times by such authors as G. E. M. Anscombe (1957) and G. H. von Wright (1971).

6   Some philosophers might object that this analysis rescues us from the quagmire of mentalism only to lead us into the Cloud-cuckoo-land of Platonic reification, home of propositions and similar monstrosities. To those philosophers, I reply that if they object to propositions on nominalist grounds, they may if they wish replace them with sentences in the above analysis.

7   The epithet is meant to distinguish them from more traditional hermeneuticians, such as Hans-Georg Gadamer. The difference between the two groups lies, *inter alia*, in the willingness to criticise and reject agents' own interpretations, a possibility on which the critical hermeneuticians insist and their opponents largely reject. Here, however, where we deal only with the critical type of hermeneuticians, I shall henceforth refer to them simply as *hermeneuticians*.

8   In fairness to the phenomenologists, it should be noted that even among 'pure' representatives of the school, the more circumspect members have tried to allow for the latter possibility. Thus, in Schutz (1972), section 28, Alfred Schutz tried to do justice to the intellectual content of cultural creations. It remains true that this point is normally overlooked by phenomenologists.

9   I cite the example of the Crusades, because the topic was used to make precisely this point in Winch (1958: 130).

10 The example is inspired by one found in Dennett (1987: 20–1). Dennett uses it to make a somewhat different point.

11 For a collection of such work, see Harré (1986).

12 Representative specimens of this work are found in Lorber and Farrell (1991) and in Ortner and Whitehead (1981).

13 At the same time, it is characteristic of gender roles that they are supposed to be *natural*, giving expression to something that the person essentially and spontaneously *is*. Gender roles require us to perform the difficult intellectual trick of accepting strict standards for our conduct, while simultaneously considering this imposed conduct to be natural and unforced.

14 I have elsewhere criticised Barthes for failing to substantiate these very strong claims for the analogies between clothing and language (cf. Collin 1985, ch. 7). Still, one need not go along with Barthes all the way to see the fruitfulness of the idea of clothes as being symbolic; the value of this idea, however, is better explored by seeing clothes not as

having propositional meaning, but rather as having a simpler representational relation to that for which they stand. Barthes, by the way,
further complicates the issue by not really taking clothes as his object,
but rather *descriptions of clothes* in fashion magazines (or, as he prefers
to say, 'written clothing').

15 We may compare this tendency towards demarcation and exaggeration
of distinctive features to the way, in natural languages, the phonetic
continuum is divided into segments, in the shape of semantically
significant sounds (phonemes). There is a tendency to place phonemes
as far as possible from each other in the phonetic continuum, to
enhance the distinctiveness of speech (see van Parijs 1979).

16 As it happens, Lewis draws a distinction between the technical notions
of 'convention' and 'social contract' on the basis of certain rather
subtle details. However, the two phenomena often coincide. We may
bypass this issue here.

PART THREE   METHODOLOGICAL IMPLICATIONS OF CONSTRUCTIVISM

1 Nothing depends on the definition of 'group' cited here, which serves a
purely illustrative purpose. It is a standard definition, for which I hold
no particular brief. In particular, my invocation of the definition is
intended not to beg the question as to the ultimate definability of
social concepts in terms of purely individualist ones, an issue I discuss
below. The point is, simply, that *even if* such definition is possible, the
reduction of laws does not follow.

References

Anscombe, G. E. M. (1957) *Intention*, Oxford: Basil Blackwell.

Austin, J. L. (1962a) *How to do Things with Words*, Oxford: Oxford University Press.

—— (1962b) *Sense and Sensibilia*, Oxford: Oxford University Press.

Barthes, R. (1990) *The Fashion System*, Berkeley: University of California Press.

Beattie, J. H. M. (1970) 'On Understanding Ritual', in B. Wilson (ed.) *Rationality*, Oxford: Basil Blackwell.

Becker, H. (1973) *Outsiders*, New York: Free Press.

Berger, P. and Luckmann, T. (1967) *The Social Construction of Reality*, Harmondsworth: Penguin.

Blackburn, S. (1984) *Spreading the Word*, Oxford: Basil Blackwell.

Bloom, A. (1971) 'Theorizing', in J. Douglas (ed.) *Understanding Everyday Life*, London: Routledge and Kegan Paul.

Brown, J. R. (1989) *The Rational and the Social*, London: Routledge.

Brown, S. C. (ed.) (1979) *Philosophical Disputes in the Social Sciences*, Sussex: Harvester Press.

Burge, T. (1979) 'Individualism and the Mental', *Midwest Studies in Philosophy* vol. 4.

Callon, M. and Latour, B. (1992) 'Don't throw the baby out with the bath school!', in A. Pickering (ed.) *Science as Practice and Culture*, Chicago: University of Chicago Press.

Collin, F. (1985) *Theory and Understanding*, Oxford: Basil Blackwell.

Collins, H. M. (1992) *Changing Order*, Chicago: University of Chicago Press, 2nd edition.

Davidson, D. (1963) 'Actions, Reasons, and Causes', *Journal of Philosophy* vol. 60.

—— (1974) 'On the very nature of a conceptual scheme', *Proceedings and Addresses of the American Philosophical Association* vol. 47.

Dennett, D. (1987) *The Intentional Stance*, Cambridge MA: MIT Press.

Denzin, N. (1971) 'Symbolic Interactionism and Ethnomethodology', in J. Douglas (ed.) *Understanding Everyday Life*, London: Routledge and Kegan Paul.

Dilthey, W. (1894) 'Ideen Über eine beschreibende und zergliedernde Psychologie', in *Gesammelte Schriften*, vol. 5, Stuttgart: Teubner (1957).

References

—— (1907–10) 'Der Aufbau der geschichtlichen Welt in den Geisteswissenschaften', in *Gesammelte Schriften*, vol. 7, Stuttgart: Teubner (1957).

Dixon, R. M. W. (1982) *Where Have All the Adjectives Gone* (*Janua Linguarum*, Series Major, 107) Berlin: Mouton Publishers.

Douglas, J. (ed.) (1971) *Understanding Everyday Life*, London: Routledge and Kegan Paul.

Douglas, M. (1975) *Implicit Meanings*, London: Routledge and Kegan Paul.

—— (1979) 'World View and the Core', in S. C. Brown (ed.) *Philosophical Disputes in the Social Sciences*, Sussex: Harvester Press.

Durkheim, É. (1915) *The Elementary Forms of the Religious Life*, London: George Allen and Unwin.

—— (1938) *The Rules of Sociological Method*, Chicago: University of Chicago Press.

Durkheim, É. and Mauss, M. (1963) *Primitive Classification*, Chicago: University of Chicago Press.

Eddington, A. (1928) *The Nature of The Physical World*, Cambridge: Cambridge University Press.

Evans-Pritchard, E. E. (1937) *Witchcraft, Oracles and Magic among the Azande*, Oxford: Clarendon Press.

Feyerabend, P. (1987) *Farewell to Reason*, London: Verso.

Foucault, M. (1965) *Madness and Civilization*, New York: Random House.

—— (1972) *The Archeology of Knowledge*, London: Routledge.

Frazer, J. (1911) *The Golden Bough, Vol. 1: The Magic Art and the Evolution of Kings*, London: Macmillan Press.

Frege, G. (1967) 'The thought: a logical enquiry', in P. F. Strawson (ed.) *Philosophical Logic*, Oxford: Oxford University Press.

Fuller, S. (1993) *Philosophy of Science and Its Discontents*, New York and London: Guildford Press, 2nd edition.

Garfinkel, H. (1967) *Studies in Ethnomethodology*, Englewood Cliffs: Prentice-Hall.

Garfinkel, H. and Sacks, H. (1970) 'On Formal Structures of Practical Actions', in J. C. McKinney and E. A. Tiryakian (eds) *Theoretical Sociology: Perspectives and Developments*, New York: Appleton-Century Crofts.

Gellner, E. (1962) 'Concepts and Society', *Transactions of the Fifth World Congress of Sociology (Washington)*, Louvain, reprinted in *Cause and Meaning in the Social Sciences*, London: Routledge and Kegan Paul (1973).

—— (1968) 'The New Idealism – Cause and Meaning in the Social Sciences', in I. Lakatos and A. Musgrave (eds) *Problems in the Philosophy of Science*, Amsterdam: North-Holland Publishing.

Gilbert, M. (1989) *On Social Facts*, London: Routledge.

Goffman, E. (1959) *The Presentation of Self in Everyday Life*, New York: Doubleday.

Goody, J. (1977) *The Domestication of the Savage Mind*, Cambridge: Cambridge University Press.

Grice, H. P. (1957) 'Meaning', *Philosophical Review* vol. 66.

—— (1969) 'Utterer's Meaning and Intentions', *Philosophical Review* vol. 78.

Habermas, J. (1972) *Knowledge and Human Interests*, Boston: Beacon Press.

—— (1974) 'Wahrheitstheorien', in H. Fahrenbach (ed.) *Wirklichkeit und Reflexion: Walter Schultz zum 60. Geburtstag*, Pfullingen: Neske.

—— (1988) *On the Logic of the Social Sciences*, Cambridge: Polity Press.

Harré, R. (ed.) (1986) *The Social Construction of Emotions*, Oxford: Basil Blackwell.

Hart, H. L. A. (1960) *The Concept of Law*, Oxford: Oxford University Press.

Hesse, M. (1980) *Revolutions and Reconstructions in the Philosophy of Science*, Brighton: Harvester.

Hollis, M. (1982) 'The Social Destruction of Reality', in M. Hollis and S. Lukes (eds) *Rationality and Relativism*, Oxford: Basil Blackwell.

Hollis, M. and Lukes S. (eds) *Rationality and Relativism*, Oxford: Basil Blackwell.

Horton, R. (1970) 'African Traditional Thought and Western Science', in B. Wilson (ed.) *Rationality*, Oxford: Basil Blackwell.

—— (1982) 'Tradition and Modernity Revisited', in M. Hollis and S. Lukes (eds) *Rationality and Relativism*, Oxford: Basil Blackwell.

Humboldt, W. von (1988) *On Language*, Cambridge: Cambridge University Press.

Hume, D. (1888) *A Treatise of Human Nature*, Selby-Bigge (ed.) Oxford: Clarendon Press.

Jarvie, I. C. (1972) *Concepts and Society*, London: Routledge and Kegan Paul.

Knorr-Cetina, K. (1981) *The Manufacture of Knowledge*, Oxford: Pergamon Press.

Kripke, S. (1982) *Wittgenstein on Rules and Private Language*, Oxford: Basil Blackwell.

Kroeber, A. L. (1940) 'Psychosis or Social Sanction', *Character and Personality* 8: 204–15.

Kuhn, T. S. (1972) *The Structure of Scientific Revolutions*, Chicago: University of Chicago Press, 2nd edition.

Lakoff, G. (1987) *Women, Fire, and Dangerous Things*, Chicago: University of Chicago Press.

Latour, B. (1993) *We Have Never Been Modern*, New York and London: Harvester Wheatsheaf.

Latour, B. and Woolgar, S. (1979) *Laboratory Life*, Beverly Hills: Sage Publications.

Leach, E. (1976) *Culture and Communication*, Cambridge: Cambridge University Press.

Lévi-Strauss, C. (1970) *The Raw and the Cooked*, London: Jonathan Cape.

Lewis, D. (1969) *Convention*, Oxford: Basil Blackwell.

Locke, J. (1970) *Two Treatises of Civil Government*, London: Dent.

Lorber, J. and Farrell, S. A. (eds) (1991) *The Social Construction of Gender*, Beverly Hills: Sage.

MacIntyre, A. (1962) 'A mistake about causality in social science', in P.

Laslett and W. G. Runciman (eds) *Science, Politics, and Society*, second series, Oxford: Basil Blackwell.

Mandelbaum, M. (1955) 'Societal Facts', *British Journal of Sociology* vol. 6.

Melden, A. I. (1961) *Free Action*, London: Routledge and Kegan Paul.

Mellor, D. H. (1982) 'The Reduction of Society', *Philosophy* vol. 57.

Newton-Smith, W. H. (1981) *The Rationality of Science*, London: Routledge and Kegan Paul.

Ortner, S. B. and Whitehead, H. (eds) (1981) *Sexual Meanings*, Cambridge: Cambridge University Press.

Parijs, P. van (1979) 'Functional explanation and the linguistic analogy', *Philosophy of the Social Sciences* vol. 9.

Pickering, A. (ed.) (1992) *Science as Practice and Culture*, Chicago: University of Chicago Press.

Pollner, M. (1987) *Mundane Reason*, Cambridge: Cambridge University Press.

Popper, K. R. (1972) 'On the theory of the objective mind', in K. R. Popper *Objective Knowledge*, Oxford: Clarendon Press.

Putnam, H. (1975) 'The Meaning of "Meaning"', in K. Gunderson (ed.) *Language, Mind and Knowledge, Minnesota Studies in the Philosophy of Science*, vol. 7, Minneapolis: University of Minnesota Press.

——(1978) *Meaning and the Moral Sciences*, London: Routledge and Kegan Paul.

——(1983) 'Why reason can't be naturalized', in *Realism and Reason. Philosophical Papers*, vol. 3, Cambridge: Cambridge University Press.

Rudner, R. (1966) *Philosopy of Social Science*, Englewood Cliffs: Prentice-Hall.

Ryle, G. (1949) *The Concept of Mind*, London: Hutchinson.

Sahlins, M. (1976) *Culture and Practical Reason*, Chicago: Chicago University Press.

Sapir, E. (1973) 'Linguistics as a science', in *Selected Writings of Edward Sapir*, Berkeley: University of California Press.

Schiffer, S. R. (1972) *Meaning*, Oxford: Clarendon Press.

Schutz, A. (1945) 'On Multiple Realities', *Philosophy and Phenomenological Research* vol. 5.

——(1962) 'Concept and theory formation in the social sciences', *Collected Papers*, vol. I, The Hague: Martinus Nijhoff.

——(1967) *Phenomenology of the Social World*, London: Heinemann.

Searle, J. R. (1995) *The Construction of Social Reality*, New York: Free Press.

Sherif, M and Sherif, C. W. (1969) *Social Psychology*, New York: Harper and Row.

Simmel, G. (1959) 'How is society possible?', in K. H. Wolff (ed.) *Georg Simmel, 1858–1918*, Columbus: Ohio State University Press.

Skorupski, J. (1976) *Symbol and Theory*, Cambridge: Cambridge University Press.

——(1979a) 'Pangolin Power', in S. C. Brown (ed.) *Philosophical Disputes in the Social Sciences*, Sussex: Harvester Press.

——(1979b) 'Our philosopher replies', in S. C. Brown (ed.) *Philosophical Disputes in the Social Sciences*, Sussex: Harvester Press.

References

Spencer, H. (1893) *The Principles of Sociology*, vol. 2, London: Williams and Norgate.

Stebbing, L. S. (1944) *Philosophy and the Physicists*, London: Methuen.

Sugden, R. (1986) *The Economics of Rights, Cooperation and Welfare*, Oxford: Basil Blackwell.

Szasz, T. (1961) *The Myth of Mental Illness*; New York: Harper and Brothers.

——(1973) *The Manufacture of Madness*, London: Granada Publishing.

Taylor, C. (1982) 'Rationality', in M. Hollis and S. Lukes (eds) *Rationality and Relativism*, Oxford: Basil Blackwell.

Thomas, W. I. (1928) *The Child in America*, Chicago: University of Chicago Press.

Trigg, R. (1985) *Understanding Social Science*, Oxford: Basil Blackwell.

Von Wright, G. H. (1971) *Explanation and Understanding*, London: Routledge and Kegan Paul.

Weber, M. (1930) *The Protestant Ethic and the Spirit of Capitalism*, New York: Charles Scribner.

——(1947) *The Theory of Social and Economic Organization*, New York: Free Press.

Whorf, B. L. (1956) *Language, Thought, and Reality*, Cambridge, Massachusetts: MIT Press.

Winch, P. (1958) *The Idea of a Social Science*, London: Routledge and Kegan Paul.

——(1964) 'Understanding a Primitive Society', *American Philosophical Quarterly* vol. I.

Wittgenstein, L. (1953) *Philosophical Investigations*, Oxford: Basil Blackwell.

——(1969) *On Certainty* , Oxford: Basil Blackwell.

Zimmerman, D. (1971) 'The Practicalities of Rule Use', in J. Douglas (ed.) *Understanding Everyday Life*, London: Routledge and Kegan Paul.

Zimmerman, D. and Pollner, M. (1971) 'The Everyday World as a Phenomenon', in J. Douglas (ed.) *Understanding Everyday Life*, London: Routledge and Kegan Paul.

Zimmerman, D. and Wieder, D. L. (1971) 'Ethnomethodology and the Problem of Order', in J. Douglas (ed.) *Understanding Everyday Life*, London: Routledge and Kegan Paul.

INDEX

action: assimilated with language 136ff; as dramaturgical self–presentation 175–6; as meaningful 103ff; as a propositional attitude 117–121; and social facts 1–2, 233–6; as symbolic-expressive 163ff

action coordination 1–2, 27–8, 201ff

aggurram 133–5

agreement: and convention 185ff; as generative of reality 3, 5, 11–12, 15–16, 144; hypothetical 42–4; and linguistic meaning 31–7; and ontological regress 37 –45; agreement that vs agreement to 196–7

Anscombe, G. E. M. 120, 136, 240n5

anti-realism 48, 52–3

Apel, K.-O. 136–7

argument from symbolism 165f, 184, 212, 222, 229

Aristotle 161, 240n5

arthritis 156–8, 181, 229

Ast, F. 137

Austin, J. L. 9, 192

Azande 55

Babel effect 161

Barthes, R. 172, 240–1

basic acts 240n4

Beattie, J. 167–8

Becker, H. 93–4

behaviourism 141

belief: and action explanation 117–20; and linguistic division of labour 156; religious 165–7; and

social reality 3, 10–11, 15–16, 20, 68 ff, 73–4, 105, 115, 122, 128f, 132f, 181–2, 206, 209, 225–6, 229, 232–4; and speech acts 179

Berbers 133

Berger, P. 4–5, 8, 20, 64f, 70f, 74f, 98–9, 127

Berkeley, G. 70

Blackburn, S. 156

Bloom, A. 238

Boas, F. 81

Boyle–Charles' law 231

bridge laws 231, 234

Broad Arguments 14, 21, 78, 87, 97, 99, 103, 115, 121, 219, 221–2, 254, 259; defined 23

Brown, J. R. 238

brute existence 74–5

Burge, T. 156

Byzantium 139

Caesar 108, 138

Callon, M. 13, 76, 78, 238

Calvinism 109

capitalism 109–110

Catholic Church 158, 162

CERN 160–1

class 64, 77, 131–3, 171–2, 175, 226

class classification 3, 31, 37, 62, 84 ff, 99, 103

closed predicament 58

coherence conditions 51–2, 63

collective intentionality 195

Collin, F. 238n3, 240n14

Collins, H. M. 13, 76, 78, 237n2, 238n7